Middle Rockies and Yellowstone

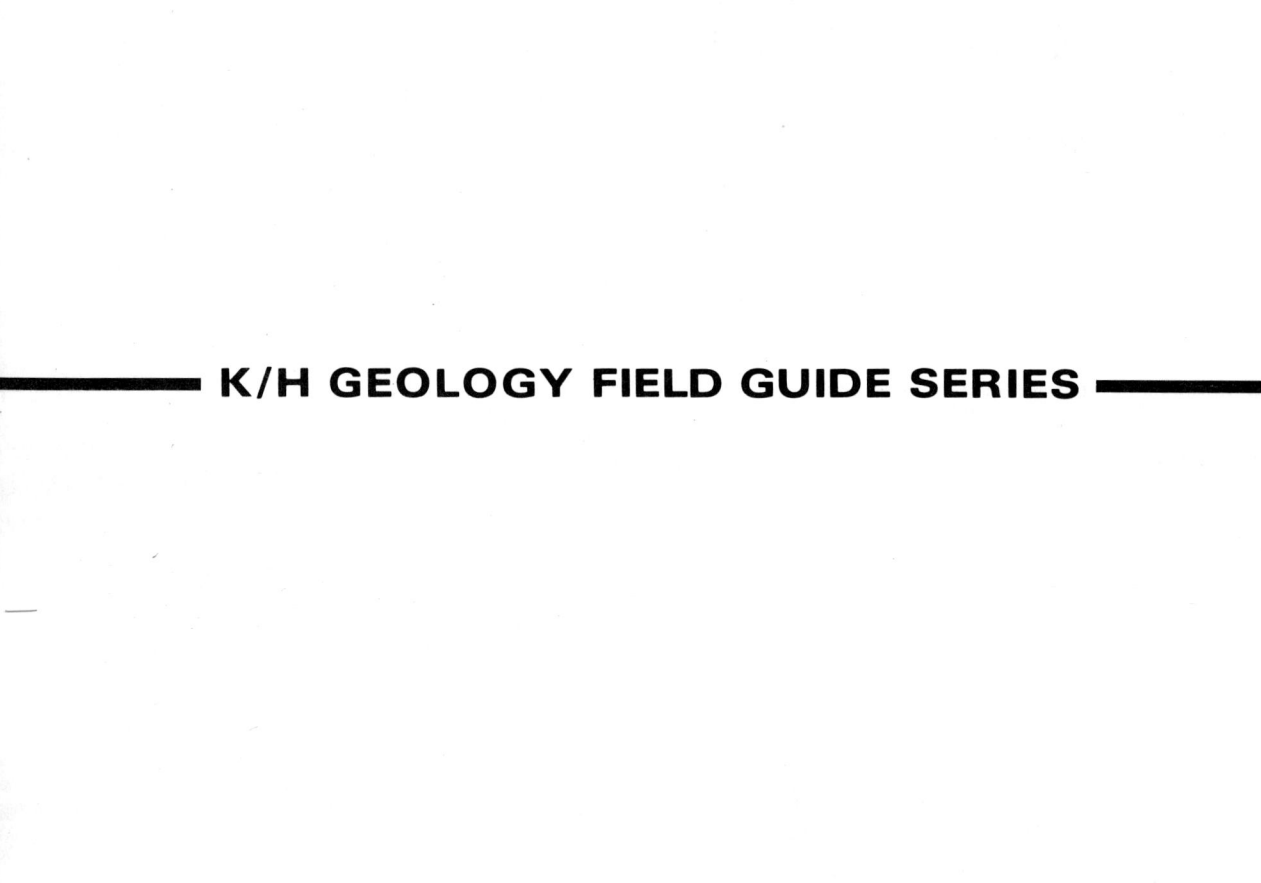

K/H GEOLOGY FIELD GUIDE SERIES

FIELD GUIDE

Middle Rockies and Yellowstone

Willard H. Parsons

Professor Emeritus
Wayne State University

KENDALL/HUNT PUBLISHING COMPANY
2460 Kerper Boulevard, Dubuque, Iowa 52001

ELMHURST COLLEGE LIBRARY

Cover photo used by permission of John Shelton.
This photo also appears in the text as Photo 2.18.

K/H GEOLOGY FIELD GUIDE SERIES

    Consulting Editor
    John W. Harbaugh
    Stanford University

Copyright © 1978 by Kendall/Hunt Publishing Company

Library of Congress Catalog Card Number: 78-57433

ISBN 0—8403—1869—3

All rights reserved. No part of this publication may be reproduced, stored in a retrieval system, or transmitted, in any form or by any means, electronic, mechanical, photocopying, recording, or otherwise, without the prior written permission of the copyright owner.

Printed in the United States of America   C 401869 01

CONTENTS

Foreword   vii
Preface   ix

CHAPTER

1. **Background** 1
   - Materials 2
   - Geologic Structures 4
   - Surface Processes 10
   - Age of Rocks and the Geologic Time Scale 12
   - Brief Summary of the Geologic History of the Middle Rockies . . . 14

2. **Natural Provinces of the Northern Middle Rockies** 16
   - Big Horn Mountains 16
   - Big Horn Basin 21
   - Owl Creek Mountains 23
   - Wind River Basin 25
   - Wind River Range 25
   - Absaroka Mountains 31
   - Beartooth Mountains 38
   - Gallatin and Madison Ranges 46
   - Yellowstone Plateau 48
   - Teton Mountains and Jackson Hole 61
   - Gros Ventre Mountains and Mount Leidy Highlands 68
   - Idaho-Wyoming Border Ranges 70
   - Northern Green River Basin 73
   - Eastern Snake River Plains 74

3. **Trip Guides** 81
   - Routes Leading to East Entrance to Yellowstone Park 83
     - Log 1: Buffalo to Worland to Cody 83
     - Log 2: Sheridan to Lovell to Cody 87
     - Log 2A: Burgess Junction to Greybull 96
     - Log 3: Shoshoni to Thermopolis to Cody 99
     - Log 4: Cody to East Entrance to Lake Junction 103

Routes Leading to Northeast Entrance to Yellowstone Park 113
    Log   5: Laurel to Red Lodge to Cooke City 113
    Log 5A: Cody via Dead Indian Hill to Cooke City 123
    Log 5B: Cooke City via Northeast Entrance to Tower Junction . 129
Routes Leading to South Entrance to Yellowstone Park 132
    Log   6: Farson via Pinedale to Jackson 132
    Log   7: Farson to Lander 138
    Log   8: Lander via Togwotee Pass to Jackson Hole 142
    Log   9: Jackson to South Entrance to West Thumb Junction . . 145
Route to North Entrance to Yellowstone Park 151
    Log 10: Livingston to Gardiner to Mammoth 151
Routes Leading to West Entrance to Yellowstone Park 157
    Log 11: Bozeman to West Yellowstone 157
    Log 12: Ennis to West Yellowstone 161
    Log 12A: West Yellowstone to Madison Junction 164
    Log 13: Blackfoot via Idaho Falls to West Yellowstone 166
Geological Side Trips Along Log 13 171
Routes from Idaho to South Entrance to Yellowstone Park 174
    Log 14: Idaho Falls via Snake River to Jackson 174
    Log 14A: Swan Valley to Jackson via Teton Pass 179
Yellowstone National Park Loop Roads 181
    Log 15A: Mammoth to Norris Junction 181
    Log 15B: Norris Junction to Madison Junction 188
    Log 15C: Madison Junction via Old Faithful to West Thumb . . 188
    Log 15D: West Thumb to Lake Junction 190
    Log 15E: Lake Junction to Canyon Junction 190
    Log 15F: Canyon Junction to Tower Junction 194
    Log 15G: Tower Junction to Mammoth 196
    Log 15H: Norris to Canyon Junction 197
Special Trips 198
    Log 16: Craters-of-the-Moon National Monument, Idaho . . . 198
    Log 17: The Crystal Ice Caves on the King's Bowl Rift, Idaho . 202
    Log 18: The Stillwater Igneous Complex, Montana 204

Appendixes

A. Geologic Time Scale and Stratigraphic Columns 211
B. Topographic Maps 215
C. Glossary 216
D. Annotated Bibliography 224

Index 227

FOREWORD

Willard Parsons' book is one of a series of books in the K/H *Geology Field Guide Series*. The objective of this series is to provide an authoritatively written layman's guide to important geologic features in each region treated in the series. Stress is placed on observations in the field. Each guide provides an overview of the geologic provinces of the region to which it pertains, and outlines a series of self-guiding field trips which will allow users to make their own firsthand observations on features that typify the provinces.

The series is directed toward diverse groups of users. The series should find use in formal classes in geology, both at the college and university level, and in high schools, in which field trips form an essential part of introductory or advanced courses. Furthermore, books in the series should be useful to professional geologists and other scientists who desire an introduction to the geologic features of particular regions. Finally, the series should find use among individuals who are not necessarily trained in science, but who do have an active interest in natural history and who enjoy travel.

Authors of books in this series all have intimate acquaintance with their respective regions and extensive teaching experience which has stressed field trip observations. Consequently, each book in this series represents a distillation of teaching experiences that have involved many students and numerous field trips.

John W. Harbaugh
Consulting Editor

PREFACE

Yellowstone is a geological park; its special wonders of hot springs and geysers are the continuing result of volcanic heat. In fact, the amount of heat coming to the surface in hot water and steam proves that hot molten rock must still exist below the Park. Its volcanoes are not extinct, only dormant! And around Yellowstone are the most spectacular mountains in our Rocky Mountain System: the Beartooth, Wind River and Teton ranges. These mountains and their adjacent basins contain rocks of all geologic ages and of almost all types. The region, therefore, is a vast natural laboratory for geologic study.

This book deals with this geological wonderland in a nontechnical manner. To follow the road logs herein it is not necessary to be a geologist, only to be interested in nature and the out-of-doors; it's a chance to know your Earth and its environment a little better, and for laymen to see the natural landscape through a geologist's eyes!

Chapter 1 gives a short introduction to geology for those who have no background in the language of this science. Geology students may skip this chapter. Chapter 2 describes the geography, appearance, and geologic history of some fourteen natural provinces including the mountain ranges and the intermontaine basins and plains that surround the Yellowstone Plateau. This section tells what kinds of rocks and mineral resources are found and how they were formed in each province.

Chapter 3 contains trip guides or road logs for all the U.S. highways and some other routes leading to Yellowstone National Park; coming from the east one may cross the Big Horn Mountains or the Beartooth Plateau; from the south, the traveler may drive along the Wind River Range; from the southwest, he can go across the Eastern Snake River Plains; and from the north, he may follow along the Gallatin or Madison valleys. These road logs point out prominent geological landmarks, unusual outcrops and cliffs as well as individual mountains and canyons. Explanations are given of the little things along the way which are like pages in the book of earth history. To follow these carefully will help to keep you awake on a hot day's drive! Many stops are suggested where one can get a view or examine rocks and other geologic features. Some are places where significant photographs may be taken. A few walks, usually short, are recommended to visit places or rocks of unusual interest or to break an otherwise long ride. A few trips of interest only to geologists, perhaps, are also included, such as the Elk Basin oil field, the Stillwater Igneous Complex, or the welded tuff on Mount Everts.

When geological terms are used they are usually defined in the text. However, a glossary of geological terms and tables of rock formation names are included in the appendix to help those new to the science. Rock names are summarized in short tables in Chapter 1.

The author has spent many summers in this region over the past 45 years. He has taken many geology students and laymen to all of the localities mentioned in this book. He has learned from many geologists over these years; men too numerous to list but a few stand out. The author was originally introduced to this area by John Rouse and Prof. Wm. T. Thom, Jr. and to these men he owes his lasting love for the Yellowstone country. William G. Pierce and Robert Christiansen of the U.S. Geological Survey and William Wilson of Wyoming and the late Armond Eardley were all very instrumental in the author's understanding of the area. But perhaps most thanks belong to Prof. Erling Dorf of Princeton University for inspiration and cooperation through many field seasons. Without the help and inspiration of these and many others the author would not have had the background to write this guide.

The author wishes to acknowledge and thank Carolyn R. Tourney of Wayne State University for drafting the maps and most of the diagrams without which this guide would be useless. The author's wife, Alice G. Parsons, served long and patiently as lay reader and grammarian. Thanks are also due to John S. Shelton for permission to use five of his outstanding aerial photographs.

Willard H. Parsons
March 25, 1978

Chapter 1

Background

Yellowstone Park and its surrounding mountain ranges are a great scenic wonder. All of us are amazed at the continuing flow of heat from within the earth in the steam of geysers and the water of hot springs. The earliest men to report on what they had seen in Yellowstone a century and a half ago were not believed, so startling were their reports. How did it all get there? What happened in the past? The Middle Rockies with Yellowstone in the center is like a giant textbook of geology, open and ready to be studied. It takes only a little understanding of rocks to read many of the facts and come away with a feeling for how mountains and hot springs and canyons were formed.

Modern geology perhaps was born in 1785 when James Hutton, a Scottish geologist, convincingly put into words the *Doctrine of Uniformitarianism* which has become the foundation of most geologic thought. This doctrine holds that earth processes in operation today have operated in the past in a similar manner. Today's processes are sufficient, allowing enough time, to explain the surface features and materials of our earth. In other words, the "present is the key to the past." Certainly, we learn about ancient volcanoes by watching modern lava flows. We understand erosion by watching rivers cutting canyons today. We discover that many mountain valleys were filled with glaciers by studying present-day glaciers in Greenland, the Alps, and Alaska. In Yellowstone many geologic events are in progress, and many other features reveal the volcanic episodes of the very near past. Nowhere is there a better outdoor laboratory than in the Middle Rockies. There are lava flows 2,000 years old, and, at the other extreme, there are mica gneisses more than three billion years old. Just look around you as you drive through this region.

The shape of scenery, or landforms, is the result of (1) rock materials and their structure or attitude; (2) surface processes eroding the rocks, for example, the work of rivers and glaciers; and (3) the stage or extent to which these processes have progressed. Rocks have formed, and are still being formed today, in many ways. But soon after they are formed they get modified, especially by movements or *deformation* within the earth's crust. The major episodes of deformation we call mountain building, and these episodes represent a complex series of events over millions of years which gradually elevate parts of the crust so that mountains are produced.

The major geologic processes of the earth may be considered in two broad categories which, in a sense, are acting against each other: one set, whose origin is within the earth's interior, and the other, whose origin is on the surface of the earth's solid part. The first group tends to deform the crust of the earth and elevate the land surface. They might be called constructive forces and are known under the headings Igneous Activity and Deformation. The second set of processes is wearing away the land areas of the world, and thus would be called destructive processes. This leveling activity is known collectively as *gradation*. Gradation is primarily work of solar energy forces acting in the atmosphere and hydrosphere. The end result of gradation alone, given sufficient time, would be the wearing down of all land to sea level.

With this concept, Uniformitarianism, geologists have been able to explain most earth features in a logical way. Past processes presumably have operated at the same slow pace as those of today. Therefore, very long periods of time must have been available for these processes to bring about what we see on the earth's surface now. This concept of almost unlimited time for the development of earth's features was a necessary outgrowth of the principle that the present is the key to the past.

MATERIALS

Matter is composed chiefly of fundamental units called *atoms*; and different kinds of atoms are called *elements*. The earth's crust is composed of ninety-two different, naturally-occurring elements, of which ten make up more than 99 percent of its mass.

Minerals are the main building blocks of the earth's crust. Minerals are formed of atoms combined as chemical compounds. A mineral is a homogeneous, natural substance of inorganic origin, having a definite chemical composition and certain characteristic physical properties. The most significant of these physical properties is a definite internal structure, or 3-dimensional atomic arrangement, which finds occasional outward expression in crystals. Two fundamental properties ordinarily characterize a mineral: its chemical composition and its distinct atomic structure. Natural glass is not a mineral; glass is a state of matter in which a disordered structure exists in a rigid state.

Some two thousand mineral species have been recognized, but most of these are very rare compounds. About two dozen minerals make up most of the crust of the earth and are known as the rock-forming minerals. Minerals may be identified by observing certain physical properties such as hardness, cleavage, fracture, specific gravity, color, streak, and luster. Most of these are probably new concepts to the average layman. Once these properties are understood, however, the recognition of mineral species should be as simple for the hobbyist as recognition of wild flowers. More positive identification can be accomplished by X-ray diffraction or chemical analysis.

Rocks are aggregates of one or more minerals, although a few exceptions are known. For example, obsidian is glass, and coal is compacted, altered organic matter; neither contains actual minerals in any quantity. A rock may be further defined as any large mass making up a part of the earth's crust. Rocks are usually solid bodies, but we also include as rocks such unconsolidated masses as gravel deposits, soil layers, or a compacted stretch of volcanic ash.

The distinction between minerals and rocks might be likened to the relationship between trees and a forest. Just as a forest is composed of many trees, sometimes all of one species, or again, of many species, so a rock is a mass containing many mineral grains, either of one kind, or of many different kinds. A typical example of a rock in which different minerals may easily be recognized in interlocking grains in a crystalline mass is *granite*.

There are three main classes of rocks: igneous, sedimentary and metamorphic, depending on the kind of environment in which they were formed. For the present we need only recognize two major environments, that within the earth's crust, and that on the surface. The chief conditions within the earth are high temperature and, often, great pressure. We distinguish two main rock groups—igneous and metamorphic—as associated with these conditions. The surficial environment, on the other hand, where materials settle out in shallow seas is characterized by low temperatures. Rocks formed under these conditions are known as sedimentary rocks.

Rock origin is never more dramatically illustrated than in a stream of red-hot molten lava rushing from a volcano. Solidified lava is an example of *igneous,* or "fire-made rock," which is best defined as rock formed by the crystallization or freezing of hot molten material, usually deep within the crust. Actually, less than one percent of all igneous rocks occur as lava; most igneous rocks have crystallized below the earth's surface in cracks and other spaces in the crust. When molten rock material cools rapidly, as in volcanic rocks, individual crystals do not have much time to grow, and consequently remain very small, giving the rock a fine-grained texture and a dense or stony appearance. On the other hand, igneous rocks forming deep within the earth's crust, crystallize more slowly, and individual crystals will grow to an average diameter of perhaps one-half inch. Such rocks are coarse-grained and granular in appearance, like granite. Occasionally rocks will have large crystals, surrounded by fine-grained material. This arrangement or texture forms a spotted material, a rock called porphyry.

Igneous rocks are classified on the basis of different textures, indicating different environments of formation, and on the basis of mineral composition. During the crystallization process of the magma, extremely complex but very definite chemical laws apply, and the classifications man has devised make allowance for these chemical relationships. A very simple classification is given in the following table.

TABLE OF IGNEOUS ROCKS

Color and Mineral Composition	Crystallized at Depth: Coarse-Grained	Solidified on or Near Surface: (Volcanic) Fine-Grained and/or Glassy
Light-colored minerals predominate: quartz, orthoclase feldspar, small amounts of mica and/or hornblende	Granite	Rhyolite Obsidian (glass)
Intermediate in color: two feldspars; hornblende	Diorite Monzonite	Andesite
Dark-colored minerals predominate: plagioclase feldspar, augite, and/or olivine	Gabbro	Basalt
Pyroxenes and/or olivine: no feldspars	Ultra-mafic rocks	—

Sedimentary rocks are formed by the accumulation of sediments in ancient seas and lakes, often now found uplifted in plateaus and high mountains. As rocks are disintegrated and decomposed at the earth's surface by weathering, their remains are carried to the seas as sand, silt, mud, and dissolved salts. Some of these are fragments of previous rocks and minerals and are compacted or cemented together to form rock layers. Others are crystallized masses of interlocking crystals formed by precipitation of the dissolved salts in ocean waters. Limestone is the most common example. Sedimentary rocks contain fossils, the evidence of life which existed at the time the rock material was being deposited. The other most distinctive characteristic of sedimentary rocks is a uniform layering or bedding called *stratification*.

Sedimentary rocks are named or classified on the basis of the size and kinds of particles or crystals which have been compacted or cemented together to form the rock, and the common ones are named in the table at the bottom of the page.

Previously formed rocks, igneous or sedimentary, which are deeply buried in the crust are gradually subjected to increasing temperature and pressure as a result of deposition of overlying sediments and progressive involvement with crustal stresses. An environment of increasing temperature and pressure brings about slow changes in mineral composition and texture in the original rock. These changes take place by atomic rearrangement in the solid state producing new reoriented mineral grains. The entire rock mass occupies progressively less and less space in response to the increased pressures and becomes chemically stable at the higher temperatures. The changes sometimes continue until the original rocks are completely altered in both physical properties and mineral composition; the changed rocks are called *metamorphic* rocks. The best known examples, probably, are *slate* and *marble*. The table at the top of the next page lists the more common types to be found in the Middle Rockies.

GEOLOGIC STRUCTURES

Structures in rocks are the presence or absence of layers and the attitude of such layers if present. We also consider under "structure" the presence of little cracks as well as great fractures or faults in the crust whose movements may cause earthquakes.

Sedimentary rocks are formed, as we have seen, by deposition of debris in oceans and are usually deposited in horizontal or flat-lying beds, or strata. Thus, geologists speak of the general rule of original horizontality of sedimentary rocks, meaning that the layers were deposited essentially flat-lying. We

TABLE OF SEDIMENTARY ROCKS

Sediments or Particles	Rocks	Composition
Pebbles, gravel	Conglomerate	Various rocks
Sand	Sandstone	Usually quartz, but various others
Silt	Siltstone	Usually quartz
Mud, clay	Shale	Clay minerals
$CaCO_3$ precipitates	Limestone and dolomite	Calcite (dolomite)
$CaSO_4$ precipitates	Gypsum	Gypsum

TABLE OF METAMORPHIC ROCKS

	Rock Name	Mineral Composition	Commonly Derived from
Foliated or Layered	Slate	Micas, etc.	Shales
	Schist	Micas, hornblende, garnet, quartz	Fine-grained igneous rocks; silt, shales
	Gneiss	Feldspar, quartz, hornblende, etc.	Many coarse-grained rocks; igneous + conglomerate
	Amphibolite	Hornblende, (trace of feldspar, quartz)	Basalts; iron-rich sediments
Nonfoliated or Massive	Quartzite	Quartz	Conglomerates and sandstones
	Marble	Calcite, dolomite	Limestones or dolomites
	Serpentinite	Serpentine	Ultramafic igneous rocks

Photo 1.1. Vertical sedimentary beds as a result of mountain uplift and deformation. The rock wall to the left of center is a sill of igneous rock, parallel to the vertical beds of sedimentary rock. The Devil's Slide seen in Log 10 along the Yellowstone River valley north of Gardiner, Montana.

may find these layers, or strata, tilted at various angles and even standing straight up and down in a vertical position as a result of deformation that has taken place long after deposition (Photo 1.1). The strata or bedding planes in sedimentary rocks may be very thin, fractions of an inch, or certain beds may be extremely thick, several tens of feet thick; so we describe the structure of sedimentary rocks in terms of thin beds or thick beds. We also speak of the angle of the tilt as the angle of dip of the strata.

Igneous rocks which have formed in the earth's crust and have been exposed at the surface by erosion represent molten material which has crystallized when it was chilled near the surface. Igneous rocks which are formed as magma comes up through cracks (sometimes very irregular cracks) to solidify and form more or less steeply dipping layers of igneous rock are called *dikes*. These dikes, being crack fillings, seem to cut across the rocks in which the crack has been formed and, of course, the igneous rock, filling a crack, must have come in after the surrounding rock had been formed. Layers of igneous rock parallel to previous strata are called *sills* (Photo 1.1). Some igneous rocks are very large and irregular masses where molten material at depth pushed up, filling a great space. These great masses of igneous rock which usually have no layering are said to have a massive structure, and such great masses are known as *stocks* or *batholiths* depending on size. Batholiths are the largest masses of igneous material which today may be exposed over tens of hundreds of square miles of a region.

Earth crustal movements taking place slowly but progressively result in deformation of rock layers. This generally results in uplift and tilting of strata, with the bending or folding of rock layers and breaking or fracturing if the rocks respond in a brittle fashion. Rock layers can be folded on a small scale of a few feet or on a scale of miles in gigantic folds. Folds are either upfolds, or domes, called anticlines; downfolds called synclines; or one-sided folds called monoclines (Fig. 1.1).

Little breaks where there has been only cracking are called *joints*. Joints may be likened to a cracked windshield where the glass is still in place but highly fractured. Almost all rocks are jointed to some extent,

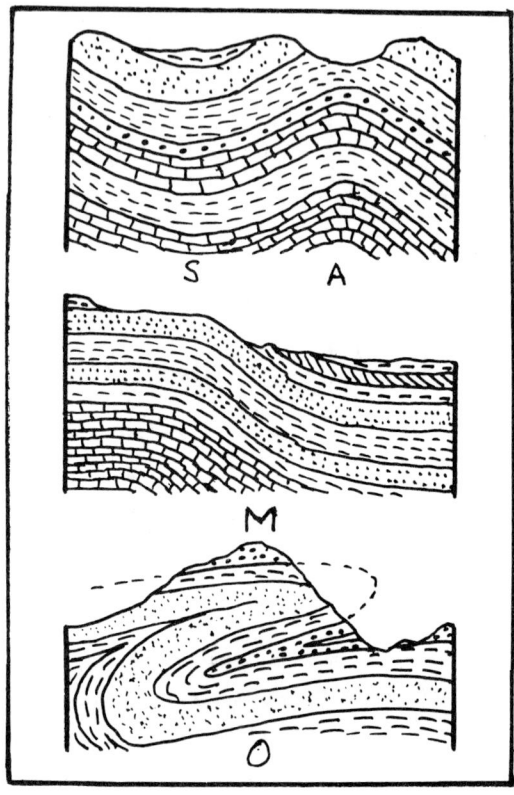

Figure 1.1. Folds. Top, symmetrical syncline (S) and anticline (A). These folds are drawn partially eroded such that ridges are found where the hard resistant beds are at the surface. Middle, a monocline (M). The erosion of such a fold may result, as diagrammed, in a mountain surface (left) adjacent to a lower plain. Bottom, an overturned anticline (above) and syncline. The overturned anticline may become a thrust fault with additional deformation.

and it is along these joint cracks that rocks break loose as can be seen along most highway road cuts (Photo 1.2).

Breaks or fractures along which there has been movement are called *faults* (Photo 1.3). Faults can result in one block of the earth's crust moving upwards relative to another block, or they can result in one block moving horizontally relative to the block on the other side of the fault. This latter is referred to as a horizontal fault and is best exemplified by the famous San Andreas fault in Cal-

Photo 1.2. Closely spaced joint planes or cracks in granite in a road cut in the Beartooth Mountains, Wyoming, seen on Log 5.

Photo 1.3. Small normal faults. The trace of steeply dipping fault planes as exposed in a road cut. Locality unknown. (Photo by H. L. Wanless.)

ifornia. Faults which result in uplift (and down-throw) can be either *normal* or *thrust*. In normal faults, one side is seen to slide down relative to the other as if the earth were being pulled apart. In thrust faults one side is shoved up over another block as though the earth were being compressed and the crust shortened. (Fig. 1.2).

Large faults which may be traced for many miles may result in sufficient uplift to produce an entire mountain range. For example, in the Middle Rockies the Teton Range is a block fault where the mountain mass has been uplifted more than five miles along a great fracture traceable for many miles at the foot of the range. The evidence is that this kind of movement takes place little by little over several million years, perhaps a few feet at a time, so it is a gradual but continuing process. When one great block is uplifted, the block on the other side is relatively dropped down, or perhaps literally dropped down, and this down-side often gets buried by sediment washed in as the up-side is being eroded. Thus, there is usually a basin at the base of the mountain range partly filled in with debris worn off the uplifted side. With the Teton Mountains, the basin on the east, known as Jackson Hole, has thousands of feet of young sediments which have been deposited slowly, layer by layer, as the mountain range was slowly pushed upwards.

Sometimes large blocks of the crust are slowly uplifted over thousands of square miles without any pronounced major folding or faulting, so that great areas of sedimentary rock deposited under ocean water come to stand thousands of feet above sea level, but with the layers more or less horizontal. Again there has been continual crustal movement, but not crustal deformation resulting in folding and major faulting.

Why does all this deformation and crustal uplift take place? How does it take place? These questions are among the most challenging in all of geology and are not fully answered today, since we do not have all the data we need about the interior of the earth where the energy must be generated. However, in the last couple of decades geologists have come to formulate an overall theory of earth deformation known as *Plate Tectonics,* which is a modification of an older idea called Continental Drift. This theory says that the earth's outer layers, perhaps a hundred-miles thick, are divided or broken up into six major plates and many smaller pieces. The plates involve not only the land, but also the rock material of the ocean floor. The North American plate, for example, extends from the middle of the Atlantic Ocean throughout North America to the border of the Pacific, or specifically, to the San Andreas Fault in California. The evidence that this is really so comes from many lines of evidence—geology, paleontology, and geophysics—and a full explanation of all this is entirely beyond the purpose of this book. However, in brief, plate tectonics shows that today several plates are very, very slowly moving relative to one another at one or two inches a year. Plates are pulling apart, and plates are colliding, or pushing against each other. The rate of movement has been measured and can be clearly demonstrated by careful study of earthquakes and so forth. Apparently, this kind of thing has happened in the past. Again, if we stick with the principle of the present as the key to the past, it appears that the great mountain systems of the world have been produced where two great plates have very slowly collided and have jammed the ocean sediments into great folds and faults. The heat of this collision has resulted in melting and development of magmas which have been squeezed upwards as igneous rocks and volcanoes.

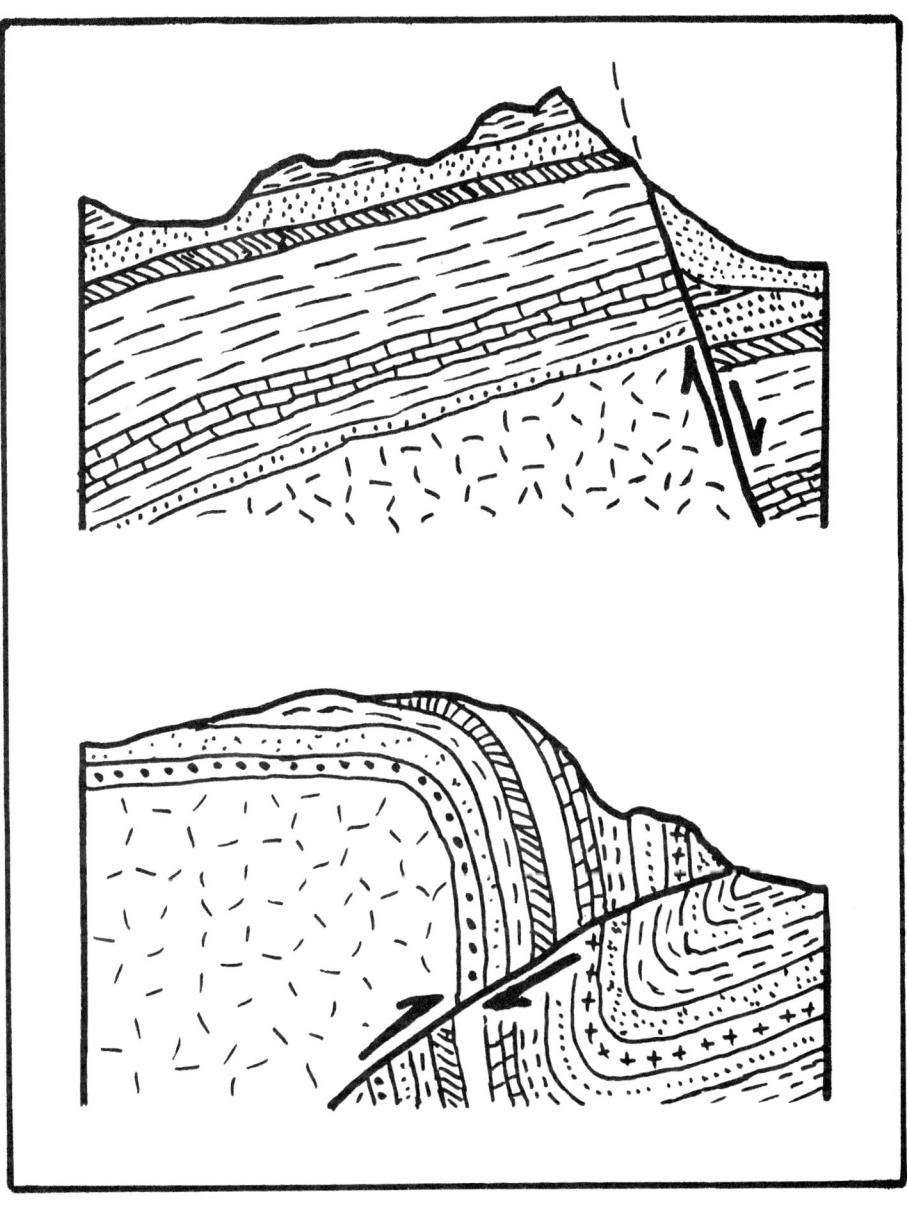

Figure 1.2. *Faults.* Top, a normal fault, in which the right side has moved down relative to the left side which has moved up. Debris has weathered off the uplifted block and is deposited as sediment and talus at the foot of the mountain to the right covering the fault plane. Bottom, a thrust fault in which the left side has moved up and *over* the down side.

Perhaps the most spectacular evidence that plates are really moving today is the coincidence that the plotting of the epicenters of all earthquakes around the world gives us a perfect picture of present plate boundaries, both pull-apart and collision boundaries, which are mapped on other bases. It's where this differential motion takes place that the great earthquakes and active volcanoes occur today.

Looking back in history some 70 million years, therefore, we suggest that the Rocky Mountains were formed by a plate collision in the past, and sedimentary rocks deposited in then existing oceans were folded and pushed up and magmas were generated which gradually worked their way up in association with the growing mountains. If we look at the Middle Rockies, (and we can extend this picture both north and south into the Northern and Southern Rockies) we find a western belt (Nevada-Utah-Idaho) of highly-folded sedimentary rocks which have been thrust faulted showing the same kind of structure we find in the Appalachians. This kind of deformation implies crustal compression, and almost certainly is the result of a plate collision, crumpling the sediments in the ocean near the margin of the colliding plates.

The more eastern ranges of the Rockies—specifically the Beartooth, Big Horn, and Wind River ranges—have a totally different kind of structure. These ranges are elongate uplift blocks, with down-thrown blocks between them. They represent a breakup of the surface of a plate near, but not actually at, the collision site. This kind of a breakup of the surface crust might be likened to the breakup of ice on a large lake or on the Arctic Ocean where blocks of ice get moved horizontally and jammed together (perhaps by wind) so that some blocks are pushed up and other blocks are pushed down.

SURFACE PROCESSES

Weathering includes all those processes whereby rocks are broken and decomposed, on or close to, the earth's surface by contact with air or water. During the processes of weathering, we observe a mechanical disintegration of solid rock into smaller particles, and a decomposition of their minerals by chemical reactions with oxygen, carbon dioxide, and water.

The debris formed by weathering—broken rock and soil—slowly, or rapidly, slumps downslope under the impetus of gravity. Eventually, the loose material reaches the valley bottoms and is delivered to rivers to become part of their load.

The most spectacular of the gravity actions are the mass movements or landslides in which great quantities of soil and bedrock suddenly break loose and rush down the mountainside. In high mountains, individual rock fragments and small rock falls occur almost continuously and build up piles of loose rock at the foot of steep slopes and cliffs. These deposits are known as *talus slopes* (Photo 1.4) and are characteristic features throughout the Middle Rockies.

The slow slump or creep of soil downslope, though not spectacular and at times not even noticeable except to students of earth science, eventually delivers a tremendous load to the transporting agents. The most important of these agents in the Middle Rockies has been running water, aided during the colder climate of the past by glaciers, and, to some extent in the dry basins, by wind blowing dust and sand from one place to another.

Photo 1.4. Talus cone of rock debris at the mouth of a gully on a mountainside. Note the variation in fragment size, with many blocks over 10 ft. in diameter. In Death Canyon, Teton Range, Wyoming. (Photo by Walter Nickell.)

We see, therefore, that rocks of all kinds are broken up by weathering and that these broken fragments ultimately are moved by running water, wind, or ice. In this process valleys are slowly cut by the running water or ice, leaving ridges or divides. Thus, landscape as we know it has been developed. Rocks that were once formed deep within the earth are now exposed at the surface as a result of this erosion continuing for millions of years. It is only as a result of this continuing erosion that we see deep-seated igneous rocks and metamorphic rocks now at the earth's surface.

AGE OF ROCKS AND THE GEOLOGIC TIME SCALE

One of the interesting and valuable contributions of the study of natural radioactivity is the determination of the approximate age in years of various minerals and rocks from the various isotopes (radiogenic forms of atoms) present in them. For example, the amount of radiogenic lead present in uranium-bearing minerals indicates their ages. It is demonstrable that a certain quantity of uranium will yield in one year $\frac{1}{7,600,000}$ of that quantity of lead. The ratio of lead to uranium in a given mineral, therefore, may be used to determine how long ago that mineral crystallized. In addition to the lead/uranium ratios, the ratio of rubidium to strontium and the ratio of potassium to argon are also used for geologic age determination. The ratio of radioactive carbon (carbon 14) to ordinary carbon (carbon 12) has been used to date materials containing carbon originally taken from the atmosphere as in wood and plant fibers. This dating method is only good for ages back to a maximum of 50,000 years ago. It has been used to date buried wood in glacial deposits and wood, charcoal, and various fibers in archeological workings.

Most of us are greatly confused by the carefree way geologists speak of millions and billions of years, and their suggestion that the earth started 4.5 billion years ago. To help put geologic events into perspective, it has been suggested that one might consider all geologic time compressed into one year and then to imagine the present moment as exactly midnight of December 31. It has been calculated that Columbus then discovered America 3.3 seconds ago; Christ was born about 14 seconds ago; and 100 seconds ago ice covered much of North America, and Stone Age man was living in caves. The great, extensive volcanic eruptions that built the Yellowstone Plateau began about eight o'clock New Year's Eve, and the Rocky Mountains were pushed up the day after Christmas. Precambrian time lasted all year till the middle of November. Thus, we see that events and rocks which we see in the Rocky Mountains have been developed in comparatively recent geologic time, compared to the entire age of the earth.

For our purposes, relative age relationships, perhaps most understandable geologic time, may conveniently be expressed as the order in which different events have taken place throughout the history of the earth. This is relative time and can usually best be determined from the position of sedimentary rocks.

As layers of sediment are deposited in lakes or in the ocean, each newly deposited layer settles on top of a previous layer in a thick section of sedimentary rock strata. Therefore, the top layer is the youngest, and the bottom bed is the oldest. This very obvious relationship is known as the *Law of Superposition* and is of the utmost importance in determining the relative ages of rock series.

Any group of rocks which have been elevated above sea level, with or without folding, will eventually be subject to erosion. This now low-lying land surface may sink and be covered by an inland sea with a gradual accumulation of a new and younger series of sedimentary rocks. The line of contact between the old, partly eroded rocks and the new rocks is called an unconformity; the latter is in reality an old erosion surface and indicates, so far as geologic history is concerned, the passage of a period of time for which no rock record is preserved (Fig. 1.3).

Igneous rocks are intruded into previously existing rocks in cracks in the crust. Obviously, the igneous bodies are younger than the rocks they crosscut. This simple relation-

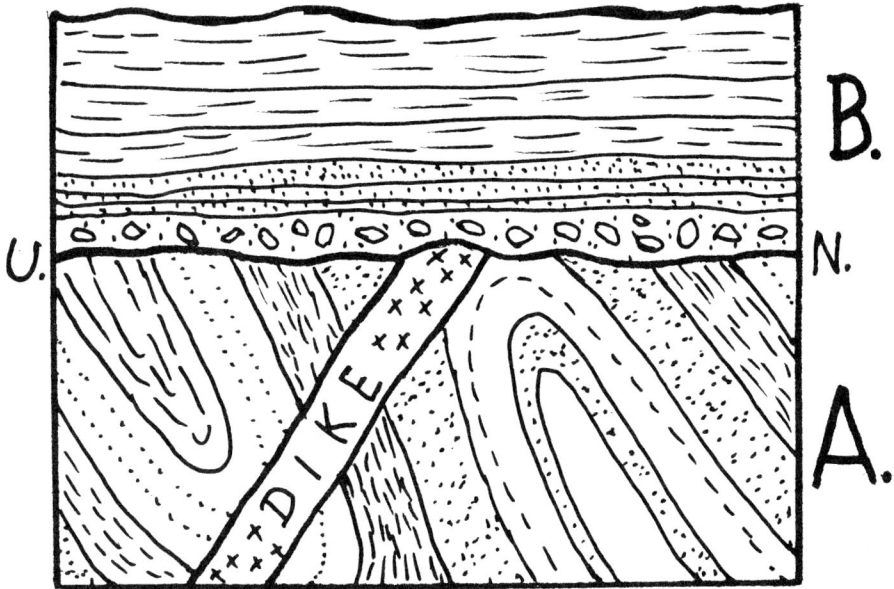

Figure 1.3. An angular unconformity. A series of older and highly folded sedimentary rocks (A) separated by a surface of erosion (U.N.), known as an *unconformity,* from the younger overlying beds of sedimentary rocks (B). The geologic events portrayed in this diagram have occurred in the following order, starting with the first, or oldest event: (1) deposition of the A series of sedimentary rocks, originally in a horizontal position, (2) folding of the A series rocks, (3) intrusion of a dike of igneous rock, (4) a long period of erosion wearing away part of the A series rocks and part of the dike to form an old land surface (U.N.), and (5) deposition in a later and younger sea of the B series of sedimentary rocks.

ship is known as the *Law of Intrusion* and makes possible a determination of the relative age of most igneous rocks. For example, in Figure 1.3 a dike crosscuts folded, older sediments (labeled A). The dike, therefore, is younger than the A beds. Erosion, represented by the unconformity, has removed part of the dike. This dike must be older than the period of erosion, and, of course, also older than the time of deposition of the B beds.

In a thick sequence of sedimentary rocks, such as the Paleozoic sedimentary rocks of the Yellowstone region, various fossil assemblages are found in different positions in the sequence. According to the Law of Superposition, we know that fossils in the uppermost layers are a record of more recent life. This superposition of recent fossils over ancient fossils is called the *Law of Faunal Succession.* Throughout geologic history this succession shows, in general, gradual development of life types from primitive organisms to the complex plants and animals of today. When we find the same fossil assemblage in rocks in widely separated areas, perhaps even in different continents, we may safely conclude that these separate rocks are similar in age. Here we have the outstanding criteria for correlating rocks in one part of the world with those in another.

When sedimentary rocks in various parts of the country were correlated by their fossil assemblages and the presence of unconformities was carefully noted, it became apparent that rock sequences in one locality interfinger in time with those in another section of the country. In this way, a composite geologic column of the sedimentary rocks and lavas has been assembled for the entire world, in which all known rock units are arranged in their chronological order from oldest at the bottom to youngest. This is the geologic column, also known as the geologic time scale. Geologists have applied various names to each period of relative time. A simplified version of this geologic time scale is supplied in Appendix A-1. In addition, geologic columns of Paleozoic and younger rocks which are found in the Middle Rockies are included in Appendix A. Don't try to memorize these names, but look at these charts from time to time as you come across geological time and rock formation names in these pages. Gradually then, you will learn something about the relative ages of the rocks you will be seeing.

BRIEF SUMMARY OF THE GEOLOGIC HISTORY OF THE MIDDLE ROCKIES

Study of the Middle Rockies indicates that sedimentary rocks were first deposited here more than three billion years ago. These rocks were buried and metamorphosed, and magmas developed to form various igneous bodies, including the famous Stillwater Igneous Complex in the Beartooth Range. For some two billion years we have no evidence of what happened here. Apparently this region was land for at least part of that time, and long-continued extensive erosion wore away a great thickness of rock, so that these older metamorphic rocks were exposed at the surface of the earth at the beginning of the Paleozoic Era.

During Paleozoic time (see Appendix A-2 for relationships) the Middle Rocky Mountain area was covered by various large long-standing inland seas in which sedimentary materials accumulated, including much limestone. The marine origin of these sedimentary rocks is indicated by their fossils.

During the Mesozoic Era the area continued to be low-lying, alternating shallow seas and swamps near sea level or deltalike areas on which much sandstone and shale was deposited. During the Cretaceous Period dinosaurs roamed the land. Their fossils have been found in the Big Horn Basin. So this part of the earth was largely flat land, but the seas came in at times, especially from the west.

Toward the end of the Mesozoic Era, the continental plates which presumably had been slowly moving, began their terrifying collision with the slow rupture, compression, and uplift of the crust which we call the Rocky Mountain uplift. This began in late Cretaceous time and continued into the early Tertiary Period (Paleocene Epoch). This period of plate collision and Rocky Mountain uplift began perhaps, ninety million years ago and lasted until sixty million years ago. As the slow uplift took place, erosion continuously removed some of the uplifted rock materials so that the Paleozoic and Mesozoic rocks, which once covered the great blocks of Precambrian rocks, now uplifted as the Beartooth, Big Horn, Wind River and Teton ranges were worn away.

Some of the material worn away was carried on to unknown oceans, but quite a bit of the sediment was deposited in the areas that were shoved down between the uplifted blocks, or in other words, some of the sediment was deposited into the basins between the mountain ranges—for example, into the Big Horn Basin, the Wind River Basin, Green River Basin, and Jackson Hole. All of these basins contain great thicknesses of Tertiary sedimentary rocks; fossils indicate they were deposited by streams or in swamps, but not in oceans. Many land animal fossils are found here, and rather extensive coal deposits are evident in the Paleocene.

As we appreciate, by studying today's earth, these plate collisions result in localizing heat, melting of rock material at depth, and developing volcanic belts. A few million years after the Rocky Mountain uplift, such magmas began to appear in western Wyoming and built up the extensive volcanic province known as the Absaroka Volcanic Field exposed in the Absaroka, Gallatin, and Beartooth mountains. This first period of Rocky Mountain volcanism began in the Eocene Epoch.

Even though the main period of plate collision and Rocky Mountain uplift was finished, there continued to be movements in the deep crust, and these movements continue even into the present time. In middle to late Tertiary time block faulting occurred, and several mountain ranges were slowly elevated. The most outstanding example is the Teton Range whose uplift continued from Pliocene to Pleistocene time.

New magmas developed as the result of some fracturing below; and during the last two million years (Pleistocene Epoch) very extensive rhyolite lavas have exploded to the surface, at times very violently, to develop the whole Yellowstone province of volcanic materials.

Finally, and perhaps contemporaneous with the Yellowstone volcanism, basalt volcanism has occurred in eastern Idaho in the area known as the Snake River Plain. This volcanism continued right down until only two thousand years ago at Craters-of-the-Moon National Monument and elsewhere to give us a third great type of volcanic activity and volcanic rocks.

Throughout all this time climates were changing. They must have been warm during Tertiary time as indicated by the life forms and fossil leaves in Tertiary rocks, but they became very cold in Pleistocene time. Rock records show that three major ice advances occurred in the Middle Rocky Mountains during the Pleistocene Epoch. The last one melted as recently as ten to fifteen thousand years ago.

Chapter 2

Natural Provinces of the Northern Middle Rocky Mountains

The Rocky Mountains have been divided into the Southern, Middle, and Northern Rocky Mountain sections for ease of reference. The Southern Rockies lie largely in Colorado and New Mexico; the Northern Rockies in Montana, north-central Idaho, and on into Canada. That leaves a group of ranges and intermountain basins in Wyoming, northeastern Utah, and southeastern Idaho as the Middle Rocky Mountains. We are concerned in this guide book with the northern part of this section of the Rockies, as outlined on the map (Fig. 2.1.). These are ranges and basins that surround Yellowstone National Park and are usually crossed by tourists and students who visit Teton and Yellowstone National Parks.

The Middle Rockies are characterized by ruggedness, high peaks, and great relief—up to 7,000 feet at the base of the Tetons. Elevations rise near or above 13,000 feet in four of these ranges. The mountainous areas have extensive bare rock with shallow soil covering so that the rocks and geologic structures are easy to see and understand. The lower slopes and valleys in most of the mountains are forested with conifers. Several of the headwaters of the Missouri River and the headwaters of the Snake River rise in this region. The several basins between ranges are filled with young sedimentary rocks and exist as semiarid desertlike areas with sparse sagebrush and bare, alkali-covered soils.

There is a moderate amount of mineral wealth here, especially the fuel minerals—coal, oil, and uranium. There are smaller amounts of phosphorus and iron; and potential chromium and molybdenum deposits are known or being developed.

The Middle Rockies may be divided into several natural provinces for convenience in description. These provinces are characterized by similar topography and geologic structures. The boundaries of provinces are quite distinct in some cases but rather arbitrary in others, as these province divisions have been outlined by man. In nature one province grades fairly rapidly or very gradually into another. Most of the mountainous provinces lie in national forest lands or in the two great national parks, Yellowstone and Teton. Even in the basins, however, much land is undeveloped and federally owned by the Bureau of Land Management.

BIG HORN MOUNTAINS

The Big Horn Range is the eastern-most of the ranges of the Rockies in Wyoming. This range stands abruptly above the plains and is the first sight of the Rockies that one sees coming from the east across the semidesert of the high plains. The Big Horn Range runs approximately north-south (slightly north-northwest—south-southeast) for almost 150 miles, although a high central part of the

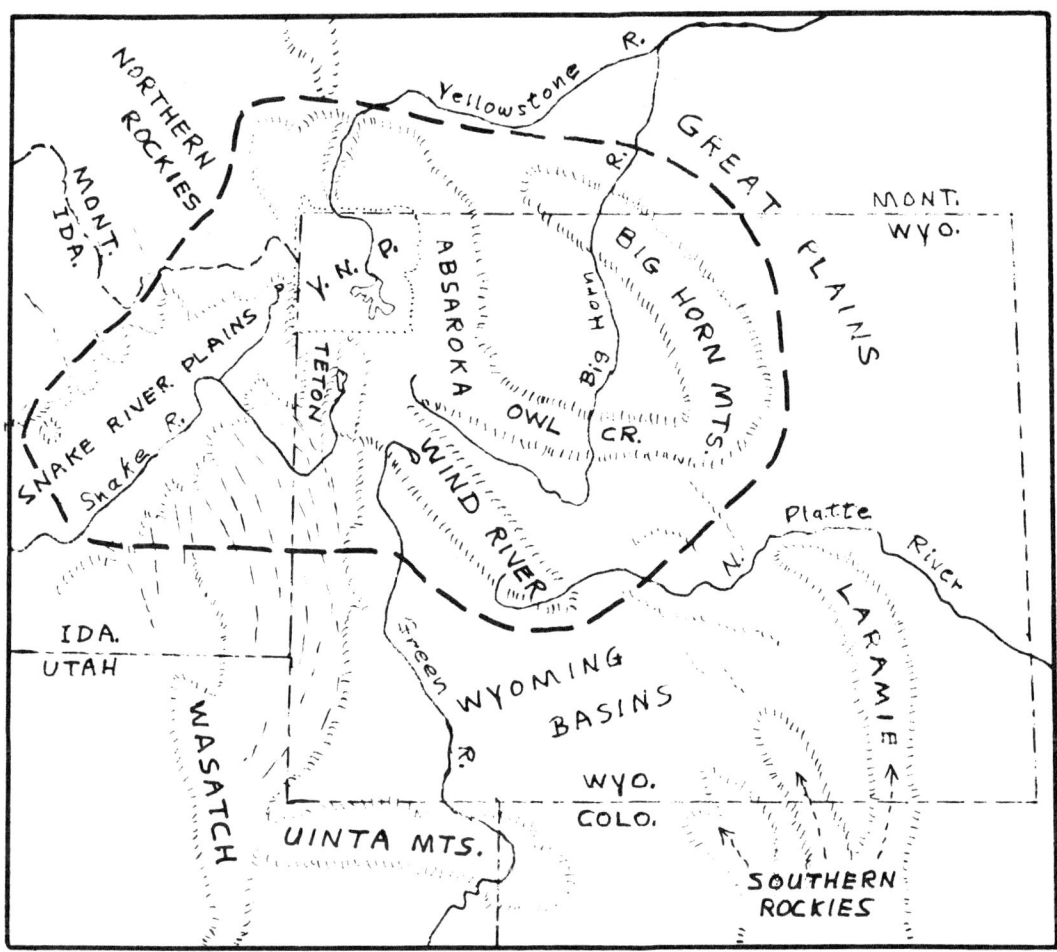

Figure 2.1. Outline map of the Middle Rockies and vicinity. Area discussed in this guide is encircled by the heavy dashed line.

range extends only about 100 miles. The range is approximately 30 miles wide where it is crossed by two U.S. highways—U.S. 14 and 16. This is illustrated in Figure 2.2 with map and ERTS photograph (Earth Resources Technology Satellite No. 1., 1972).

General Description

The Big Horn Mountains rise steeply on both sides from the plains or the Big Horn Basin without foothills as such. The elevation of the plains on the east and of the Big Horn Basin on the west is in the range of 4,000 to 4,500 feet, whereas the average summit level of the main range is 9-10,000 feet. This area is a rolling plateaulike topography which is easily traveled by highways and has a relief of about 1,000 feet. There is a steep, very rugged alpine central area in the range located between the two highway crossings, where peaks rise appreciably above the 10,000 foot level, culminating in Cloud Peak at 13,165 feet (Photo 2.1). This central, rugged area has

Natural Provinces of the Northern Middle Rocky Mountains

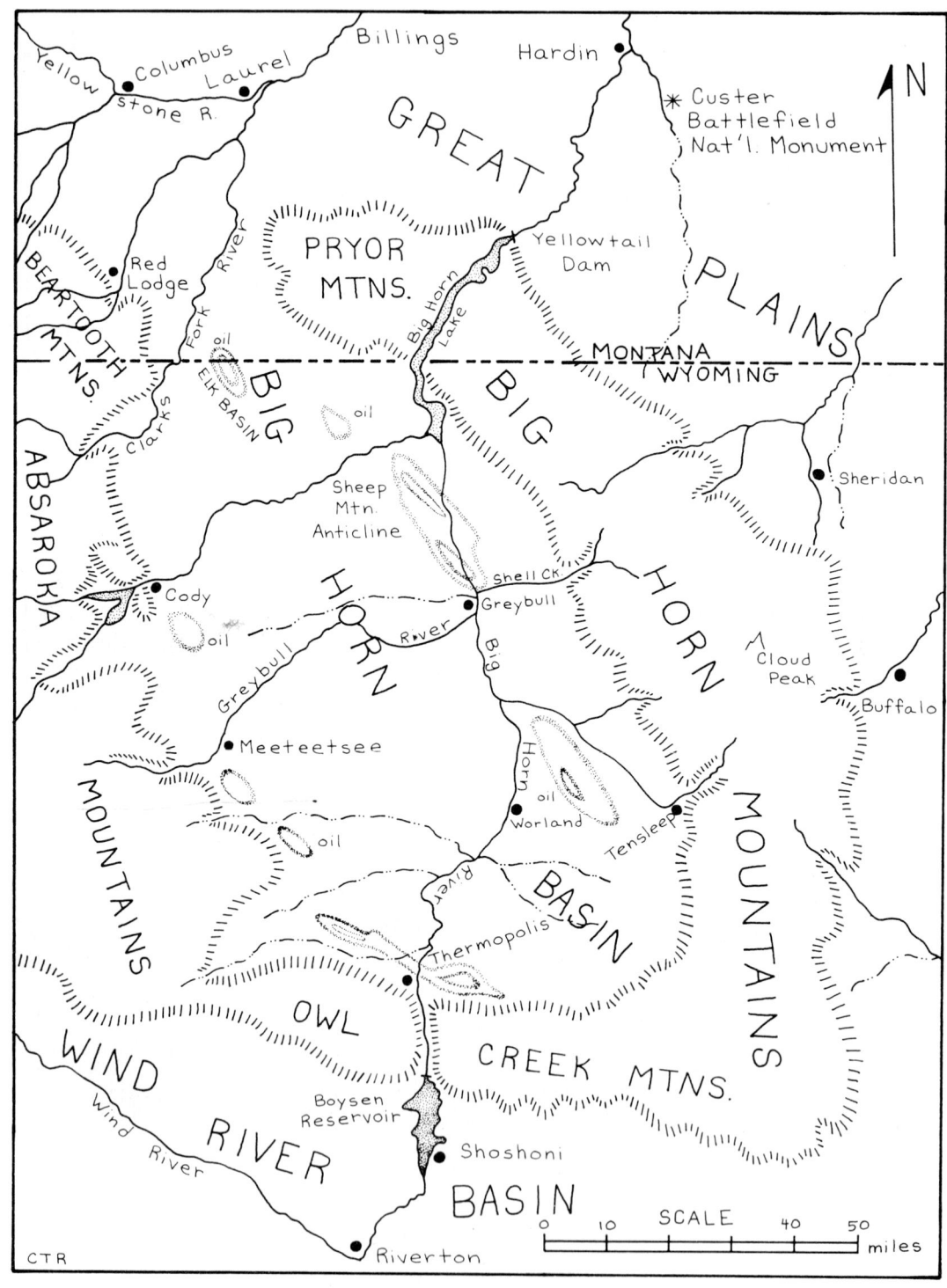

Figure 2.2. (On left page) Map of the Big Horn Mountains, Big Horn Basin, and Owl Creek Mountain Provinces and vicinity. (Facing page, on right) ERTS photograph of the same area.

Photo 2.1. High central peaks of the Big Horn Mountains rising above the forested plateau surface at about 9,000 ft. View on Log 1.

been cut into U-shaped canyons and sharp, glacial ridges and horns by ice during the Pleistocene period of glaciation. Valleys that lead down, both east and west, from this central area are well filled with glacial moraine and outwash deposits.

Rocks

The main central part of the range is cut in Precambrian gneisses, schists, and granites of rather monotonous appearance. The northern and southern parts of the range are almost completely covered by Paleozoic sedimentary rocks.

On the flanks of the range on both east and west sides, steeply dipping Paleozoic and Mesozoic rocks stand, sometimes in nearly vertical triangular spurs called *flatirons,* and rise abruptly from the plains areas (Photo 2.2). The most obvious rocks are great massive limestones and sandstones, inasmuch as the interbedded shales are usually covered by soil and talus deposits.

At present, there is no important mining activity, and no major mineral resources are known in the Big Horn Range.

Structure

The main part of the Big Horn Range is an elongate uplifted block about 100 by 30 miles in size which has been lifted a maximum of four or five miles above the plains and basin blocks. This means, or is evidenced by the fact, that the Precambrian rocks at 10,000 to 13,000 feet above sea level in the mountain range are some 10,000 to 12,000 feet *below sea level* under the plains and Big Horn Basin. As this block of Precambrian rocks was uplifted, the overlying sedimentary rocks were draped and tilted on either side to form the steeply dipping flatirons previously mentioned. And most of some 15,000 feet of sedimentary rocks have been worn off the uplifted block, which 15,000 feet of material still lies in the basins. On the top of the mountain block the remains of Paleozoic sedimentary rocks lie essentially flat. The major uplifted block is warped and broken into sections. The high central part or block is most uplifted on the east and is overthrust a little in that direction, that is, shoved out slightly over the plains block. The major blocks of the moun-

Photo 2.2. Flatiron erosional effect along the east side of the Big Horn Range near the mouth of Shell Canyon; view on Log 2A. Limestone beds are nearly flat on top of mountain but dip steeply down towards the observer in a giant monocline-type fold.

tains next north and next south are most uplifted on the west. The northwesternmost part of the range up in Montana is broken up into four fault blocks and is usually known as the Pryor Mountains. As a result of these differences in segments, as you drive across the most northern road (14A), the sedimentary rocks are dipping about 20–25 degrees to the east on the east side, but after you cross the range and come down into the Big Horn Basin the rocks are standing vertically. On the southern crossing of the range (U.S. 16), as you start up on the east side you cross vertical sedimentary rocks; but as you come down on the west, the sedimentary rocks are dipping rather gently under the Big Horn Basin.

The Big Horn River flows northward through the Big Horn Basin, then turns northeastward and cuts a canyon through the northern end of the Big Horn Range in Montana. On the eastern side of the range at the mouth of this canyon, the Yellowtail Dam has been built, backing the water up through the canyon to form Big Horn Lake. The area surrounding this lake is a national recreation area, although the dam and most of the lake lies within the Crow Indian Reservation.

BIG HORN BASIN

The Big Horn Basin is a low-lying area west of the majestic Big Horn Range and is surrounded on three sides by mountains. To the south is the relatively low Owl Creek Range, and to the west are the Absaroka and Beartooth ranges. The Big Horn Basin is almost 150 miles long from southeast to northwest and is up to 75 or more miles wide in its central portion, although it narrows to only about 30 miles wide at its open, northern end, where the surface of the Big Horn Basin is continuous with the northern high plains of Montana (Fig. 2.2).

The Basin is a low-lying semiarid desert, quite featureless in its central portion. However, there is considerable relief around the margins of the Big Horn Basin in a belt up to 20 miles wide. This marginal zone has been eroded out of folded Mesozoic rocks so that there are long continuous and zig-zag ridges of bare sandstones, sometimes as much as several hundred feet high. The Mesozoic rocks in this zone have been folded into long narrow anticlines and synclines trending northwest-southeast. The most spectacular of these folds is known as Sheep Mountain (Photo 2.3) near Greybull. Sheep Mountain is a compound anticline with relief of more than a thousand feet.

Many of the other small anticlinal fold structures around the margins of the Big Horn Basin contain oil deposits, and there are several producing oil fields. Perhaps the most accessible and productive of these is known as the Elk Basin Oil Field on the Wyoming-Montana border in the northern part of the Big Horn Basin. This oil field may be reached by a paved road from Powell, Wyoming.

The center of the Big Horn Basin is filled with Tertiary sediments, Paleocene, Eocene, and Oligocene in age. These sediments are

Photo 2.3. Zig-zag sandstone ridges of eroded anticlines and synclines in Mesozoic rocks just north of the Sheep Mountain anticline in the western part of the Big Horn Basin, Wyoming. The nose of the Sheep Mountain anticline lies in the right foreground. (Photo by John S. Shelton, with permission.)

sands and muds formed by the weathering-down of the mountains on either side after Rocky Mountain formation and uplift.

The basin is crossed by a few rivers, along which are narrow belts of irrigated land in distinct contrast to the desertlike character of the rest of the Basin.

Most spectacular and unusual of the rivers is the Big Horn River itself (see Map, Fig. 2.2). This rises as the east-flowing Wind River to the south in the Wind River Basin, but the river turns abruptly northward through a canyon in the Owl Creek Mountains—the Wind River Canyon. At the mouth of this canyon where the river flows into the Big Horn Basin near Thermopolis, it becomes known as the Big Horn River and flows northward along the east side of the Big Horn Basin almost to the Montana line. Here the river turns abruptly northeastward in a steep canyon cut across the northern end of the Big Horn Mountains. It looks as though this river should have continued to flow northwestward up the open flat land of the northern part of the Big Horn Basin right out onto the plains. Why does it turn abruptly through a canyon? In fact, two canyons, one to the south and one to the north? Geologists say that in the middle of Tertiary time, after sediments had been deposited filling the Big Horn Basin well up onto the flanks of the mountains, an ancestral river began to flow and, of course, by the law of gravity it had to flow down a slope. This slope took it across the relatively low, then buried, Owl Creek Mountains to the south and the completely sediment-covered northern end of the Big Horn Mountains to the north, so that the river did not know in those early days that it was flowing across buried uplifted hard rock and would have to, someday, cut canyons to maintain its course. The soft, unconsolidated sediments of the Big Horn Basin were very rapidly eroded away in later Tertiary time, but the river found itself cutting these steep canyons!

OWL CREEK MOUNTAINS

The Owl Creek Mountains separate the Big Horn Basin to the north from the Wind River Basin to the south. The Owl Creek Mountains are moderate in heighth, and their topographic relief is not as great as other ranges in northwestern Wyoming. The mountain trend from east to west is approximately 75 miles in the main part of the range. The range averages only about 15 miles wide. It is sparsely forested and rather semiarid and rocky, certainly not the kind of majestic mountains that we see in the Big Horn, Absaroka, and Wind River ranges (Fig. 2.2).

The range is reasonably inaccessible except to four-wheel drive vehicles, largely because most of the land is quite useless except for rangeland, and there has been no need to put in roads.

The range is dissected by a number of canyons of which the most outstanding is the Wind River Canyon. Most of the rocks in the main part of the range are Paleozoic sedimentary rocks which dip gently toward the north. However, there are several sizeable areas of Precambrian rocks along the south side of the range. These are igneous and metamorphic rocks of various types and are cut by small granite pegmatites. The structure of the range is that of a long, narrow block gently dipping to the north with the Paleozoic sedimentary rocks dipping under younger rocks of the Big Horn Basin. However, the block is steeply uplifted along the south, along irregular faults with one major thrust. The structure suggests that the crustal block of the Big Horn Basin has been shoved southward up over the crustal block of the Wind River

Basin. This overlap has produced the uplift which we call the Owl Creek Mountains. A diagram across this structure is presented in Figure 2.3.

The outstanding feature of the Owl Creek Mountains is the canyon cut from south to north directly across the middle of the range by the Wind River. This canyon provides access for railroad and highway and also presents excellent exposures of all the Paleozoic formations, gently dipping and well exposed at road level over a several mile stretch as outlined in the Trip Guide of U.S. 20.

At the southern margin of the range the Boysen Dam has been erected across the river with its foundations on an exposure of Precambrian rock on the north side of the boundary fault. This dam forms a reservoir southward into the Wind River Basin.

The eastern end of the Owl Creek Mountains merges both with the Big Horn Mountains to the north and with the Casper Arch to the south, which are the major uplifts separating the plains to the east from various basins within the Rocky Mountain Province.

To the west, the Owl Creek structure continues (as the Washakie uplift) for another 75 miles as foothills of the southern Absaroka Mountains, swinging northwestward into Yellowstone Park, perhaps almost as far as the south arm of Yellowstone Lake. This trend is evidenced by scattered and highly-faulted outcrops of Paleozoic sediments and Precambrian metamorphic rocks, largely covered by the prominent volcanic rocks of the Absaroka Range deposited after Rocky Mountain formation. This thick volcanic rock covering makes it difficult to be certain that the structure actually continues; but almost certainly there must be both mountain uplifts and basin structures buried beneath the extensive volcanic complex of the Absaroka Mountains and Yellowstone Park.

Near Dubois the Wind River structure and this western extension of the Owl Creek structure (Washakie uplift) are quite close, Wind River structure to the south of the town and the partly-buried Owl Creek rocks a few miles to the north.

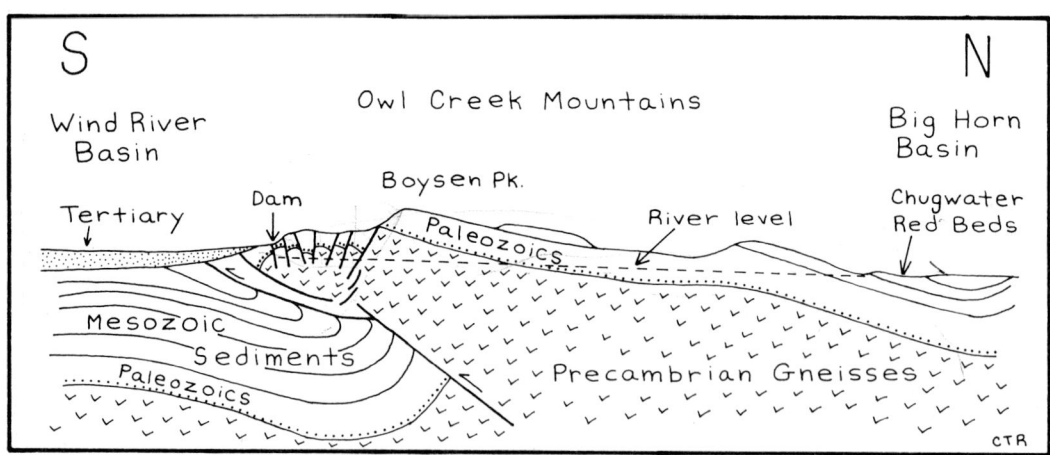

Figure 2.3. Diagrammatic cross section of the Owl Creek Mountains showing how a slab or block of the earth's crust has been pushed southward up and partially over the Wind River Basin along a thrust fault. The vertical scale is not exaggerated.

WIND RIVER BASIN

To the south of the Owl Creek Mountains an east-west trending basin of semiarid to desert land extends at least 100 miles. The Basin is 30 to 50 miles from north to south at its widest but thins to a very narrow valley to the west between the Wind River Range and the Owl Creek Mountains near Dubois. To the east and south there is no clear, obvious boundary to the Wind River Basin but there's a continuation for miles and miles of semiarid terrain with low hills, occasionally with sparse tree clusters, such that most of central Wyoming is very arid and unappealing to the traveler. Actually however, from the south end of the Big Horn uplift to Casper, Wyoming, there is a crustal uplift known as the Casper Arch. At the surface, this brings up Mesozoic rocks from which all Tertiary rocks have been eroded. However, the terrain does not look any different than in the Wind River Basin, as previously mentioned (Fig. 2.4).

To the south the semiarid terrain is the deeply eroded remains of the Sweetwater uplift, a structural uplift some 120 miles from east to west. In the center of this uplift Precambrian rocks have been exposed over a belt 20 to 30 miles wide and are known as the Granite Mountains. However, these are low hills by comparison to neighboring mountain ranges.

Along the north side of this uplift the sedimentary rocks make small uplands known as the Rattlesnake Hills, whereas along the south side of the Sweetwater uplift the sedimentary rocks form the Green Mountains along an east-west fault zone. This Sweetwater uplift, characterized by its low semiarid hills, is a major crustal block, although not expressed as high mountains in the Wyoming sense. This crustal block has been shoved up to the south and is similar in a structural sense to the Wind River or the Big Horn Mountain blocks. All sedimentary rocks were eroded down to the Precambrian metamorphic rocks at a fairly low level.

The Wind River Basin proper, that is, the area south of the Owl Creek Mountains and north of the Sweetwater uplift, is a deep structural basin filled with thick Tertiary sedimentary rocks, these sediments having been formed by the wearing down of the Owl Creek Mountains and Sweetwater uplift ranges.

As in the Big Horn Basin, this basin has some minor fold structures, such as small anticlines, a few miles long. These are especially noteworthy, trending northwest to southeast past Lander, and contain small oil-producing reservoirs.

In the south-central part of the Wind River Basin in the Tertiary sediments, extensive deposits of uranium have been located. The most important uranium district is the Gas Hills region.

A large part of the western half of the Wind River Basin has been set aside as the Wind River Indian Reservation. The Reservation includes a section of the Wind River Mountains as well as the Wind River Basin.

WIND RIVER RANGE

The largest of the Rocky Mountain uplift blocks and the highest mountain range in Wyoming is the Wind River Range. These are probably the most rugged and least developed mountains in the state. Most of the area is virgin forest and has been set aside as various primitive areas within the national forests that make up the range. The central high part of the range is almost 100 miles from northwest to southeast and is not crossed by any road, not even a four-wheel drive trail.

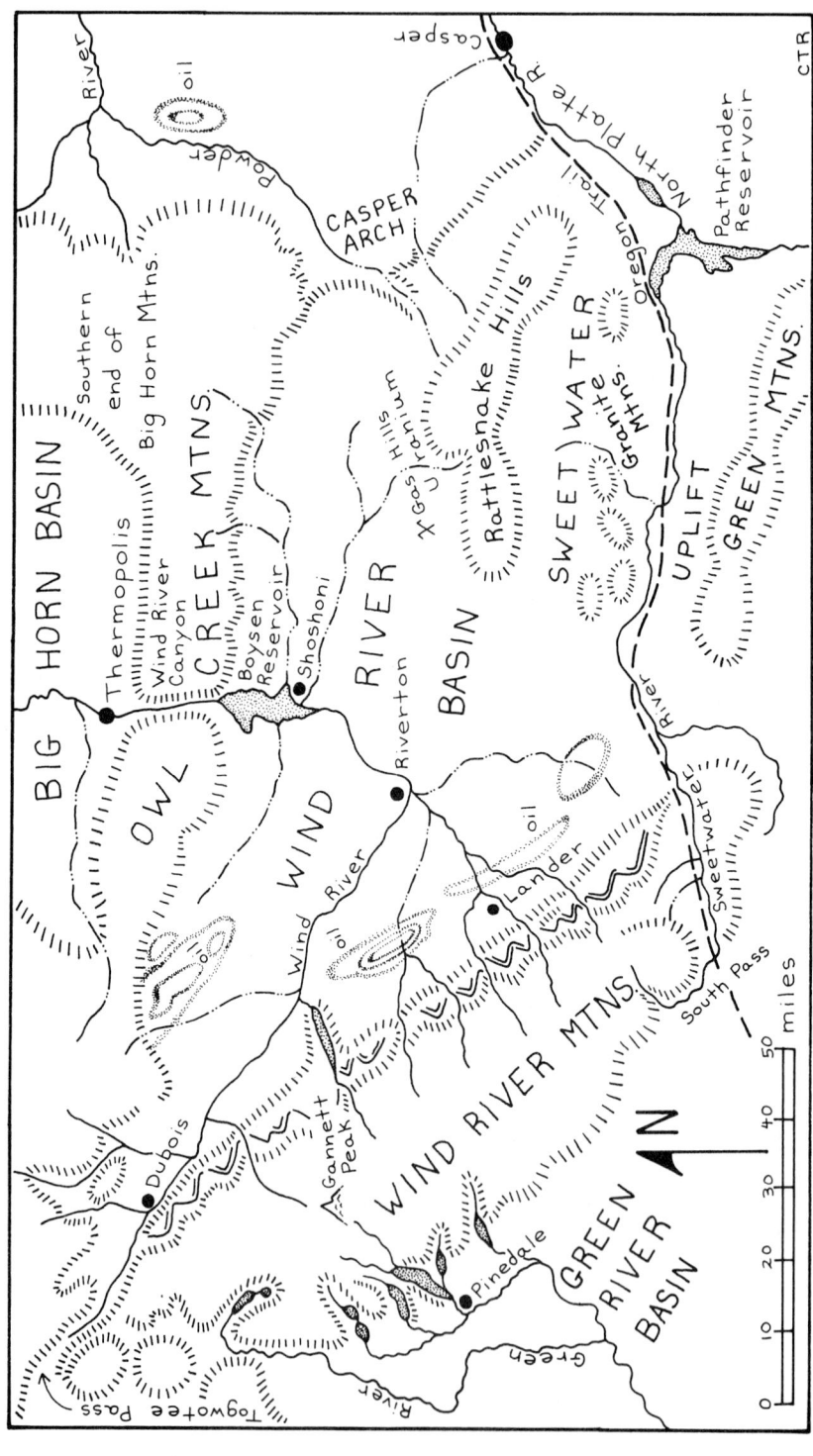

Figure 2.4. (on the left page) Map of the Wind River Basin and Wind River Range and vicinity. (facing page, on right) ERTS photograph of the same area.

General Description

The Wind River Range trends from northwest to southeast and is highest in its northwestern half. It has a maximum length of perhaps 125 miles and an average width of 30 miles. Most of the central part of this range is carved into steep ridges, jagged peaks, and deep canyons. The valleys and lower slopes are in spruce, fir, and pine forests. There are a couple of dozen peaks over 12,000 feet and, perhaps, ten peaks over 13,000 feet. Gannet Peak at 13,804 is the highest point in Wyoming. Fremont Peak is the second highest, 13,745, and was once thought to be the highest point. There are thousands of small lakes in the high alpine part of the range which fill ice-carved basins or cirques, and half a dozen active existing glaciers, especially on the northeast slopes (Fig. 2.4).

In the Wind River Basin elevations range from 5,300 feet at Lander to 6,900 feet at Dubois, whereas on the south side of the range at Pinedale the elevation is 7,175. We see, therefore, that the range rises seven or eight thousand feet above the flat basins on either side. Especially from the west and southwest, the range makes a very impressive sight with its great, snow-covered peaks towering above dark forests on the lower slopes.

Rocks

The main part of the range is composed of Precambrian rocks: granites, granite-gneisses, hornblende and biotite-gneisses, and interbedded schists of various kinds. Throughout most of the range these gneisses present a monotonous similarity.

Along the northeast side of the range Paleozoic sedimentary rocks stand as giant hogbacks showing the whole range of sandstone, limestone, and shale which characterizes the Paleozoic rocks of the Rocky Mountains.

In the very southeast end of the range at fairly low elevations, the schists and slates of the Precambrian rocks are cut by veins of pyrite and quartz carrying gold in limited quantity. These gold-bearing veins were mined during the latter part of the last century and up into the early part of this century near South Pass City and Atlantic City. In this same area just north of Atlantic City a large deposit of Precambrian iron formation has been found recently, and this is now being mined as a major iron ore deposit. The iron is primarily hematite and, in association with metamorphosed sedimentary rocks, something like the Lake Superior iron ores.

Structures

The Precambrian core of the range represents the main part of the uplift block. All along the northeast side for over 100 miles, Paleozoic sedimentary rocks dip gently to the northeast under the Wind River Basin. The average dip is perhaps 15 to 20 degrees. These sedimentary rocks form very prominent hogbacks or dip-slopes, sometimes called flatirons. Rivers coming out of the mountains have cut canyons across these hogbacks so that the sedimentary rocks are very well exposed on the canyon walls. Some of these are accessible from local roads going part way up the mountain flanks.

All along the southwest and south sides of the range, however, Precambrian rocks are exposed right down to the foot of the mountains where they are covered by Tertiary sediments and glacial deposits, with absolutely no trace of sedimentary rocks. It is generally assumed that this is the side of the range that was uplifted along a fault, probably very steeply dipping. (See diagram, Fig. 2.5). In effect, the range seems to be an elongate block that has been uplifted and shoved slightly to the southwest over the northern end of the Green River Basin.

On the northwestern end of the range

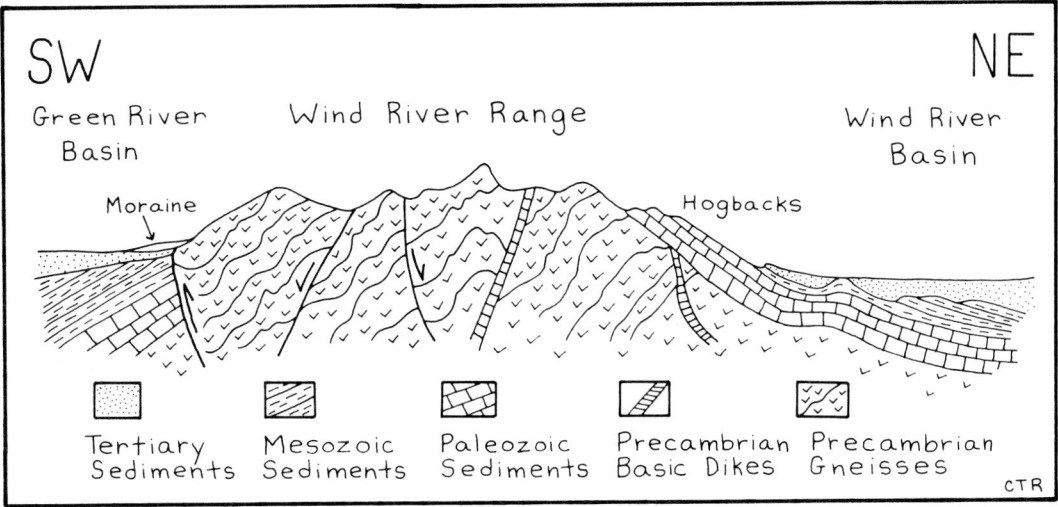

Figure 2.5. Diagrammatic cross section of the Wind River Range showing the limestone hogbacks and flatirons along the northeast or Wind River Basin side and a covered fault along the southwest side of the range.

there is a very complicated structure of highly folded Paleozoic and Mesozoic rocks at the headwaters of the Green River on either side of the deep valley which holds the Green River Lakes. Here, the structures in the sedimentary rocks are adjacent to the structural trend of the Gros Ventre Range. However, the latter range is offset from the Wind River Range and so is not a direct continuation.

Special Features

The crest of the Wind River Range is the Continental Divide with most of the rivers on the east side flowing into the Wind River, and thence into the Missouri system. On the southwest side most of the streams flow out into the Green River, and thus into the Colorado River system. However, there are peculiarities at both ends of the range in the drainage pattern. At the north end a limited amount of the drainage goes due westward into headwaters of the Gros Ventre River, thus into the Snake and Columbia system, so that in the northern end of the range there is a triple divide between these three drainages about halfway between the Green Lakes and Dubois.

At the south end of the range another unusual feature has developed. The headwaters of the Sweetwater River, which flows eastward into the North Platte River, actually come out on the southwest side of the range. This stream flows out of the mountains and then southward, and finally eastward across the very southern end of the range, where there is no longer much true mountain but where there is an exposure of the Precambrian rocks. The divide between the eastflowing Sweetwater River and intermittent streams flowing southwest into the Green River is actually just southwest of the mountains proper. This is known as South Pass, and this pass made it possible for the early settlers to come steadily up the North Platte and the Sweetwater rivers and pass by the end of the Wind River Mountains without really ever climbing any mountains.

They then had access to the Green River Basin. This was the site of the old Oregon Trail and many other trails.

The very low topography on the southeastern extension of the range along the south of the Sweetwater River is an area of sagebrush and a few scattered trees, but it is an area of Precambrian rocks which are a part of the Wind River uplift. Tertiary sedimentary rocks lap up onto these Precambrian rocks on all sides, southwest, south, and southeast. It is in this low, semiarid, hilly country, south of the mountains proper, that gold was found in the early days and where the thriving mining communities South Pass City and Atlantic City were part of the Old West story. Actually, gold was mined here well up into the middle of the twentieth century. These towns are currently being restored by local historical societies as tourist attractions. They are interesting bits of history.

This southeast end of the range is totally different in appearance from the northern part of the range, but it is properly considered part of the Wind River Mountain system from a geologic point of view. Erosion has worn away the Precambrian rocks, perhaps because they are more easily-eroded schists and slates and perhaps, also, because the mineralization partly altered the rocks so that they eroded more easily.

The most spectacular process in determining the present appearance of the Wind River Mountains, both along their crest and along their foothills, has been glaciation. Even today, a half dozen or so small glaciers exist along the highest part in the northern half of the mountain range, mainly on the northeast side near Gannet Peak. These glaciers are accessible by hiking trails from either side of the range, although, perhaps, Pinedale, is the center of the trail access. The high mountains have been carved by ice in recent geologic time with deep, U-shaped valleys running off either side of the Continental Divide with spectacular, well-developed cirque basins, most of which contain a few small tarn lakes with steep jagged ridges on three sides. Maximum glaciation occurred perhaps ten to fifteen thousand years ago.

The major valleys leading out of the mountains are carved U-shaped way out to the edge of the range and, characteristically, are a half mile wide with very steep canyon walls at least 2,000 feet high.

At the maximum extension of glaciation ice tongues extended out onto the basin surfaces, both east and west of the range, with several glaciers extending out into the Wind River Basin towards the Wind River itself and many ice tongues extending out into the north end of the Green River Basin. This is especially true in the northern half of the Wind River Range, with ice tongues also extending northward and northwestward. As a result of this, very extensive moraine deposits exist out beyond the mountain front on the north, west, and east sides. These moraines are not only terminal, but lateral, and serve as natural dams on long valleys out beyond the mountain front itself, such that a number of big, long lakes have formed behind these morainal dams: particularly, Fremont Lake, Half-Moon Lake, the New Fork Lakes, and the Green River Lakes along the west side. On the east side, most important is Bull Lake whose heighth has been increased somewhat by a man-made dam, adding to the natural moraine dam. Around the ends and sides of all these lakes are parallel ridges or recessional moraines showing successive stands of the ice. Large lateral moraines slope up onto the rocks of the mountain mass itself. At the upper end of Fremont

Lake, for example, this lateral moraine is 1,500 feet above the lake level. A scenic road runs for 20 miles from Pinedale up this lateral moraine from near lake level at Pinedale to 1,500 feet above lake level, where the lateral moraine is against granite gneiss. Consequently, this is one of the outstanding displays of terminal and lateral moraines to be seen anywhere in the Rocky Mountains! Some of the side trips from Pinedale are, therefore, well worth taking to examine these features as described in the Trip Guides.

Among all the mountains in the Middle Rockies, the Wind River Range is the most outstanding for backpacking and hiking, without the mountaineering-experience needed in the Teton Range. An extensive trail system is maintained back into the wilderness areas of the Wind River Mountains with many campsites under the control of the Forest Service. In a general way, the many peaks are not too difficult to scale; the hiking trails are long and require overnight camping for several days, since the access roads penetrate only a very short distance into the lower parts of the range. An area of spectacular valleys and great peaks and rock ridges lies above timberline at 10,000 feet with peaks up over 13,000 feet and thousands of small lakes at and above timberline in the cirque basins.

ABSAROKA MOUNTAINS

The Absaroka Mountains are a Range of high, impressive looking mountains lying east of Yellowstone National Park, although part of the range lies within the eastern boundaries of the Park. The range also extends south of Yellowstone to merge with the Owl Creek Mountains. The Absaroka Range is an impressive sight from over in Yellowstone Park, from up on the Beartooth Plateau looking southward, from out in the Big Horn Basin looking westward, or along the south side from Togwotee Pass.

General Description

The Absaroka Mountains are characterized by high peaks and steep ridges separated by broad U-shaped valleys. In the northern part of the range there are essentially no flat top surfaces; two or three peaks rise slightly above 12,000 feet, of which Trout Peak is the highest at 12,259 feet. The southern part of the range is the most extensive and most primitive and, in part, is a very high plateau above timberline, dissected by deep canyons. Here are several peaks over 12,000; the highest is Frank's Peak, 13,140 feet.

In the entire Absaroka Range there are relatively few lakes up in the high mountains, that is, very few tarn lakes in the cirque basins. This is in abrupt contrast to the thousands of lakes in the Wind River Range and the hundreds of lakes in the Beartooth Mountains above timberline. The reason for this difference is the character of the rocks in the Absaroka Mountains. The rocks are more easily eroded, more fractured, and more porous; consequently, lake basins were not scooped out. Instead, more sloping valleys were developed by ice erosion.

The range is separated into a northern and southern division by the north fork of the Shoshone River which cuts across the range somewhat north of its actual center. The valley of this river is followed by the main highway from Cody to the east entrance of Yellowstone National Park.

In general, the valleys are well timbered, and the rocky ridges are various shades of dark brown, usually with some snow drifts on the higher peaks throughout the summer (Photo 2.4).

Rocks

The Absaroka Range is composed largely of a great thickness of very extensive volcanic rocks, largely the rocks made of fragments which we call pyroclastic rocks. These are andesitic in composition with some basalt lava flow sequences. These volcanic rocks are of Eocene Age (approximately 44-49 million years) and make up what is called the Absaroka Volcanic Field (see Fig. 2.6). This field covers 9,000 square miles including not only the Absaroka Range, but the southwestern part of the Beartooth uplift and the northern half of the Gallatin Range in Montana. To the south this volcanic field extends down abruptly to the western end of the Wind River Basin, where the volcanic rocks cover the older, sedimentary rocks of the Owl Creek Mountain uplift.

These volcanic rocks have, today, a total thickness in excess of 10,000 feet, but much has been worn away by erosion. Some of the original volcanoes were probably at least 5,000 feet higher than any present mountain.

These pyroclastic volcanic rocks along with some lavas were thrown out from a considerable number of both large and small volcanic centers. There were at least a dozen such centers, and several of those had many subcenters (Fig. 2.6). We can picture during

Photo 2.4. View over the central Absaroka Range from near Sunlight Peak. Note typical rocky cliffs and talus covered slopes.

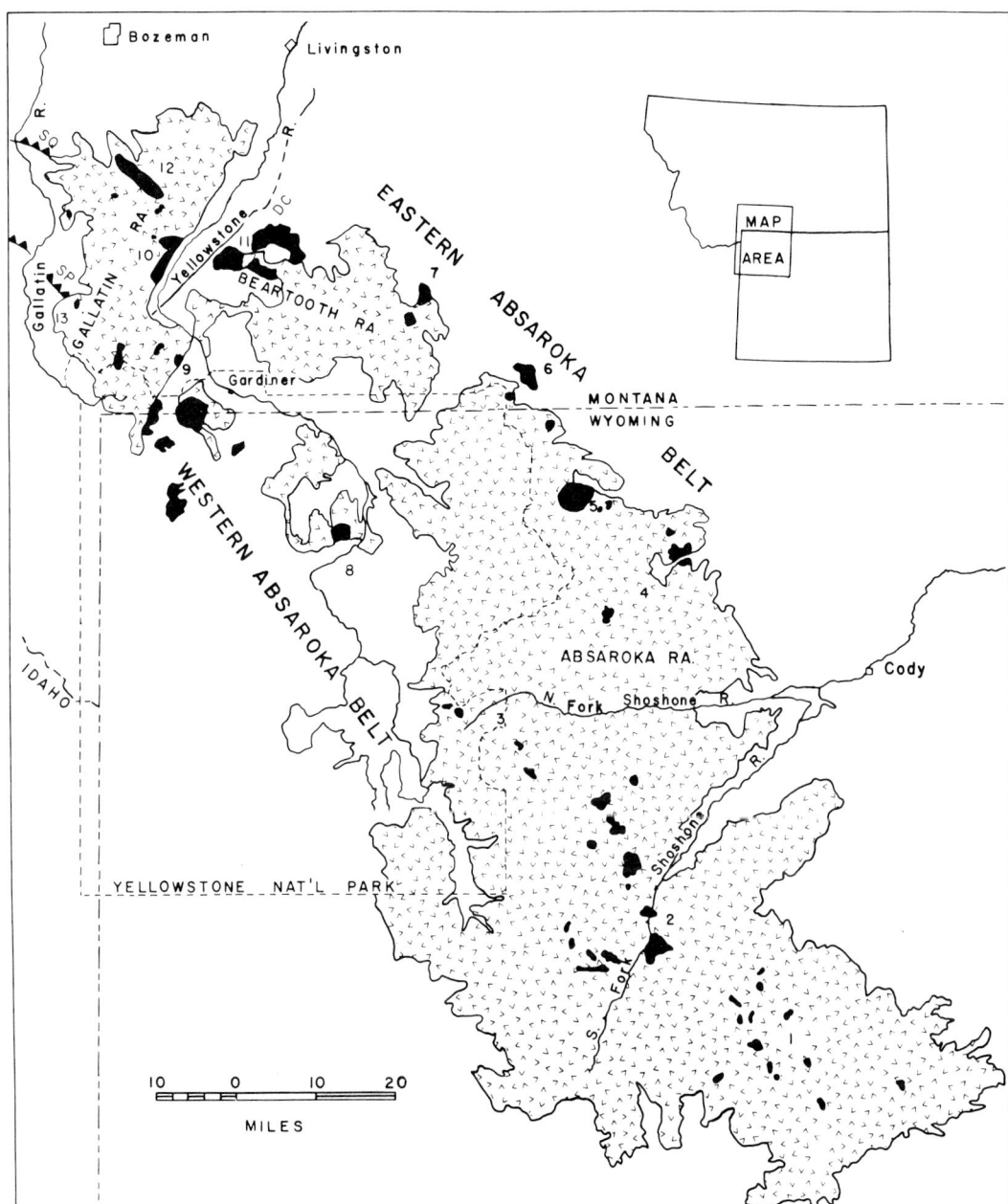

Figure 2.6. Geologic map of the Absaroka-Gallatin Volcanic Field. (Chadwick, R. A., 1970, Geol. Soc. America Bull., p. 268). V pattern = Eocene-Oligocene volcanics; black = principal vent complexes and intrusives in and between eruptive centers. Principal recognized eruptive centers are aligned along two subparallel belts and are numbered as follows: *Eastern Absaroka belt:* (4) Sunlight; (5) Hurricane Mesa; (6) Cooke City; (7) Independence; (10) Point of Rocks; (11) Emigrant Peak; (12) Northern Gallatin Range dike swarm. *Western Absaroka belt:* (1) Kirwin; (2) Ishawooa; (3) Sylvan Pass; (8) Mt. Washburn; (9) Electric Peak; (13) Porcupine Creek.

Eocene time large clusters of high volcanic cones of various ages and shapes separated by broad, lowland areas, valleys or basins, with very poor stream drainage. As lavas and fragmental rocks were erupted from one or more centers, material slid downward and was washed by streams out into these lowland basins where it was redeposited as fragments of various sizes. From the character of fossil leaves found in the fine-grained volcanic tuffs we postulate a warm, moist climate during the volcanic period. In such areas today, in Central America, the Andes, and East Indies, following extensive eruptions, loose fragmented materials and ash become saturated in rainy periods and begin to slide in mud flows. In Indonesia and Ecuador such mud flows have been observed to travel 50 miles down valleys away from the volcanoes. The character of the Absaroka volcanic material suggests that this mechanism was very common (Photo 2.5). The broad, lowland basins gradually became filled in with these mud flow deposits. Forests would grow up and flourish for hundreds of years, and then a tremendous mud flow would sweep down into a lowland forest, smashing the trees and burying everything under tens of feet of debris.

There were two major environments of deposition of these volcanic rocks: the one environment was in the cluster of volcanoes where fragmental material and lava flows were extruded and helped build up the vol-

Photo 2.5. Coarse bouldery volcanic breccia that is very common in the Absaroka Volcanic Field. This is probably a mud flow-type breccia.

canic peaks; the other environment of volcanic deposition were the basins or lowlands where the broken, explosive debris was washed down from the volcanoes by streams and mud flows and deposited in these basins. Geologists speak of the first environment as the "Vent Facies," and the second environment, as the "Alluvial Facies."

The actual rocks in the vent areas are made up of angular fragments of volcanic material cemented together in a coarse-grained rock called volcanic breccia. These rocks may be interlayered with scattered lava flows, but in many areas the layering is not very obvious or is very irregular. On the other hand, in the so-called alluvial areas, where material has been deposited after being moved by water, the fragments in the rocks were not quite so angular, and the layering of the units becomes somewhat more regular. Vent area rocks can be seen on the high cliffs above Cooke City and at Sylvan Pass. An excellent exposure of the alluvial materials, stream and mud flow deposits, are exposed along much of the length of the Cody to East Entrance road and along Soda Butte Creek in Yellowstone Park proper, as will be mentioned in the Trip Guides.

In the deeply eroded clusters of old volcanoes many small intrusive masses and vent fillings and hundreds of vertical dikes are common (Photo 2.6). These are well seen near Sylvan Pass and elsewhere as men-

Photo 2.6. Dikes cutting volcanic breccia and overlying lava flows in a vent area in the high part of the Absaroka Range, Wyoming.

tioned in the Trip Guides. These major eroded volcanic centers are outlined on the map (Fig. 2.6).

None of the old volcanoes really stand today as great volcanic cones. They have been deeply eroded and are now simply part of the overall mountain range. They cannot be recognized by their shape, only by the difference in rock types.

Around the margin of the Absaroka Range, especially on the northeast and south sides, older rocks which were buried by the volcanic materials in the range are now exposed. These areas are probably best classified as foothills of the Absaroka Mountains. Along the east and south there are various Paleozoic sedimentary rocks, sometimes folded and faulted complexly. These are best described in the Trip Guides. Along the north and northwest side of the range Precambrian rocks immediately underlie the volcanic materials. This is part of the Beartooth Plateau and the Gallatin Range, which was largely buried by this volcanic material.

The age of these volcanic rocks has been determined by potassium argon isotope methods as ranging from 49 million for the start of volcanism, to about 44 million years ago for the end of this period of volcanic activity. However, the age of this volcanic activity has also been verified by a careful study of fossil leaves found in a number of localities. One hundred fifty species or so of trees and plants have been identified, and these all indicate a Middle Eocene Age by the relative dating techniques of correlating with other parts of the world.

Moderately small ore deposits are found associated with perhaps a half dozen of the major volcanic centers. These represent mineral matter brought in by hot solutions as the very last phase of volcanic activity in the deep root area of the old volcanoes. The 45 million years of erosion since volcanic activity has removed the upper part of the old volcanoes, and these metallic mineral deposits are now exposed. The ores are primarily sulphide minerals of copper, lead, and silver. There has been a small amount of successful mining for gold and silver in the Cooke City area, but elsewhere it has been mostly prospecting. A few ore bodies do seem to have possibilities for the future, although they are low grade. In the northern Absaroka Range these ores are found not only in Cooke City, but also around the old Sunlight volcano. In the southern Absarokas such ore deposits are known near the headwaters of the Wood River at Kirwin, where a copper-molybdenum deposit is under development, and near the headwaters of the south fork of the Shoshone River at Ishawooa. On the western Beartooth Plateau, associated with volcanic rocks, there are ore deposits at the head of the Boulder River, in the Independence area, and on the east side of the Yellowstone Valley near Emigrant Gulch.

Structures

Structures in the volcanic rocks are primarily the intrusive dikes and small plugs associated with the root areas of the old volcanoes as previously mentioned. Some dips in the pyroclastic rocks and lavas may represent outward dipping layers of old worn-down volcanoes.

Other structures are folds and uplifts produced during the period of Rocky Mountain formation before the volcanic rocks were erupted. These structures are partially buried.

A major uplift trending to the northwest may be an extension of the Beartooth Block which cuts across the northern part of the Gallatin and Madison ranges. This is largely buried in the Gallatin Range.

The Beartooth Block from Cooke City to near Gardiner dips gently southward, and these dipping rocks are buried by the volcanics.

Along the south side of the Absarokas the volcanic rocks bury a western extension of the Owl Creek uplift (the Washakie uplift). In the Owl Creek Mountains proper this uplift dips gently under the Big Horn Basin. Such a gentle northeastward dip under the southern Absarokas may be present but completely buried. Between this partially buried Owl Creek uplift and the partially buried Beartooth uplift on the north is the main part of the Absaroka Range. Here, a shallow basin may be completely buried and unknown.

Since the period of volcanism there has been some faulting and minor folding of the volcanic rocks, although the general attitude of most of the beds of stream and mud deposits in the alluvial volcanic areas is still nearly horizontal.

Special Features

One of the most exciting aspects of the alluvial fragmental volcanic rocks is the presence of fossil forests buried in mud flow deposits and well-preserved fossil leaves buried in volcanic ash fall deposits. There are two regions where such buried forests occur in great profusion. One is in northeastern Yellowstone Park along the south side of the Lamar River Valley in an area called "The Fossil Forest" which is further described in the Yellowstone section. However, fossil forests are found in many of the nearby ridges in that part of Yellowstone. The other area of extensive fossil forests lies just northeast of Yellowstone in the Gallatin Range, best developed at the head of the Tom Miner Basin extending into the northeast corner of the Park.

In both areas twenty or thirty successive fossil forests are buried one above another. As a forest grew up after a volcanic eruption it came to full size in perhaps a 2,000-year period; then, in a particularly violent period of eruption, mud flows swept down from the high volcanoes and buried the forest-covered basin, smashing small trees and burying bigger trees as they stood, up to ten or twenty feet above their base. This happened again and again to give the succession of fossil forests, exposed today on 2,000-foot-high mountainsides.

Another extremely interesting structure which lies between the Absaroka volcanic rocks proper and the Big Horn Basin is an anticline known as Rattlesnake Mountain which has a gentle dip towards Cody, but a very steep faulted side toward the volcanics. The Shoshone River has cut a canyon across this fold and it is crossed on the highway leading from Cody through the Absaroka Mountains to the east entrance. This structure is really a small block which has been tilted on a vertical fault in the Precambrian rocks, draping the Paleozoic rocks over it. It is further described in the Trip Guide, Cody to East Entrance.

Along the boundary between the Beartooth Range to the north and the Absaroka Mountains to the south, from the Big Horn Basin to Cooke City, Paleozoic rocks are exposed along the Clarks Fork River, starting with the spectacular Clarks Fork Canyon at the edge of the Big Horn Basin, and following westward up the Clarks Fork River and its numerous tributaries such as Sunlight Creek. Here Paleozoic rocks and volcanic rocks are found together and there are many interesting relationships described later as a special trip off the main highway (Log 5A).

In this vicinity are the remains of an extremely unusual geologic feature, the Heart Mountain Gravity Fault, as it is called by geologists. Great blocks of limestone up to 3,000-feet thick and several miles long seem to have moved horizontally over the underlying rocks just before volcanic activity began. Why? Nobody knows, and exactly how is not fully understood, but the evidence that such movement took place is quite dramatic at a number of places along the Clarks Fork Valley, from Cooke City all the way to the Sunlight Basin area, and up Dead Indian Hill. Another of these blocks moved out over the lower Eocene rocks in the Big Horn Basin, and its eroded remnant sits out there as Heart Mountain. This mountain serves as a challenge to geologists to try to understand the kinds of things that have not happened in historic times, and which are therefore difficult to imagine. (You may be glad to know that we geologists do not have all the explanations for the earth events of the past, even though we sometimes speak too authoritatively!)

BEARTOOTH MOUNTAINS

The Beartooth Range is the largest and highest mountain mass in the Middle Rockies and is located in southwestern Montana and northwestern Wyoming (Map, Fig. 2.7). The range is about 80 miles long with a northwest-southeast trend, and is 30 miles wide in its eastern segment and nearly 50 miles wide in the west. It is a very rugged range with hundreds of square miles of wilderness area, accessible only by pack and foot trails. Only one road crosses the range, the famous Red Lodge-Cooke City Highway across the southeast end of the mountains. This is one of the most spectacular mountain highways in the country winding for almost a dozen miles above 10,000 feet.

General Description

The Beartooth Mountains are characterized by high alpine topography, much of it above timberline. Granite Peak at 12,799 feet is the highest point in Montana. The eastern part of the Beartooth uplift is a dissected plateau, with gently rolling relief between 10,000 and 12,000 feet; this is a tundra-covered terrain with areas of permafrost. Deep canyons have been cut into this surface, first by streams and then by glaciers, to form U-shaped valleys 3,000 to 4,000 feet deep (Photo 2.7). At the head of a few of these canyons small cliff glaciers still remain, but they are inaccessible and out of sight from any road. One such small glacier north of Cooke City can be reached in a one-day hiking or horseback trip. Much of the scenery of the Beartooth Plateau is the result of glacial erosion. Steep-walled cirque basins indent the plateau at the heads of hanging valleys and the U-shaped canyons, such as that of Rock Creek. In these cirque basins and valleys are dozens of small lakes in ice-carved basins; several are visible along the Red Lodge-Cooke City Highway.

The northwestern segment, or North Snowy Block, of the range is a wild mountainous area without the upland plateau character. A southwestern part, the South Snowy Block, is similar and is separated from the northwestern unit by a fault zone to be described later. These western segments are the most inaccessible and least known; these areas are the habitat of most of the remaining grizzly bears in the 48 conterminous states. Valleys are deeply forested, while the rocky ridges and peaks stand high above timberline. The timberline is at about 9,500 feet on north-facing slopes, while scattered patches of scrub trees may be found to almost 10,000 feet on south-facing and otherwise protected slopes.

The Beartooth Range rises abruptly, without foothills, above the Big Horn Basin to the east and above the high plains to the north and northeast. The average elevation at the foot of the range is about 5,000 feet above sea level, and the mountains rise immediately to 9,500 or 10,000 feet before leveling out to the plateau surface, which

Photo 2.7. High Beartooth Mountains with a deep U-shaped valley as seen from the Red Lodge-Cooke City Highway, Log 5. Note rolling plateaulike surface on the right, above timberline.

then slopes gradually upward to several peaks over 12,000 feet.

The boundary of the Beartooth uplift is less obvious to the south, inasmuch as the Absaroka Mountains are more or less continuous, especially near Cooke City. Along the southeast, this boundary is the valley of the Clarks Fork River. West of Cooke City the mountains merge gradually into the Yellowstone Plateau. At the southwest corner and north, along the west side, the Beartooth uplift is delimited by the wide valley of the Yellowstone River from Gardiner to Livingston. Along the northern 30 miles or so of this valley, the mountains rise abruptly above the valley with an average 6,000 feet of relief to form a majestic range of sharp peaks.

Rocks

Most of the Beartooth Range is composed of Precambrian igneous and metamorphic rocks: specifically, granites, gneisses, and schists which have been dated by *radiogenic methods* at 2 1/2 to 3 billion years old. The lighter-colored rocks contain feldspars and quartz, while the darker rocks have biotite mica or hornblende. Other rock types are present in small quantities.

This whole complex of Precambrian rocks is cut by a system of long, dark-colored dikes of basalt or fine-grained gabbro of three dif-

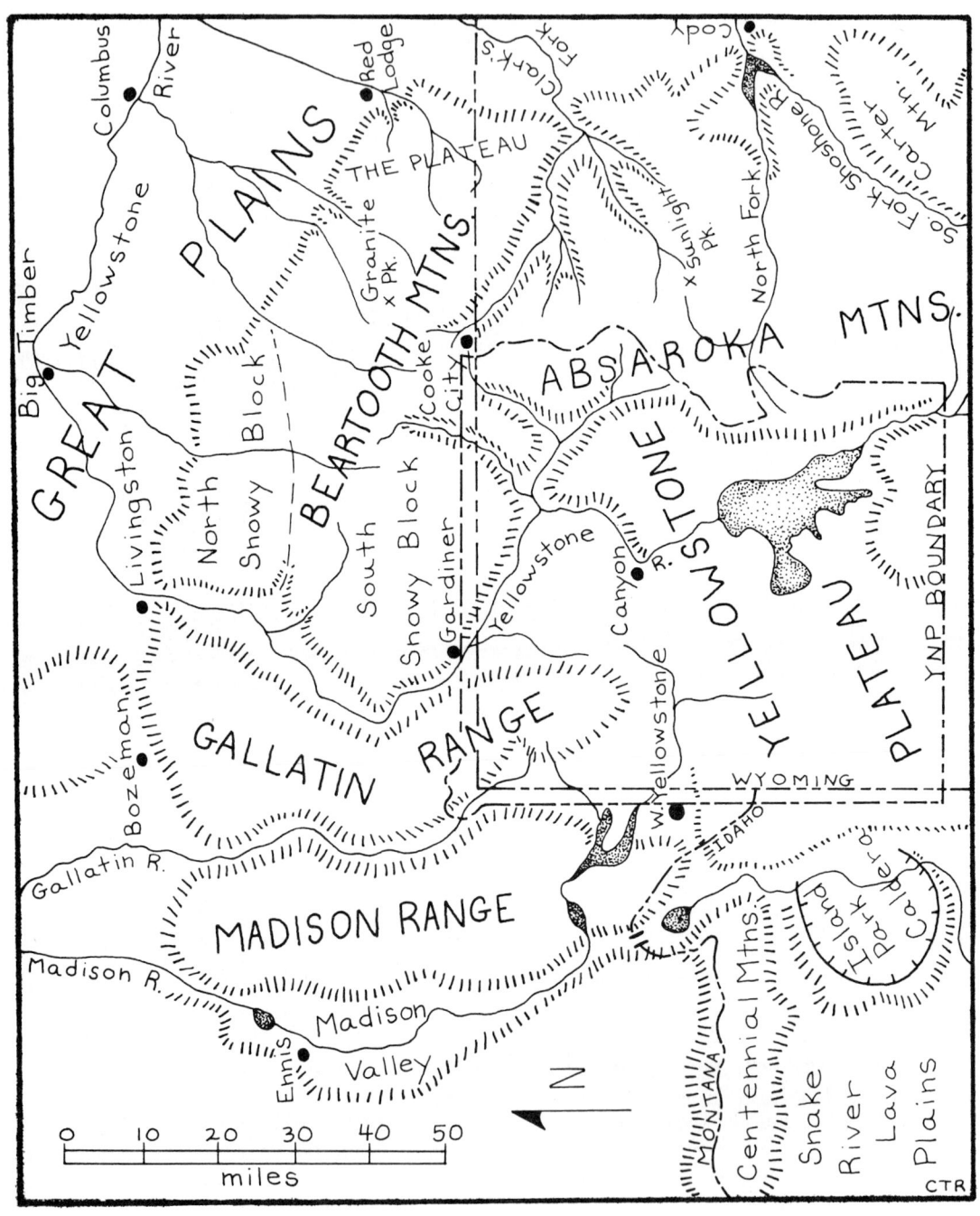

Figure 2.7. (on left page) Map of the Beartooth Mountains, Gallatin and Madison ranges, northern Absaroka Mountains and the Yellowstone Plateau. (facing page, on right) ERTS photograph of the same area.

ferent ages. Some of the dikes can be traced for tens of miles across the plateau. The dikes average in width from 20 to over 100 feet. Several of these dikes can be seen along the Cooke City Highway (Photo 2.8).

Around the margins of the Beartooth uplift, Paleozoic sedimentary rocks, most commonly limestones, are present, generally standing in near vertical palisades. Such palisades are well exposed near Red Lodge, at the mouth of the Clarks Fork Canyon to the southeast, and in the Devil's Slide, north of Gardiner. Along the south central part of the range, the same sedimentary rocks have a very gentle dip beneath the volcanic rocks of the Absaroka Mountains.

A few areas of essentially flat-lying sedimentary rocks occur on top of the Beartooth Range as erosional remnants of the strata that covered the entire area before the mountains were uplifted. The most prominent of these erosional outliers is Beartooth Butte.

The South Snowy Block has a considerable covering of Tertiary volcanic rocks and associated intrusive igneous rocks which are part of the Absaroka Volcanic Field. These volcanic rocks lie on top of the Precambrian granites and gneisses with some Cambrian sedimentary rocks. These relationships are well exposed in the Independence area at the head of the Boulder River.

An unusual complex of coarse-grained,

Photo 2.8. Beartooth Plateau surface just below timberline. Surface rises in a series of steps to a high summit erosion surface. Note dark-colored basalt dike near center of picture cutting across ice-smoothed outcrops of whitish granite gneiss. On Log 5.

dark-colored, igneous rocks rich in pyroxene, olivine, and plagioclase feldspar occurs within the northern part of the range and is known as the Stillwater Ultramafic Complex. Chrome ore has been mined in these rocks.

The youngest rocks within the Beartooth Mountains are dikes and irregular masses of igneous rocks of *monzonite porphyry* composition. These rocks were intruded at about the time the Beartooth Mountains were being uplifted at the end of Cretaceous time. These porphyries have large feldspar crystals in a grayish groundmass, and are well exposed along the switchbacks of the Red Lodge-Cooke City highway above Rock Creek.

Mineral Resources

At the present time there is no mining within the mountains, but a number of metals have been mined or are being prospected for the future. Especially noteworthy are the chrome (chromite) deposits associated with the Stillwater Complex. This complex also contains rather extensive, although low grade, masses of copper-nickel and platinum ores which have been carefully explored over the last dozen years by several major mining companies. These are a valuable reserve for the future and will be discussed later.

In several localities in the range, gold has been mined in the past. These include the Independence area at the head of the Boulder River where a thriving mining town existed at the turn of the century; the Emigrant Gulch area east of the Yellowstone Valley; and the Jardine district about 5 miles from Gardiner. Mines in this latter district were producing gold and tungsten until the mill burned down in the 1930s. At Cooke City both gold and silver have been mined, but this ore is associated with the volcanic rocks of the Absaroka Range and will be discussed later.

Structures

The Beartooth uplift is a compound block where the upward movement has been along vertical or steep thrust faults. This is another of the large blocks of basement complex shoved up above the Big Horn Basin and Great Plains blocks. The differential uplift between the top of the Beartooth block and the level of the Precambrian rocks under the Big Horn Basin is at least 25,000 feet. Paleozoic and Mesozoic sedimentary rocks once completely covered this part of the crust. These strata were broken as the basement block rose and became "draped" over the faulted margins of the block during the Rocky Mountain orogeny about 70,000,000 years ago. The sedimentary rocks have been almost completely eroded away from the top of the block but remain as near vertical palisades around the margins of the uplift (Fig. 2.8).

The near vertical faults and palisades of sedimentary rocks are especially noteworthy along the northern and eastern fronts of the range. At the corners of the block, where faults in different directions intersect, the structures are quite complex. This is seen at Red Lodge, the northeast corner, where the uplifted block has spread laterally on thrust faults and split on normal faults into several units which have moved by different amounts. At the southeastern corner the relatively simple intersection of the north-south fault on the east and the northwest-southeast trending faults on the south have elevated the Beartooth Plateau with a rectangular corner above the Big Horn Basin and the Clarks Fork Valley. As a result spectacular structure in the sedimentary rocks can be seen at the mouth of the Clarks Fork Canyon. Also, the sedimentary layers are

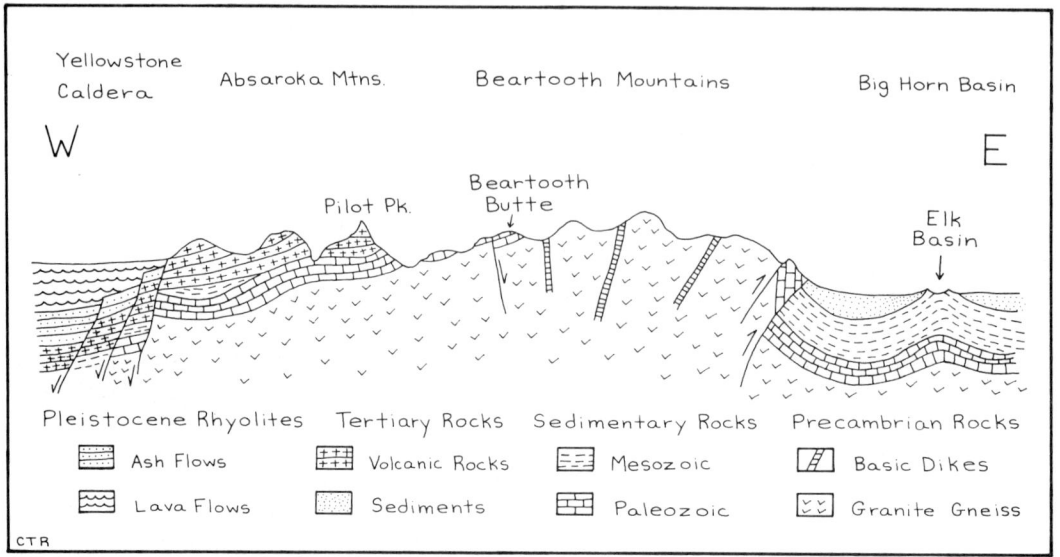

Figure 2.8. Diagrammatic cross section from the Big Horn Basin across the Beartooth Mountain Block and the Absaroka Mountains to Yellowstone, vertical scale is exaggerated. (Modified after E. Dorf).

folded into several large faulted anticlines for a dozen miles to the south. Most noteworthy of these is Rattlesnake Mountain, just west of Cody, Wyoming.

At the northwestern corner the structure is also complex. The Yellowstone River cuts a comparatively narrow canyon through a faulted, anticlinal structure a few miles south of Livingston. This structure in the sedimentary rocks extends for several miles to the west. South of this corner along the west side of the North Snowy Block, the mountains rise abruptly above the wide Yellowstone Valley. A vertical fault and tilted sedimentary rocks are almost completely covered by thick river alluvium in the valley.

Along most of the southern side of the Beartooth Mountains, the uplift is more gradual, and the Precambrian metamorphic rocks and Paleozoic sedimentary rocks dip gently under Absaroka volcanic rocks deposited after the uplift. This is the situation along the Clarks Fork Valley and into the Cooke City area (Photo 2.9 and Fig. 2.8).

The North Snowy Block of the Beartooth Range is separated by an east-west fault zone, the so-called Mill Creek Fault, which cuts diagonally across the range. This zone apparently controlled the rise of magma along its western end, as many bodies of Eocene igneous rocks occur here in the Emigrant Gulch and Mill Creek areas.

Special Features

During the Ice Age the Beartooth Plateau must have been covered by a continuous sheet of ice with only a few high peaks projecting above the ice. From this continental-type ice sheet, tonguelike glaciers extended down all main valleys, carving them into the present U-shaped canyons as typified by Rock Creek. These valley glaciers at the maximum ice advance extended a short distance out onto the plains beyond the mountain front. The evidence for this is the

Photo 2.9. View Across the Clarks Fork Valley to Hurricane Mesa just south of Beartooth Butte, Wyoming. Foreground outcrops are Precambrian granite gneiss overlain, just beyond the valley bottom, by nearly flat Cambrian sediments. The long horizontal white ledge is a 100 ft. cliff of Pilgrim limestone. Absaroka volcanic rocks lie above this to the skyline. Compare to cross section of Figure 2.8.

presence of extensive lateral and terminal moraines which today are great piles and ridges of boulders. Flat outwash deposits of smaller boulders and cobbles extend for miles downstream from the moraines.

Moraines are well developed north of the mountains in the valleys of the Stillwater River and the East and West Rosebud Creeks. A terminal moraine system also exists just east of the mouth of Clarks Fork Canyon, on the edge of the Big Horn Basin. Outwash gravels are especially well developed for miles beyond these latter moraines, and 10 or 20 square miles of *terrace* is covered by boulders and gravel in an area northwest of the Clarks Fork River.

Three different ice advances have been recognized in the Middle Rockies during the Ice Age or Pleistocene Epoch. Associated with the melting and retreat of each of these glacial advances, large quantities of melt water carried boulders and pebbles from the ice, depositing them as outwash sheets in valleys many miles beyond the mountains. During the interglacial periods streams continued to cut their valleys deeper, but the extensive boulder-covered surfaces resisted erosion. As a result, new valleys were formed leaving the old boulder and gravel covered surfaces as benches, or terraces, above the new stream valleys. This has happened three times so that today there are bench remnants at three different levels, each associated with one of the ice advances. These are well developed in the Red Lodge area and also down near Cody, Wyoming.

GALLATIN AND MADISON RANGES

A mountainous area lies to the northwest of Yellowstone National Park about 30 miles wide on the south, and 50 miles wide on the north. The eastern part of this region is the Gallatin Range, about 50 miles from north to south; and the western part of this mountain area is the Madison Range, about 70 miles from north to south. These are mountains of moderate height rising to elevations between 10,000 and 11,000 feet, with the highest peak of 11,286 in the Madison Range. There is no major topographic separation between the two ranges. The division is arbitrarily set along the Gallatin River which flows northward from the northwest corner of Yellowstone National Park. Along this river is Highway 191 leading from West Yellowstone to Bozeman. Other than this road and a few side roads, most of this mountain area is inaccessible to automobile traffic. Several areas in the range have been set aside as primitive areas.

The mountains are bordered on the east by the broad valley of the Yellowstone River from Gardiner to Livingston, and on the west by the very wide valley of the Madison River leading north past Ennis (Fig. 2.7).

Rocks

These ranges include a wide variety of rock types. There are Precambrian granites and gneisses, Paleozoic and Mesozoic sedimentary rocks, and volcanic rocks of several periods. These are similar to the rocks we have seen in other ranges where they are much better exposed than here, for example, in the Wind River Canyon. No significant mineral deposits of economic importance are being mined here at the present time.

Structures

This mountainous area has rather complex structural relationships. The major folds and faults formed during the Rocky Mountain uplift cut across the ranges with a northwest to southeast trend, so that neither range is a separate structural unit.

A major belt of Precambrian rocks, bordered by faults, cuts across the northern part of the region and may be a northwestern extension of the Beartooth uplift to the east. The northern two-thirds of the Gallatin Range is completely buried under volcanic rocks of the Absaroka Volcanic Field so that structures cannot be traced from the northern Madison Range to the Beartooth Range.

The southern end of the Gallatin Range extends into northwestern Yellowstone Park. Here are Precambrian and Paleozoic rocks cut by many medium-size Tertiary intrusive rocks. Some of these intrusive areas were source areas for some of the Eocene Absaroka volcanics. This southern end of the Gallatin Range is a fairly impressive landmark in northern and northeastern Yellowstone Park, climaxed by Electric Peak.

The Madison Range extends southward from its Precambrian northern part with a long, central area composed mainly of Mesozoic rocks in a very broad, complex, synclinal fold. These structures, again, have a northwest-southeast trend.

The southern end and highest part of the Madison Range is, again, a high block of Precambrian rocks with a limited border of Paleozoic and Mesozoic rocks along the northeast and southern ends. Most of this Precambrian area lies due west of Yellowstone Park.

Faulting was renewed in this area long after the period of Rocky Mountain uplift. Major block faults occurred in middle to late Tertiary time, and several have continued active to the present. The most impressive of these is the Madison Fault which uplifts the entire Madison Range along its west side. East of this fault the Madison Range rises abruptly above the wide Madison Valley as a very impressive mountain range (Photo 2.10).

There is a somewhat similar, but shorter, fault along the east side of the Yellowstone Valley which is the western edge of the Beartooth uplift. Both Madison and Yellowstone valleys have been dropped down by this faulting and are partially filled with Miocene and Pliocene sediments, visible in the Yellowstone Valley.

Special Features

The Madison River rises in Yellowstone Park, flows westward north of the town of West Yellowstone, and then cuts a canyon across the southern end of the Madison Range. The river then comes out in a broad down-faulted valley (the Madison Valley) and flows northward for twenty or thirty miles. Then it again cuts a small canyon across the northern end of the Precambrian structure of the Madison Range. Here again, as in the Big Horn Basin, we have a river which seems to do the impossible, that is, cuts canyons across ranges instead of flowing around them.

The West Yellowstone area was the location of the famous Madison Canyon-Yellowstone earthquake. This earthquake, called the Hebgen Lake earthquake, occurred at 11:35 p.m. on August 17, 1959. It had a magnitude on the Richter Scale of 7.1. This quake was felt over an area of 60,000 square miles, being noted as far as 500 miles from its epicenter near Hebgen Lake.

Several new fault scarps were formed and a rather large area was abruptly dropped as

Photo 2.10. Madison Range near its southern end rising abruptly above the alluvial plain of the Madison Valley along the Madison Fault. Note absence of any hogbacks of sedimentary rocks.

much as 22 feet. Many landslides were initiated as far away as 25 to 30 miles. The largest of these was the great landslide in the Madison Canyon, and many landslides in Yellowstone Park blocked roads, even in the eastern side.

Fault scarps are still visible in the Madison Canyon as high as 20 feet. These scarps are mostly in unconsolidated material, but must reflect displacements of the underlying bedrock.

Careful study by the Coast and Geodetic Survey has shown that a block of the crust, including the Hebgen Reservoir, dropped some 22 feet. This set up great waves in the reservoir which swept across the top of the dam, causing severe damage but not failure of the dam. The north shore of the reservoir dropped the most and was flooded. The south shore rose relatively, and docks have been left on dry land. Some of these features can still be seen along U.S. 287 through the canyon as described in the Trip Guides.

A disastrous landslide was triggered by the earthquake in the canyon of the Madison River, six miles downstream from Hebgen Dam. Thirty-seven million cubic yards of broken rock slid suddenly into the canyon, burying a mile of the river and the highway to depths of 220 feet (Photo 2.11). At least twenty-six people in a campground along the river were buried by the slide. The river waters were pounded by the slide and formed Earthquake Lake which became 200-feet deep within three weeks. Shortly after the slide the Army Corps of Engineers worked to cut a new river channel across the slide, and the level of Earthquake Lake is about fifty feet less than it was shortly after the event.

YELLOWSTONE PLATEAU

About 600,000 years ago a series of deafening explosions suddenly threw tremendous quantities of volcanic ash and pumice high into the sky. Great black clouds of ash and vast sheets of volcanic material spread across thousands of square miles in a matter of minutes and left behind a giant caldera more than 35 miles across in the central Yellowstone region. Thus, in one moment of geologic time there began an incredible chain of events which led to the creation of the fascinating wonders of Yellowstone National Park as we know it today. The major part of Yellowstone Park is a forested plateau, partly occupied by Yellowstone Lake. This plateau region contains most of the geysers, hot springs, and other marvels of the Park which were formed by the great volcanic events, not so long ago as the earth measures time.

General Description

Yellowstone Plateau is a relatively flat, forested surface with an average elevation over 8,000 feet. There are occasional open meadows, especially in the so-called geyser basins where hot waters have killed all trees.

Only a few hills or mountains of older rock stand up above the plateau surface. Most important of these is Mt. Washburn (10,243 feet) and its associated range. The plateau is surrounded by mountains which are parts of other natural provinces extending into Yellowstone Park; for example, the Gallatin Range runs southward into the northwestern corner of Yellowstone Park, and the Absaroka Mountains lie within the eastern border of the Park in all their wild splendor. But these mountains are outside the plateau itself. Yellowstone Lake occupies a central position in the Park and is the largest freshwater lake in the United States outside of the Great Lakes. Its level is 7,733 feet; the lake has 110 miles of shore line (Fig. 2.7 and its ERTS picture).

A number of rivers drain the area of this high plateau and, in flowing outward, have

Photo 2.11. The Madison Canyon Landslide seen a few days after its occurrence in August, 1959. Note that the landslide debris completely fills the Madison River Valley (U.S. Geological Survey photo).

cut canyons of various sizes. Most spectacular, of course, are the several canyons of the Yellowstone River as it flows to the north, but the Snake River and its tributary, the Lewis River, have cut canyons to the south, and the Madison River has cut one to the west.

Rocks and Structures

Yellowstone Plateau proper is composed almost entirely of volcanic rocks of the composition rhyolite. There are two main varieties of this rhyolite: welded tuffs and actual lava flows. Some of the older rocks which project up through the plateau rhyolites, as in the Washburn Range, are andesites of the Absaroka volcanic province which have been previously described. Mt. Washburn, itself, is part of an old volcanic vent.

The Yellowstone Plateau area, after the period of Rocky Mountain uplift, must have been a lowland or basin with the Gallatin and Beartooth mountains to the north and the Absaroka and Washakie uplifts to the east and south. During Tertiary time this lowland may have continued to sink at the times of the formation of Jackson Hole and of the eastern Snake River Plains downwarp. Therefore, at the end of the Tertiary period, the Yellowstone Plateau was a wide, broad lowland area surrounded by mountains.

At the beginning of the Quarternary period, a little over two million years ago, a giant reservoir of molten rock was building up beneath this basin and slowly rising to within a few thousand feet of the surface. As pressures increased the overlying surface was stretched and began to crack. Rumblings of coming volcanic eruptions must have sounded ominously across the Yellowstone Basin. At first, small amounts of lava came out through cracks in some places, but finally, the underlying magma burst through a series of ringlike fractures in rapid, violent, continuing eruptions. Great fountains of hot pumice and ash were spewed into the air. (See Fig. 2.9, A, B, C, D). This red-hot, fragmented material with its contained gases, spread out across the countryside in rushing flows of ash particles. These quickly filled valleys and canyons and then swept out horizontally across the lowland surfaces, piling up to thicknesses of more than 1,000 feet in a relatively short time. Simultaneously, great quantities of ash and dust were blasted high into the atmosphere and carried by the wind eastward over much of central United States. Such ash has been found in Kansas, Nebraska, and Texas, for example.

The ash flows, however, were not thrown as high into the air and quickly became surface flows. They moved around higher mountains, like the Washburn Range and Bunsen Peak near Mammoth, building up plateaulike surfaces as the material was deposited (Photo 2.12). This material came to rest as a thick layer of still red-hot particles, which settled down and fused together in a process geologists call "welding," thus forming compact rocks of rhyolite composition called welded tuffs. However, under a microscope this solid rhyolite can be seen to consist of flattened ash and pumice particles, fused and partially crystallized together.

The amount of material thrown out in one short eruption, in only a few weeks' time, represented hundreds of cubic miles of molten rock from underground. As a result, the roof of the underground magma chamber collapsed and a giant crater, or caldera, was formed at the surface, an irregular circular depression many miles across and perhaps a few thousand feet deep. The subsidence took place along near vertical, circular or ringlike fractures, so that the caldera was roundish or oval in shape.

This process of fantastic explosion of ash flows and caldera collapse has occurred three times: first in Yellowstone two million years ago; then in the Island Park Caldera in

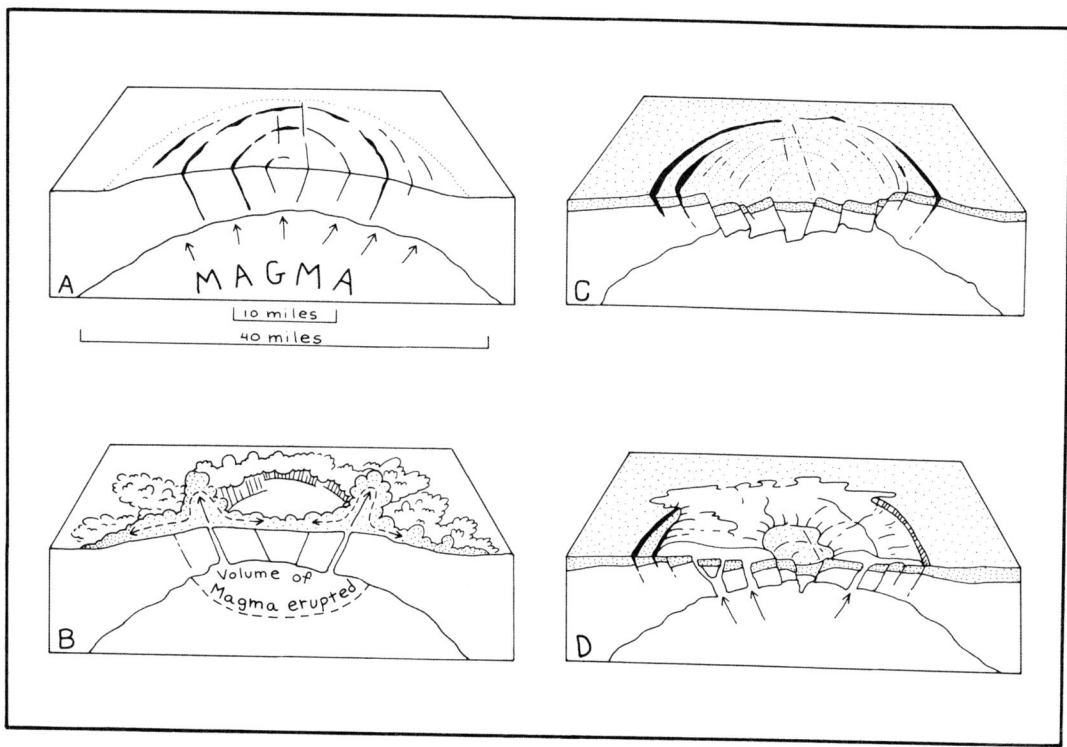

Figure 2.9. CALDERA DEVELOPMENT. Schematic diagrams showing stages in the development of the Yellowstone caldera 600,000 years ago. (A) A large magma chamber began to force its way towards the surface, arching the overlying rocks and forming a series of concentric fractures. The fractures extended downwards towards the magma chamber. (B) The ring fractures eventually tapped the magma chamber which contained a high proportion of dissolved gases. With the sudden release of pressure, tremendous amounts of hot gases and molten rock were erupted instantly. The liquid solidified into pumice, ash particles, and dust as it was blown out and much of the debris moved outward across the landscape as vast ash flows, covering thousands of square miles very rapidly. (C) The area overlying the blown-out part of the magma chamber collapsed to form a gigantic caldera. The collapse took place along normal ring faults probably to several thousand feet. (D) Renewed rise of molten magma, now poor in gas, domed the caldera floor and a series of rhyolite lava flows poured out from the ring fractures and spread slowly across the caldera floor. (Modified after Christiansen and Blank, U.S. Geological Survey).

Idaho 1.3 million years ago; and finally, for a second time in Yellowstone, 600,000 years ago. This last great eruption and caldera collapse took place simultaneously from two overlapping centers, apparently over two magma chambers. Note the sort of double shape on the trip map (Fig. 3.18) of the resulting caldera which is 45 miles by 30 miles in overall size, or about 100 square miles.

Because the Yellowstone Caldera is now partly filled by thick lava flows, the appearance of the caldera is not as impressive and obvious as it must have been immediately after formation. However, it is possible to recognize the caldera wall along the south side of the Washburn Range north of Canyon Village, and the caldera wall also stands up in highlands north of Madison Junction as Purple Mountain.

Photo 2.12. Layer of the Yellowstone welded tuff (Huckleberry Ridge member) capping Mt. Everts near Mammoth Hot Springs. The entire lower part of the mountain is composed of Cretaceous sandstones and shales. Two million years ago the valley in the foreground was not yet formed and the ash flow spread out on a then low, flat surface or plain.

After this violent caldera-forming eruption, much molten material remained deep below the surface, but it had lost much of its explosive energy through the loss of gases. Molten material continued to rise, however, and domed up the caldera floor over the two magma chambers. One of these low roof domes lies just east of the Old Faithful area. Over the next few thousand years, this remaining magma pushed out onto the surface from time to time as thick lava flows which eventually filled in the caldera and actually spread over the western wall of the caldera into Idaho. The first of these lava flows came shortly after the collapse 600,000 years ago, whereas the latest of such flows came about only 60,000 years ago. These rhyolite lava flows were extremely thick and sticky, very viscous, as scientists say, and the lava piled up 500 to 1,000 feet in thickness before it began to flow, and then most of the flows moved for less than 10 miles. This is quite in contrast to very fluid basalt lavas which can move for 30 or 50 miles and not be more than 100 feet thick.

The volume of the caldera, 45 by 30 miles by probably a half a mile deep, roughly matches the amount of material poured out in the ash flow eruptions. Later as extensive lava flows filled in this 2,000-foot caldera, continued slow sinking of the whole caldera complex occurred to compensate for the flow material filling in above. Therefore, the thickness of rhyolite in the caldera must be a mile or two at the present time.

Recently geologists have found evidence that molten magma is still located only a few miles beneath the surface of Yellowstone. This is partly proven by the behavior of earthquake waves passing through the presumed liquid rock and by measurements of low density and low magnetism under the plateau. Finally, the heat flow from the various geyser and hot spring basins in Yellowstone is 800 times the normal heat flow through the earth's crust. Geological evidence shows that this heat flow has been continuing for at least 40,000 years. All this adds up to indirect, but fairly conclusive, proof that the magma chamber still exists under Yellowstone and that further eruptions are not impossible! Since this magma chamber has existed for two million years, it may continue to exist for another million.

The Yellowstone area is continually shaken by small earthquakes, and the most abundant epicenters extend from Hebgen Lake west of West Yellowstone down to the Norris Geyser Basin. Norris is also the hottest area in the Park. Perhaps this is where another lava flow, something like Obsidian Cliff, will break through in another few hundred years.

The ash flow deposits, now welded tuffs, were thrown out of the caldera and are found today beyond the old caldera rim. The rocks are solid and light-colored, sometimes with a pinkish or purplish hue (Photo 2.13). Good places to see these rocks will be mentioned in the Trip Guide section.

The lava flows filled in the caldera and are therefore exposed in the Central, Madison, and Pitchstone plateaus. They may be seen around the Yellowstone Canyon, and along the Firehole Canyon, south of Madison Junction. The flow rhyolites are often dark-colored rocks, because they contain some glass as streaks or patches of obsidian. In other places they are light-colored, grayish rocks often with a few scattered glassy crystals of quartz and feldspar. In the vicinity of geyser and hot spring areas these rhyolites have been altered by hot chemically active waters and are now very white, yellowish, or sometimes even reddish, as in the Grand Canyon of the Yellowstone.

Grand Canyon of the Yellowstone River

The Grand Canyon of the Yellowstone is the outstanding scenic feature of Yellowstone Park. Just how and when did this canyon develop?

Prior to the catastrophic volcanism beginning two million years ago the Lamar River, flowing westward out of the Absarokas and crossing the northern part of Yellowstone Park, must have been in existence, but flowing in an appreciably higher valley. An ancestral Yellowstone River was a small tributary of the Lamar. The first great ash flow event two million years ago partially filled in this river system. By subsequent erosion, the valley was reestablished, and a short Yellowstone Canyon was developing beside Mt. Washburn at the time of the last great volcanic event, 600,000 years ago. These ash flows filled in the young canyon, and the entire basin north of Mt. Washburn now drained by Tower Creek.

The newly-formed caldera of central Yellowstone being a depression, must have filled in with rain waters to become a very large lake. As this lake began to overflow to the north, water was supplied to begin recutting the Yellowstone Canyon. Even as the early lava flows formed in the caldera, this overflow apparently continued, and the new canyon became longer and deeper.

At a time about 300,000 years ago the head to the canyon was probably near the present falls, but it was only about half as deep as now. This was the time of the Bull

Photo 2.13. Cliffs of Yellowstone welded tuff (Huckleberry member) at Golden Gate, on Log 15A. This rock is very dense and solid even though it is composed of tiny fused particles.

Lake glaciation, and all of the Yellowstone Plateau was completely buried by ice with the exception of the high peaks on either side of the Park. During the gradual melting of this ice, sediments filled in the newly cut canyon. Therefore, no down-cutting of the canyon occurred until perhaps 125,000 years ago, when water again flowed freely, and the canyon began to be cut deeper and deeper, perhaps to its present depth.

But canyon cutting was interrupted again by the advance of glaciers during the Pinedale glaciation, and again the canyon was partly filled with lake sediments as it was dammed up near Tower Falls by moraines from the Lamar Valley glacier. This last ice finally melted about 12,000 years ago, and the Yellowstone was able to wash out most of the lake and glacial sediments to assume its present shape and depth.

Some of the glacial deposits that partially block the canyon can still be seen in the Tower Falls area and in the Lamar River valley; and traces of the lake beds which formed during this last period are still preserved on the canyon walls close to the lower falls as partial evidence for this story.

The actual falls at the head of the canyon are located where very hard, resistant rhyolite is immediately next to altered rhyolite, the latter being softer and very quickly eroded (Photo 2.14). This alteration

Photo 2.14. View of the Yellowstone Canyon looking downstream from Artist's Point Lookout. The rock is rhyolite lava flow altered by hot springs activity such that it is brightly colored in reds and yellows and weathers in small pinnacles.

was caused by hot, rising water and will be discussed in the next section.

Hot Water and Steam Phenomena

Certainly, the great concentration of geysers, hot springs, mud pots, and fumaroles, provide the special reason that Yellowstone Park was set aside as a park. To count all the thermal features in Yellowstone is practically impossible. It is estimated that there are between 2,500 and 10,000 such features, depending upon how many of the small features are included. These are scattered throughout the Park but most are clustered in a few areas, called geyser basins, which have a continuous and spectacular display of hot water phenomena. Most of these geyser basins are located above the zone of old ring fractures within the caldera.

The steam that can be seen in these areas is actually a fog of water droplets condensed from steam. Therefore, much more of this "steam" appears on cold days and very early in the morning. This is for the same reason that you see your breath on a cold day.

The essential for hot water phenomena is heat. As we have seen, evidence exists for a shallow magma chamber under Yellowstone, and this is certainly the source of the heat. Normally, rock temperatures increase 1° F per 100 feet of depth in the earth's crust, but in Yellowstone the rate of temperature increase is much greater—about 40° per 100 feet.

A second essential for hot water phenomena is the presence of water. Studies show that nearly all the water involved originates as rain or snow, which penetrates into the ground. Only a very little may come from the underlying magma.

Cold surface waters descend along fractures to considerable depth, perhaps as much as five or ten thousand feet. These deep fractures are present in the ring fracture zones, as a result of the original caldera collapse.

Because of the magma below, the water is heated at depth. A research drill hole in Yellowstone by the U.S. Geological Survey found that the temperature at about 1,100 feet was 465° F. Water, at this temperature, is expanded and lighter in weight than the cold, descending water. Therefore, the lighter hot water tends to rise towards the surface along other fracture zones. In fact, the descending cold heavy water from the surface tends to push the hot water back up, and a giant convection system is developed. (See Fig. 2.10). In the major geyser basins convection systems of this kind have developed on the order of magnitude of ten miles in diameter and one or two miles deep.

The effect of pressure on the boiling temperature of water plays an important role. Under atmospheric pressure, water boils at 212° F at sea level and at about 199° F at the elevation of Yellowstone's geyser basins. However, water at depth is not only under atmospheric pressure, but under the pressure of the overlying water; and, therefore, at depth the boiling point is much higher. In fact, water at 500° F, down 1,000 feet, will not boil, because of this greater pressure which prevents the formation of steam. Now, as this hotter than boiling water begins to rise again towards the surface, and the pressure on it is gradually released, boiling will begin. The boiling will be rather slow if the pressure is released gradually as in most hot springs, but if the pressure is released rapidly, boiling may take place suddenly enough so that water flashes explosively into steam and shoots up in geyser eruptions.

The hot waters in circulating downwards dissolve mineral material and, in turn, carry it upwards, where it is deposited at the surface to make hot spring and geyser terrace deposits. Where waters circulate deeply through limestone, they bring up calcium carbonate and form travertine terraces, as at

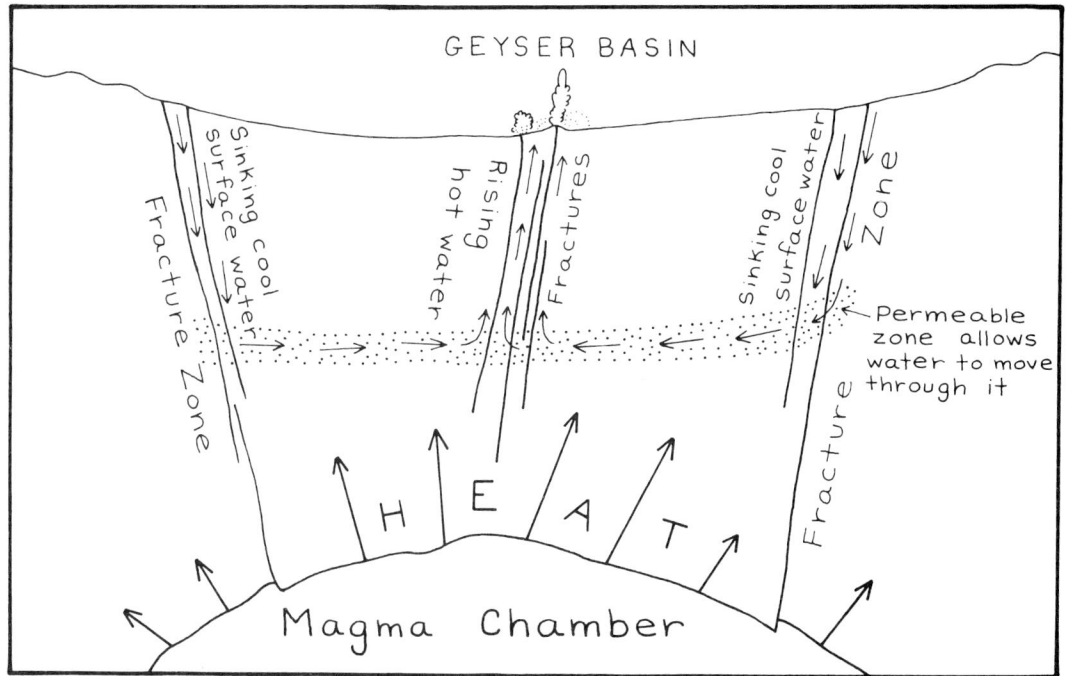

Figure 2.10. Heat flow and surface water. Diagram showing a thermal system below a geyser and hot spring basin, according to the explanation that water of rainfall origin circulates and is heated at great depths and rises to the surface again. (Modified after D. E. White and others, U.S. Geological Survey).

Mammoth Hot Springs. Almost everywhere else in Yellowstone the waters circulate through rhyolite, which has a lot of silica. This is dissolved and is brought up and deposited as geyserite deposits: chemically, silicious sinter, or silica (Photo 2.15).

Most of these deposits are white in color when dry, whether of calcium carbonate or silica. However, at many hot springs bright colors are seen. Most of these colors are due to the presence of algae that can live in hot waters up to 170° F. Depending on the temperature, the algae are green, yellow, or brown. Colors in a few places are due to mineral oxides of iron and manganese. The delicate blue color of the hot pools, however, results from the reflection of light off the pool walls, and back through the deep clear water. Some pools are yellow due to the presence of microscopic particles of sulphur. Others are green from the combined influence of sulphur and the blue water effect mentioned above.

Hot springs occur when the rising hot water of the thermal circulation systems can move up readily through fairly large ground openings and the steam can bubble out easily, sometimes with a small continuous boiling (Photo 2.16). This is by far the commonest occurrence. Fumaroles occur when only steam issues from cracks at the earth's surface. Mud pots and mud volcanoes occur where steam bubbles up through water-saturated silt, clay, or other fine sediment (Photo 2.17). Geysers are a special kind of hot spring from which there is an occasional violent expulsion of steam and water.

A geyser tube usually has some large ir-

Photo 2.15. Castle geyser and its cone in the Upper Geyser Basin. An impressive amount of geyserite (silica) has been deposited around the mouth of this active geyser. On Log 15C.

Photo 2.16. Punch Bowl Spring, a continuously flowing hot spring with steam bubbling up quietly in the center. The deposit is silicious sinter or geyserite. In Upper Geyser Basin on walking tour in Log 15C.

regular openings or reservoirs not far below the surface in which water can accumulate and be heated. After an eruption the partly emptied tubes and chambers gradually fill with water, hot water coming up from below, colder water flowing in from near the surface. The hot waters from below with their steam bubbles bring up heat energy. The steam bubbles, however, are condensed and dissolved in the somewhat cooler water in the geyser chambers. Gradually, however, these rising steam bubbles are bringing in more and more energy, and the entire volume of water becomes hotter and hotter until it is in effect slightly above the surface boiling temperature. When this happens, steam bubbles will no longer condense or dissolve and will begin to move up through the opening to the surface. This first rush of steam will push up some water which will overflow, or form a preliminary spurt as so often happens at Old Faithful. A few of these preliminary spurts results in pushing out enough water to reduce the pressure on the remaining water in the geyser plumbing system. Now the water, at this lower pressure, is superheated or above its boiling temperature. Therefore, some water flashes into steam, and the resulting surge upwards is the beginning of the geyser eruption. As

Photo 2.17. Fountain Paint Pots, a bubbling depression where steam comes up through wet clays and muds building small mounds around the sides sometimes called mud volcanoes. Wet area in right center and dried out mud in front and back with shrinkage cracks. In Lower Geyser Basin on Log 15C.

the water is erupted water below is now under a lower pressure and it flashes into steam, and so a chain reaction is set up whereby more and more water suddenly flashes into steam and the whole geyser plumbing system, tubes and chambers, are emptied upwards in a full eruption. Towards the end of the activity with most of the water expelled, only steam comes out in a so-called "steam phase" for a short time after the hot water eruption. In this case, the geyser has run out of water, and gone into a steam eruption. On the other hand, some geysers first run out of extra heat, and remaining water is not hot enough to flash into steam, so the eruption stops with water still present in the geyser system. The eruptions of some geysers are extremely complex and difficult to explain. No two geysers behave exactly alike.

The time periods between eruptions vary greatly from geyser to geyser. Some geysers erupt only a few times in a season; others every two or three days; some every few minutes. Contrary to popular belief, all geysers are very irregular in their behavior; even Old Faithful does not behave once an hour, as advertised. The interval between its eruptions varies from 30 to 90 minutes, with an average of about 65 minutes.

TETON MOUNTAINS AND JACKSON HOLE

The Teton Mountains are the most famous and spectacular of all the mountain ranges in the Middle Rockies, largely because of their abrupt rise above the flatlands of Jackson Hole. The latter is the natural complement of the great mountains and, therefore, both the mountain range and Jackson Hole have been set aside as Teton National Park (Fig. 2.11).

General Description

The jagged Teton Mountains have been carved by ice erosion from a geologically recent crustal block uplifted along a near vertical fault. Several of the peaks stick up as giant horns and challenge the best mountaineers. In between the various great peaks are deep, U-shaped canyons carved out by glaciers flowing down into Jackson Hole. All of this can be seen dramatically from the roadways in the Hole and spectacularly from the air (Photo 2.18).

The western or backside of the Teton Range has a much more gentle slope as will be described under *Structure*. This is still a wild area of steep ridges and cliffs and deep canyons. Glaciated valleys trend westward on this side also.

Photo 2.18. The Teton Range from the air looking southwest from over Jackson Lake. The abrupt rise of the mountains along a straight line marks the location of the Teton Fault. (Photo by John S. Shelton with permission).

Natural Provinces of the Northern Middle Rocky Mountains

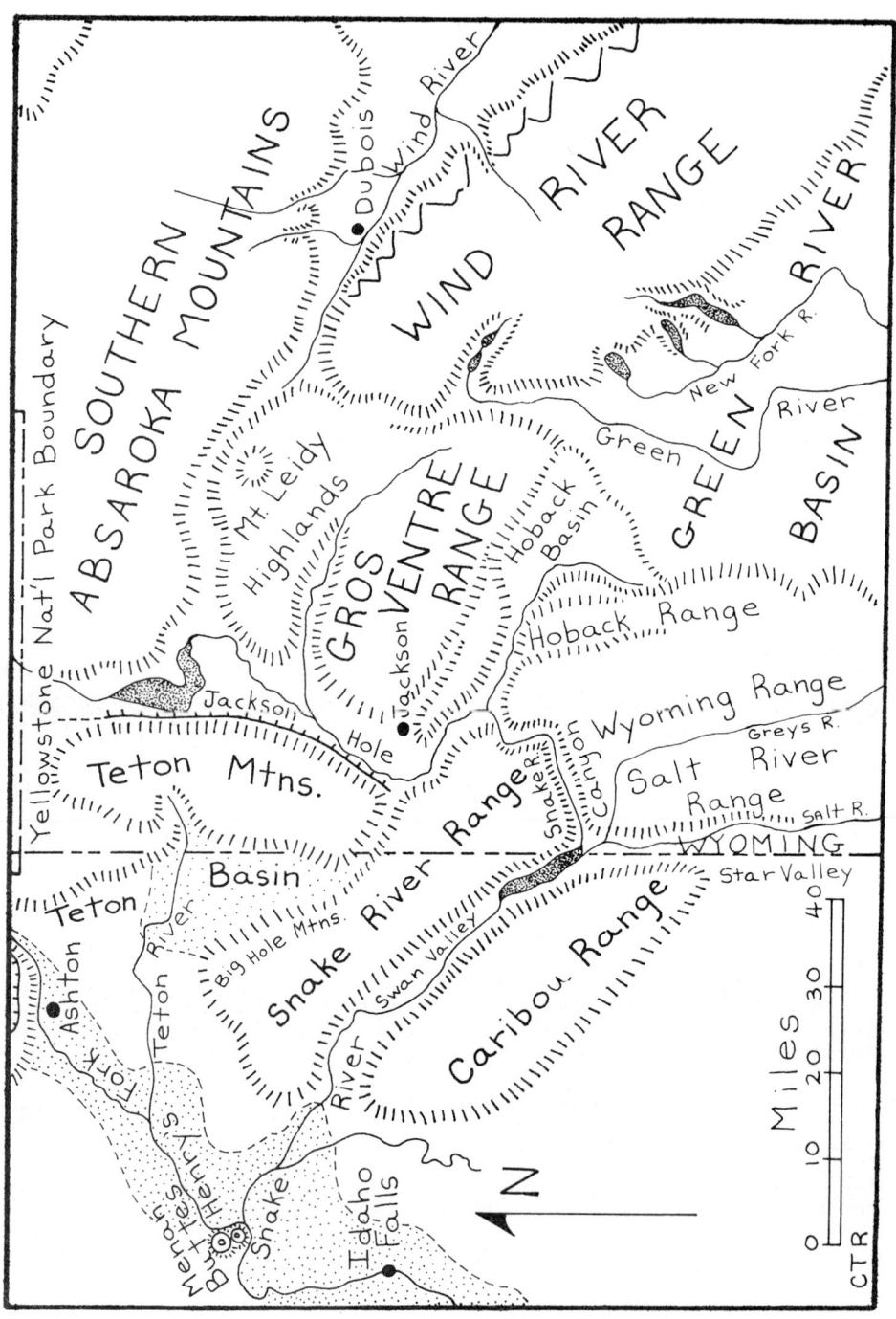

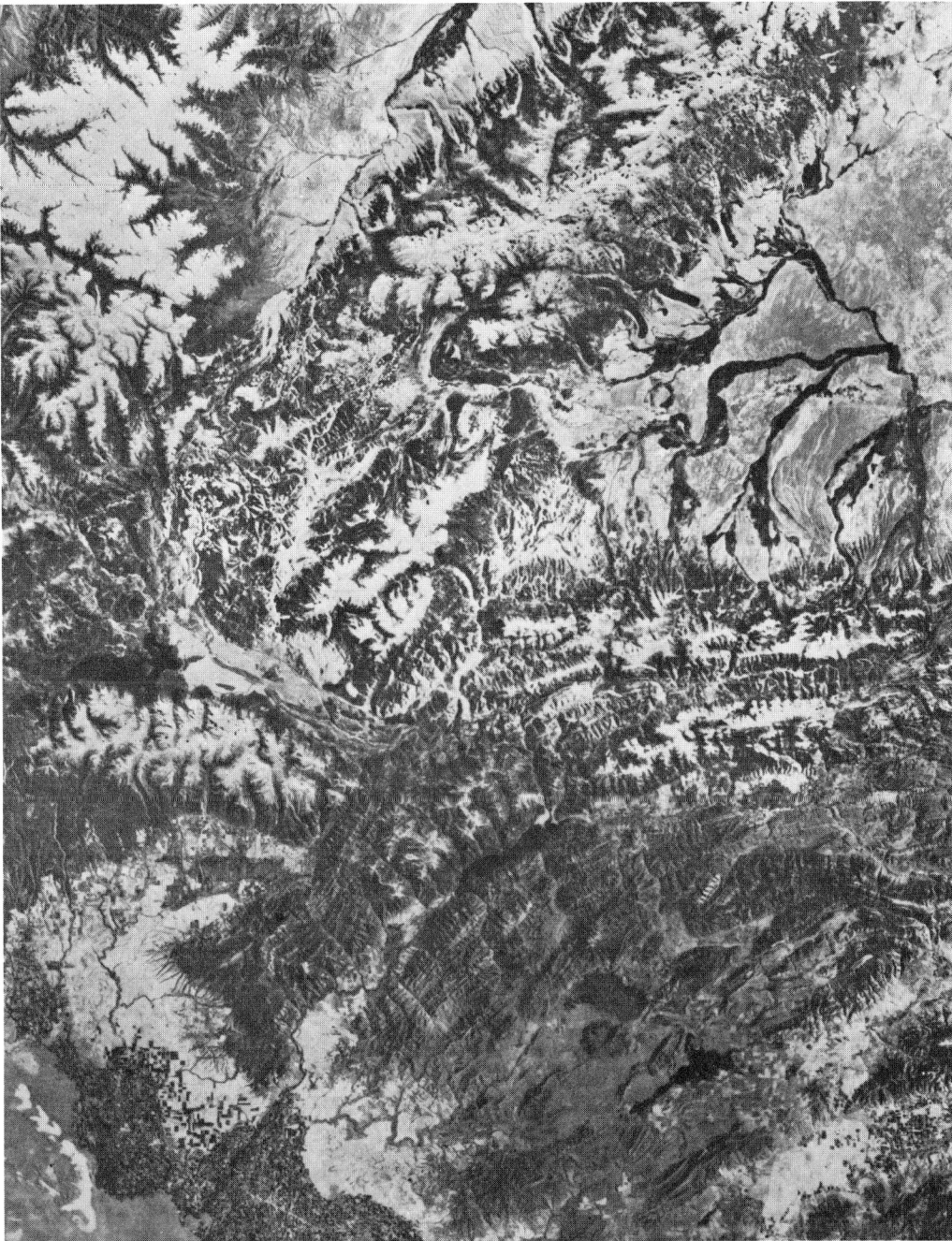

Figure 2.11. (on left page) Map of Teton Range and Jackson Hole, Gros Ventre Mountains, Idaho-Wyoming border ranges and the northern Green River Basin. (facing page, on right) ERTS photograph of the same area.

The Teton Mountain area is a hiker's paradise. There are numerous hiking and horseback trails up into the mountains reaching about 10,000 feet which are open to anybody with some energy. However, the high, spectacular peaks are a challenge to mountaineers, and it is necessary to have mountaineer training and experience and to register your climbs with the Park Service before attempting them.

Up in the high mountains there are still a half a dozen small glaciers in cirques on the Grand Teton and Mount Moran, for example. These can be seen if you look carefully and use field glasses from down on the floor of Jackson Hole. Teton Glacier is the largest and is about a mile long. There are also a few tarn lakes high up in the cirque basins near timberline which can be reached by hiking and horseback trails.

Several lakes occur at the foot of the mountains, of which Jackson Lake is the largest; but the smaller lakes like Jenny, Leigh, and Phelps are also real gems. All these lakes are contained by terminal and lateral moraines.

Jackson Hole is the flat basin at the foot of the mountains and extends the entire length of the range. It varies in width from five to ten miles. Out in the flatland there are a few buttes which stick up as much as a thousand feet. One of these, Signal Mountain, can be ascended by a paved road. From here a spectacular panoramic view of Jackson Lake and the entire Teton Range can be obtained.

Much of the floor of Jackson Hole is covered with sagebrush, although there are ridges which are forested.

Rocks

The Teton Range proper is composed mostly of Precambrian gneisses and schists. These were originally sedimentary rocks which were metamorphosed about 2.8 billion years ago, according to radiometric dates. There was some intrusion of granites and pegmatites. The latter are light colored and form a series of dikes a few feet thick which form a complex network of light-colored streaks on some of the canyon walls through the darker colored gneisses. The whole complex must have been very hot and plastic at one time, because in many places the gneisses and schists are extremely folded and contorted on a very small scale (Photo 2.19). These Precambrian rocks can only be seen by hiking up into the range. On Death Canyon Trail, for example, an area of extremely interesting contorted gneisses and pegmatites is exposed. Interesting rocks may be seen on some of the other trails as well.

Late in Precambrian time large, long, near-vertical dikes of dark-colored basic rocks were intruded. A couple of these dikes may be seen from the foot of the range, most notably on the very top of Mt. Moran, where a dark dike is seen as a vertical streak (Photo 2.20). This dike is actually two hundred feet wide, although it doesn't look like that from the foot of the mountains. Another one can be seen cutting vertically up the base of the middle Teton. Some of these dikes can be traced completely across the area of Precambrian rocks in the Teton Range.

At both the northern and southern ends of the Teton Range, highly-folded Paleozoic sedimentary rocks are exposed and may be seen from the main road in their steeply dipping attitude.

In Jackson Hole itself, a tremendous thickness of Tertiary sediments and volcanic tuffs underlie the surface, completely hidden from sight. However, in the foothills to the east on the Mt. Leidy highlands and the Gros Ventre Mountains, various of these Tertiary rocks are exposed, along with Mesozoic sedimentary rocks and various kinds of volcanic

Photo 2.19. Biotite gneiss with irregular and folded bands of white quartz and feldspar cut by tiny veins of pegmatite in various directions. A block of coarse-grained pegmatite may be seen in the lower right of the picture. Seen along the Death Canyon trail.

rocks. Most of the rock on Signal Mountain is volcanic material. These rocks, however, are not seen along the main roads, and it takes an excursion back up into the foothills to find them.

Northeast of Jackson Hole in an area sometimes called the Pinyon Peak Highlands, there are some early Tertiary conglomerates and sandstones which, according to Dr. Love of the U.S. Geological Survey, carry a small amount of gold. While this is not visible to the naked eye it occurs in so many hundreds of cubic miles of rock that the total volume, he estimates, is quite

Photo 2.20. Black diorite dike on top of Mt. Moran as seen from the air. On the summit of Mt. Moran, the dike is unconformably overlain by about 50 ft. of Cambrian Flathead sandstone. The dike is 150 ft. thick. Mountains beyond the dike (top of photo) are carved out of Paleozoic sedimentary rocks on the backslope of the Teton Range. (Photo by John S. Shelton, with permission).

tremendous. It has never been mined, however.

Structure

The Teton Range is a long fault block, tilted to the west, and steeply uplifted along the east side. Thus, the abrupt rise of the mountains is along the fault plane. At the same time as the block was being uplifted, Jackson Hole was being tilted downward. The Jackson Hole Block also dips to the west so that its deepest part is adjacent to the foot of the mountains (Fig. 2. 12).

The structural history of this area began during the period of Rocky Mountain uplift with an ancestral Teton-Gros Ventre uplift which trended northwest-southeast across what is now Jackson Hole and the Teton Range. This uplift was parallel to another one to the east, the ancestral Washakie uplift, which has previously been described as a westward extension of the Owl Creek Mountains. These two uplifts gradually rose as blocks, steepest on their southwest side, with a broad syncline between them. The maximum deformation probably occurred

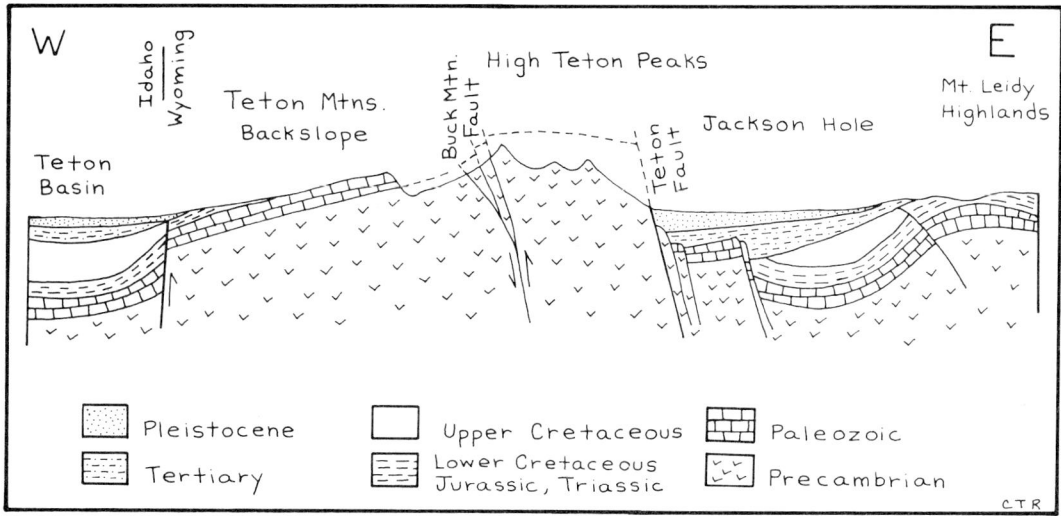

Figure 2.12. Diagrammatic cross section of Jackson Hole and the Teton Range to Teton Basin. Vertical scale not appreciably exaggerated.

during Paleocene time as revealed by careful mapping of relationships in this area.

At the same time, south of Jackson, thrust plates were being shoved eastward in an entirely different kind of deformation as will be described later. These thrust plates moved up until they abutted against the Gros Ventre uplift block.

In Pliocene time, that is, late Tertiary, this ancestral uplift broke apart along faults across the original trend of the uplift, and this was the start of the sinking of Jackson Hole and the rise of the Teton Block. This faulting has continued to the present and has completely changed the appearance of the country.

The Teton Fault Block continued to rise throughout Pleistocene time, such that rhyolite ashflows coming out of Yellowstone Park two million years ago are offset two to four thousand feet; and glacial deposits are offset by this fault. There has apparently been movement on this fault since the Ice Age, but none in historic time. It could happen again, however!

From the amount of offset of the ash flows which are known to be two million years old, it has been estimated that in the last two million years the Teton Fault Block has risen, or been displaced, perhaps as much as 4,000 feet relative to Jackson Hole. This is an average of 0.1 to 0.2 feet per century. This was probably not a continuing slow movement, but a series of periodic movements of from ten to twenty feet such as take place in active faults in California. Altogether, since the Teton Fault began in Pliocene time, displacement along the fault has been at least 30,000 feet, elevating the range as the basin went down.

The Teton Fault is not one single crack in the earth, but is a series of parallel fractures a few miles apart. This is typical of many great faults, which consist of not one major crack, but many more or less parallel cracks, so that the displacement takes place in a zone. Some of the secondary faults are buried beneath Jackson Hole and their position is known from geophysical measurements. Several of the buttes in Jackson

Hole—specifically, Black-Tail Butte and the Gros Ventre Buttes in the south—are probably projections along these subsidiary faults.

Part of the story of the whole region is the volcanic history exposed in the northern part of Jackson Hole. To the northeast is the southern extension of the Absaroka volcanic rocks, which came out in Eocene time and more or less buried the original Washakie uplift and filled in whatever basins existed at that time. Then, more recently, the period of volcanism of Yellowstone Park, the outpouring of rhyolite ash flows and lava flows, has extended southward into the northern part of the Teton Range. The main structures and the fault at the northern part of the Tetons are buried by these rhyolite lavas, the youngest of which are only about 100,000 years old. These same lavas extend down on the west side of the Teton Range, covering up part of the gentle dip slope, and extend far out in Idaho.

Glaciation

The spectacular scenery of the Tetons is due to ice erosion. Separate glaciers carved out great U-shaped canyons and left jagged ridges and horns between the glaciers. During the Pleistocene ice period there were at least three periods of glaciation. Not much is known about the oldest period, since most of the deposits of the later periods have destroyed the early records. However, some of the moraines of the early period are exposed in high valleys in the Gros Ventre Range.

Jackson Hole has moraines and outwash plains of the last two ice periods. During the last ice advance, some ten to fifteen thousand years ago, ice tongues came down the main canyons and formed small fan-shaped masses of ice out onto Jackson Hole as much as a mile or so. Around the edges of these fan-shaped glacial tongues, moraines were pushed up as great piles of boulders and shattered rock with fine-grained material in between. When the ice melted the space occupied by the ice was a hollow or lowland with a ridge around it. These have filled up with water to become the numerous lakes such as Jenny and Phelps lakes, two spectacular examples of lakes contained by lateral and terminal moraines at a canyon mouth. A still larger ice sheet spread out with its moraines, and when this larger ice melted its site gradually filled up with water as Jackson Lake itself.

Eastward and southeastward, beyond these moraines, the melt water from these glaciers poured outwards into the ancestral Snake River and on southward through Jackson Hole. This melt water was loaded with sand and gravel, particularly during the short summers when rapid melting meant great floods that carried much material; this material was deposited in outwash deposits, relatively flat plains covered by sands and gravels. These are the flat surfaces covered by sagebrush which you see in central Jackson Hole between the two main roads. You will notice that there are flat outwash plains at various levels. The highest level is related to an older glaciation, and the lower level to the last glaciation. Currently, the Snake River has cut down to a still lower level below the two outwash levels.

In general, moraines are tree-covered and outwash deposits have only grass and sagebrush. The sand and gravel in the moraines is full of silt and clay which hold moisture longer; this is ideal for tree growth. The sand and gravel of the outwash deposits have no clay, so are well drained and do not hold the moisture which trees need; only grass and sagebrush will grow.

GROS VENTRE MOUNTAINS AND MOUNT LEIDY HIGHLANDS

Various mountains and highlands rise on the east side of Jackson Hole making it truly a basin surrounded by mountains. Some of these are high mountains in their own right but are dwarfed by being opposite the Tetons. The high peaks in the Gros Ventre Range rise a mile above Jackson Hole level.

General Description

The Gros Ventre Mountains trend northwest to southeast opposite the southern part of Jackson Hole. To the south they merge topographically into the mountains of the northern Hoback Range. Within the Gros Ventre Range there are more than a half dozen peaks over 11,000 feet; Darwin Peak at 11,645 feet is the highest in the range. Much of this range is above timberline, and this high mountain country has been carved by glacial erosion into cirque basins and U-shaped valleys like the high mountain country in other ranges of the Middle Rockies. Most of the range is inaccessible except to hikers (Fig. 2.11).

The Gros Ventre Range is separated from the Mount Leidy Highlands to the north by the relatively wide valley of the Gros Ventre River and some of its tributaries. A road up the Gros Ventre represents the main access to this mountainous country.

The Mount Leidy Highlands are relatively low mountains compared to their neighbors to the south, most peaks being only 9,000 feet, although Mount Leidy itself is 10,317. The higher country is almost entirely forested, but many of the lowlands in the Mount Leidy section are sparsely timbered with many slopes in sagebrush, especially along the Gros Ventre River Valley.

Rocks

The Gros Ventre Range is composed of uplifted, folded, and faulted Paleozoic sedimentary rocks around a couple of areas of Precambrian granites and gneisses. Actually, the very highest peaks are in the massive limestones rather than the gneisses.

The Mount Leidy Highlands are composed largely of Mesozoic rocks. Near the Gros Ventre Range and especially along the Gros Ventre River Valley many of the rocks are Triassic and Jurassic sandstones and shales. The northern part of the Highlands is carved from Cretaceous rocks and some Tertiary volcanic sedimentary formations.

Structure

These two mountain areas, the Gros Ventre and Mount Leidy Highlands, together form a complex block trending northwest-southeast. This block is steep and fault-uplifted along the southwest side and then slopes gradually northward, although it is complicated by many small faults and secondary folds. The block actually dips under the Washakie uplift structure, which is largely buried under the Absaroka volcanic rocks to the north. This block, steep on one side and gentle on the other, is typical of the Middle Rocky mountain type of uplift. These ranges are part of the ancestral Teton-Gros Ventre uplift discussed under the Teton Range, which developed at the time of Rocky Mountain formation.

Along its southeast fault the Gros Ventre Mountains are nearly continuous with the west side of the Wind River uplift, although slightly offset. However, the width of the Gros Ventre-Mount Leidy tilted block is considerably less than the width of the Wind River structure, so the two blocks must be considered as separate uplifted units.

Along the steep southwest side of the Gros Ventre Block, the Hoback and other ranges are jammed up against this uplifted edge of the Gros Ventre Block. Structures of these ranges to the southwest are entirely different from those of the Gros Ventre and Wind River blocks, as will be seen in the next section. Immediately southeast of the city of Jackson along Cache Creek, the steep reverse fault along the south side of the Gros

Ventre Range trends along the north side of the valley, whereas the low angle overthrust fault of the ranges to the south, the so-called Jackson Fault, trends along the south side of this same creek. These two faults are within a mile of each other for several miles, representing the juxtaposition of two entirely different types of structure.

Special Features

Like most mountainous areas in the Middle Rockies the Gros Ventre Range is characterized by high relief. Erosion of the valleys has exposed areas of incompetent shales often beneath more resistant rocks. Rapid stream undercutting and frequent earthquake shocks cause slopes in such areas to be extremely unstable, and a principal natural erosion process is landsliding. Actually, landslides are numerous in all ranges of the Middle Rockies, but the presence in the Gros Ventre River Valley of several rather large slides seems to justify mention here of these general processes.

Wherever there are vertical cliffs, frequent rock falls occur from them. Most of the fallen blocks accumulate along the base of the cliff with the development of a talus slope, or, in some cases, scattered fallen blocks remain visible below the cliff. These are common relationships in all mountainous areas.

Major rock slides, however, where millions of cubic feet of material break away suddenly, are rather rare. Such a major rock slide took place in the lower part of the Gros Ventre Valley in 1925 after an extended period of heavy precipitation and some earthquake tremors (Photo 2.21). A section of Tensleep sandstone nearly two miles long, dipping down the mountain side, gave way suddenly and came down in a tremendous landslide, producing a pile of debris which dammed up the Gros Ventre River. Fortunately, this was an uninhabited area and there was no loss of life. However, two years later the lake formed behind the natural dam of the landslide was suddenly partly drained by rapid erosion through the dam; this produced a flood downstream in the Gros Ventre River, which hit the town of Kelly without warning, and there was some loss of life due to drowning. The slide is still a dramatic sight, although vegetation is now beginning to grow over the debris piles in the valley.

Another widespread type of landslide is the so-called "earthflow," in which a large amount of soft material, usually shales, slowly slumps down a moderate slope (5 to 10°). Such earthflows may continue to move for several years; they can advance tens of feet during a wet period and then be stationary for months before moving again. They are not the kind of landslide that suddenly can bury a town, but in the long run they cause plenty of trouble. Many large earthflows have occurred in the upper part of the Gros Ventre Valley, some of them being two or three miles long. These continuing earthflows cover up bed rock and proceed down valleys as long, tonguelike slides. Some entire hillsides are covered by a series of earthflows for many miles, each sliding at a different time. The slides in the Gros Ventre Valley were probably most active during the last glacial stages when lower temperature had increased precipitation, but many of these slides are continuing today. Slides are often reactivated by undercutting of the toe of the slide by highway construction. In the Gros Ventre Range most of the earthflows have developed in soft Mesozoic shales.

IDAHO-WYOMING BORDER RANGES

A series of parallel ridges and ranges quite different from any others in the Middle Rockies lies just south of the Teton and Gros

Photo 2.21. The Gros Ventre landslide of 1925. The rock debris in the near foreground has rushed across the Gros Ventre Valley and up the opposite slope.

Ventre mountains. They form an arcuate belt about 60 miles wide with overthrust faults and tight folds usually called the *"overthrust belt"* of western Wyoming. The belt lies in southeastern Idaho and western Wyoming and continues southward into Utah. Actually, the belt continues north of the Snake River lava plains as northwest trending ranges in southwestern Montana and east-central Idaho. We're concerned here, however, only with those ranges along the Idaho–Wyoming border (Fig. 2.11).

General Description

The various ranges are long, fairly narrow, and close together. In general, they have maximum elevations from 9,500 to 10,500 feet, the highest peaks being on the Wyoming side. Most of these ranges are forested with relatively little terrain above timberline. The lower slopes of parts of the ranges are below timberline down in the area of sagebrush and scrub trees.

In Idaho, as seen on the map (Fig. 2.11), the Snake River Range runs northwest to southeast along the north side of the Snake River with the Caribou Range on the south side. The northernmost edge of the Snake River Range is known as the Big Hole Mountains, just west of the Teton Basin. This is a low range which merges southward into the Snake River Range.

Southeastward into Wyoming the trend of the ranges curves southward and becomes, more or less, north-south. As a rule, the ranges are named differently south of the Snake River Canyon; the southern extension of the Snake River Range is the Salt River Range west of the Greys River. Next eastward is the Wyoming Range which extends many miles to the south; its highest summit is Wyoming Peak, 11,363 feet. East of these two is the Hoback Range, a rather short range with a north-south extension. In all three ranges several peaks rise to over 10,000 feet. Southward into both Wyoming and Idaho the continuation of the mountain trends have other names with which we are not concerned.

Rocks

The border ranges in both states are composed entirely of sedimentary rocks, Paleozoic and Mesozoic. In general, the Paleozoic rocks make up the highest parts of the main ranges, and Mesozoic rocks occur in the lower parts of the ranges or along the valleys between ranges.

In this part of the Rocky Mountain province the Phosphoria formation contains a considerable amount of phosphate rock, a type of material which is lacking in this formation in the mountains to the east and north. As a result quite a few phosphate-rock mines are operating in an area south of the Snake River in Wyoming and southeastern Idaho. Phosphate rock is used in the manufacture of fertilizers.

Structure

The general structure of these border ranges is similar to that in the southern Appalachian mountains: that is, roughly parallel folds, often largely overturned, and low angle thrust faults. Nearly all of these subparallel mountain ranges are bounded on the east by a major overthrust fault which dips westward, whereas the ranges tend to be bordered on the west by a high-angle normal fault that has down-dropped the western side of the range (Fig. 2.13). The folding has involved the sedimentary rocks only, not the underlying Precambrian metamorphic rocks.

Careful study of the dips and rock sections indicates that the lateral movement on each of about four or five major overthrusts was in the range of ten or fifteen miles. This suggests that these overthrusts must be, at depth, essentially bedding plane type faults. A conservative study of the whole belt shows that a segment of crust originally two hundred miles wide is now only one hundred twenty miles wide. Figure 2.13 is a diagrammatic cross section of the Snake River and Wyoming ranges to show the kind of structure which occurs here.

A suggestion as to the origin of this kind of structure holds that eastern Idaho was near the site of plate collision 70,000,000 years ago. A major plate moving from the west against thick sedimentary rocks shoved them into overlapping slices. This process took place very gradually over several million years, during the period of major Rocky Mountain deformation at the end of

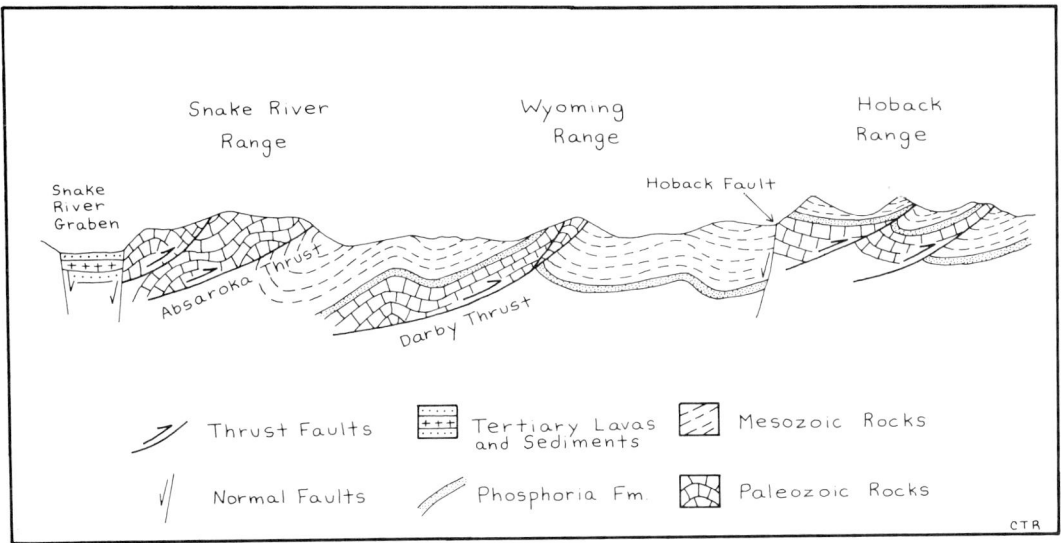

Figure 2.13. Diagrammatic cross section of the Snake River, Wyoming and Hoback ranges showing the low angle thrust faults typical of the Border Range Province.

the Cretaceous and beginning of the Tertiary period.

Much later, during the past 5 or 10 million years in late Tertiary time, crustal motions have been reversed with the tendency to stretch or pull apart this part of North America. This pulling apart has resulted in the development of normal faults forming wide basins like Jackson Hole and the Madison Valley to the north. Also this pulling apart has developed long, narrow grabens, which are down-faulted areas between two parallel normal faults. The Swan Valley section of the Snake River Valley in Idaho is one of these graben valleys. This graben extends and curves southward along the line between Idaho and Wyoming as Star Valley.

NORTHERN GREEN RIVER BASIN

The Green River Basin is an extensive area of Tertiary sediments east of the Wyoming border ranges and south of the Wind River Range extending all the way to the Uinta Range in Utah. In this guidebook the concern is with the northern triangular-shaped tip of this basin only, as seen on the map, Figure 2.11.

This part of the Green River Basin is a generally featureless plain. It is semidesert with scattered sagebrush and other desert-type vegetation. Along the Green River and some of its tributaries water is available for irrigation, resulting in green farmlands. Here and there on the basin surface are small scattered buttes and insignificant badlands.

The basin is filled with thick, Eocene sedimentary rocks that are largely sandstones and shales. These rocks are rarely very obvious in surface exposures, as they crumble and become part of the desert soil.

The famous Green River Formation with its important oil shales, sodium bicarbonate mines, and fossil fish is many miles south of the area under discussion here.

A considerable part of the Green River Basin near the Wind River Range is covered with Pleistocene alluvium, much of which is actually glacial outwash sand and gravel.

The very northern tip of the Green River Basin is the Hoback Basin (Fig. 2.11), which is quite different from the Green River Basin proper. The Hoback Basin is separated by The Rim, which is really a continental divide between the Snake River and the Green River. The rocks of the Hoback Basin, Paleocene in age and known as the Pass Peak formation, consist of coarse-grained sandstones and conglomerates. These rather coarse sediments were deposited rapidly by streams eroding the Hoback and Gros Ventre ranges as the latter were slowly rising in very early Tertiary time.

The Hoback Basin has considerably more relief than the Green River Basin proper. The Hoback River and its tributaries have cut valleys a few hundred feet into the Paleocene sedimentary rocks. As one drives up the Hoback River Valley onto The Rim, he has the feeling of coming from a hilly country onto a flat surface.

Not only does the Green River Basin have a few thousand feet of Tertiary sediments, but beneath them is the entire thickness of the Mesozoic and Paleozoic sedimentary sequence. Therefore, just west of Pinedale, in the northern Green River Basin, the Precambrian rocks are probably 13,000 feet below sea level, whereas a few miles to the east they are 13,000 feet above sea level along the crest of the Wind River Range. Therefore, the relief of the earth's crust from a geologic point of view, is at least 25,000 feet (five miles) between the Wind River Range and Green River Basin blocks.

EASTERN SNAKE RIVER PLAINS

A wide basalt lava plain in eastern Idaho trends from southwest to northeast from near Twin Falls almost to Yellowstone National Park, a distance of more than 200 miles. This lava plain is 40 to 60 miles wide.

General Description

The eastern Snake River Plains is a nearly level surface of semidesert, characterized by dark lava with scattered sagebrush and wind-blown soil. Actually, in many places irrigation has made excellent farming land, especially along the borders of the plain where water from rivers coming out of the mountains is abundant. In such irrigated farming land sugar beets, potatoes, and wheat produce excellent crops. In recent years a number of areas away from the rivers have been irrigated from deep well waters, so the area of semidesert is shrinking.

On the plains there are three large areas of recent lava flows which are bare lava surfaces without any soil, and only rare scattered bushes or grassy clumps (Fig. 2.14).

A few buttes and lava cones stick up here and there on the otherwise rather monotonous surface of these plains.

All towns and cities are on the margins of the plains where water is available; in the center of the plains between Idaho Falls and Arco, the United States Government maintains a Nuclear Reactor Research site.

Rocks

The most characteristic rock of the eastern Snake River Plains is basalt lava. Most of the surface is covered with brown weathered lava, partly buried under wind-blown soil. The three areas of geologically recent lavas, dated at about 2,000 years old, have very fresh, mostly pahoehoe-type surfaces (Photo 2.22). These three are the Craters-of-the-Moon lava complex, the smaller Wapi flows, and the Hell's Half Acre flow just west of Idaho Falls. These three areas are interesting because the lava surfaces and vent structures are fresh enough that the visitor may see what basalt lavas really look like. Since the lava plains are dry and cold in winter,

Photo 2.22. Pahoehoe lava flow surface. The lava flow in the immediate foreground was overrun by a later flow unit of large toelike masses which extended to where the man is standing. Craters-of-the Moon, Idaho.

weathering is very slow, and these 2,000-year old flows look almost like yesterday's flows in Hawaii (Photo 2.23).

Winds howl across the Snake River Plains from the west, always blowing dust derived from the mountains and river valleys of central Idaho, and carrying it across the plains to be deposited in numerous low places, as behind lava mounds. Such extremely fine silt-size particles form a wind-blown soil called "loess." This makes excellent soil for crop-growing on the low foothills along the southeastern side of the plains. The loess deposits have accumulated to a thickness of many feet there, and excellent wheat crops are grown, even without water.

A wide belt along the Snake River, on the southeast side of the plains, is covered by thick river sand and gravel floodplain deposits of the present and ancestral Snake River. A large area of such alluvial sands and gravels also occurs along the northwest side of the plains, where river waters from central Idaho disappear under the lavas.

East of St. Anthony, near Ashton at the eastern end of the plains, coarser wind-blown material has accumulated as well-developed, crescent-shaped sand dunes.

Structure

The Snake River Plains are a broad lowland between mountains to the northwest

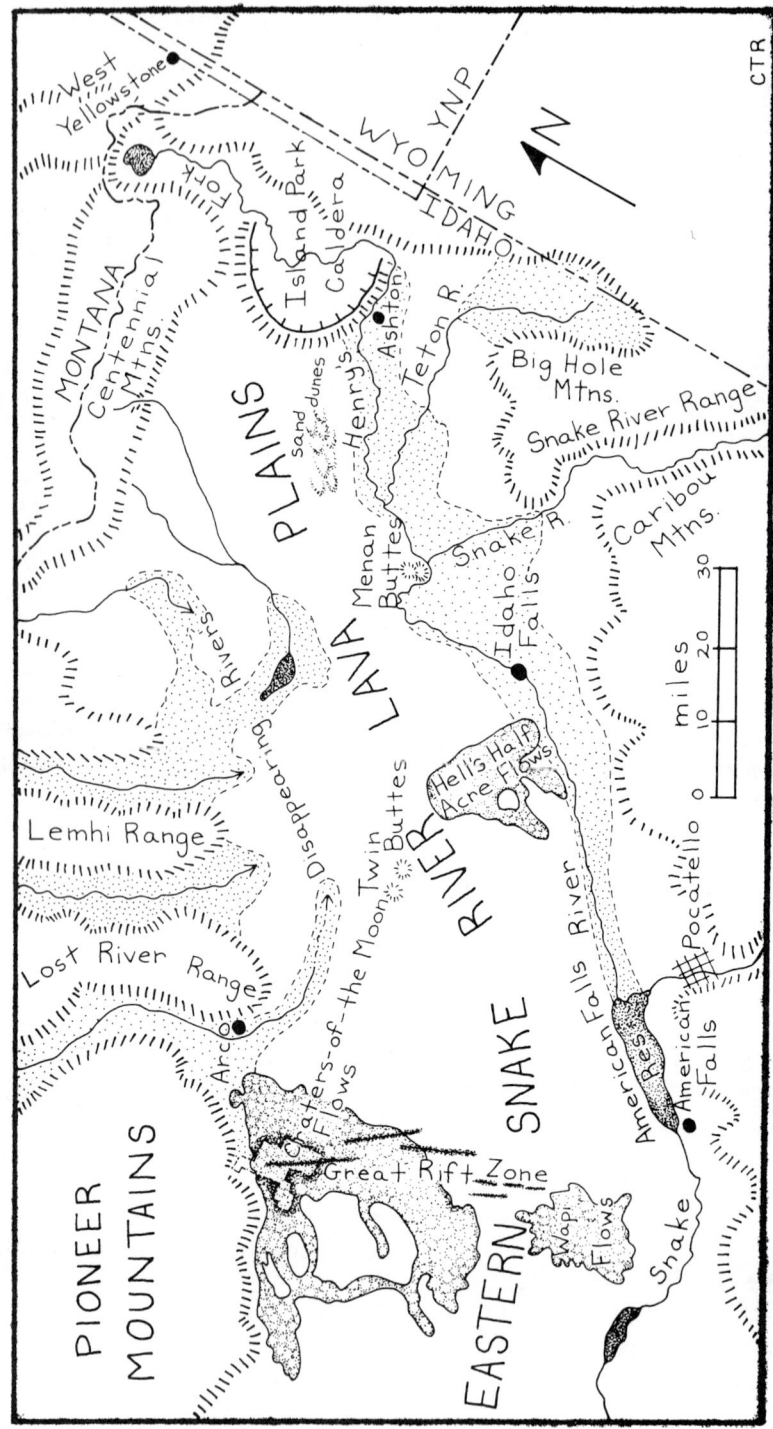

Figure 2.14. (on left page) Map of the Eastern Snake River Lava Plains. (facing page, on right) ERTS photograph of the same area.

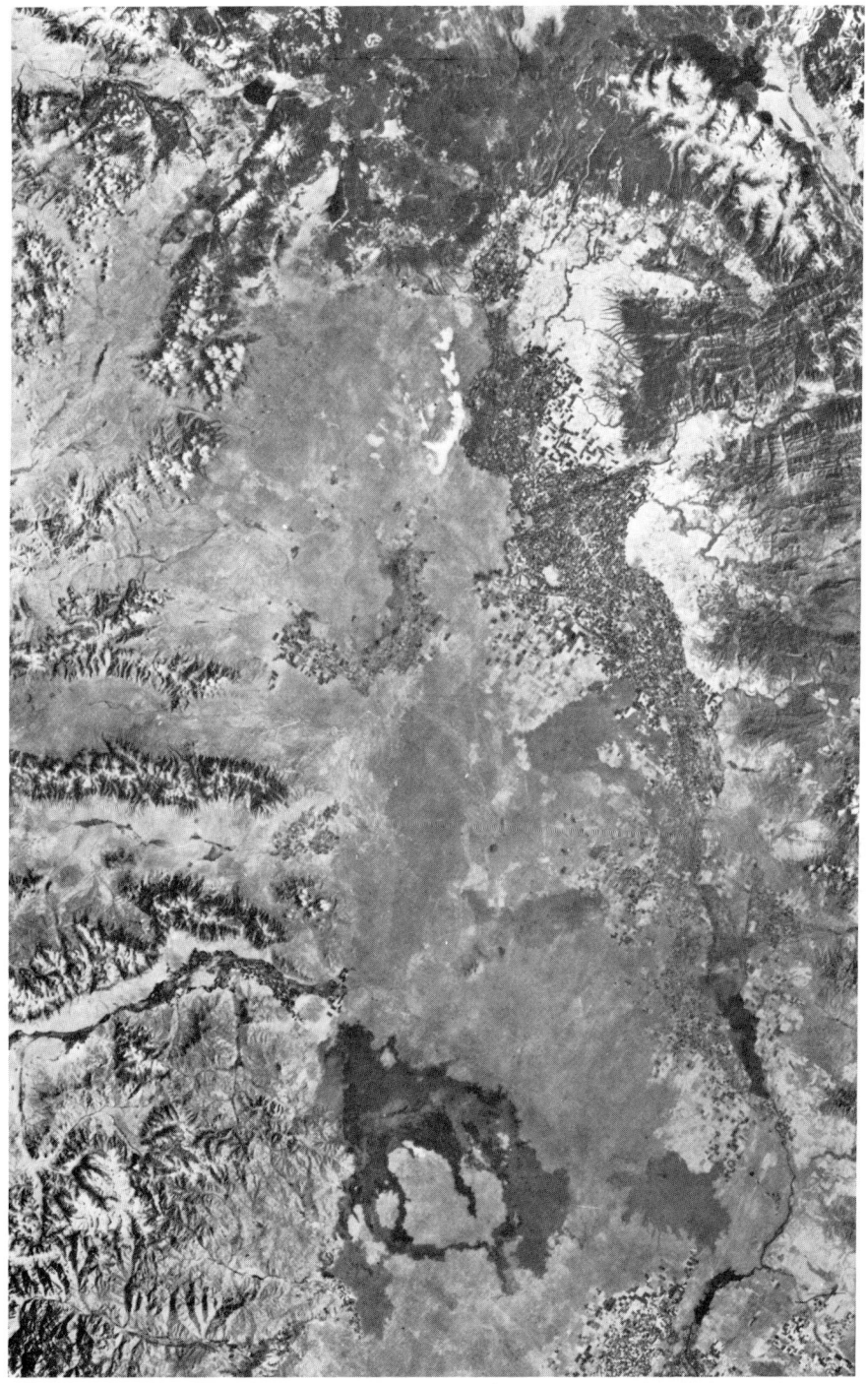

Photo 2.23. Wrinkled pahoehoe formed as a still plastic crust on a flow was carried along on the underlying moving lava until friction against the interior of the floor caused the surface to wrinkle as a rug sliding along a smooth floor! Craters-of-the Moon, Idaho.

and to the southeast. This is a basinlike structure or downwarp of the crust. The various mountain structures along the border between Idaho and Wyoming, which trend northwestward up to the southern side of the plains, apparently continue on the northern side of the plains trending in the same direction, after an interruption of 40 or 50 miles. Either the crust has been bent down, or faulted down, or both along the sides of the lava plains. This is best called a downwarp and occurred in late Tertiary time, long after the period of mountain formation.

Out on the plains holes have been drilled for various reasons, through at least 2,000 feet of lava. Geophysical studies under the center of the plains suggest that the lavas may be 5,000 feet or more in thickness. The lavas have accumulated over the past 5 or 10 million years.

On the surface of the eastern plains are some 300 known source areas for lava; that is, 300 little volcanoes! The majority of these are small, very gently sloping lava cones from which lava has flowed out in all directions for 2 to 10 miles. These little lava cones are small shield volcanoes with slopes of 2°

to 5°. When driving across the plains, many of these can be seen as gentle rises here and there on the horizon.

At some centers, cinder and ash cones have been formed by more explosive types of eruptions; these have much steeper slopes. Several cinder cones, one up to a thousand feet high, occur in the Craters-of-the-Moon National Monument near Arco. Two very unusual cones, known as Menan Buttes, on the south side of the plains, have been formed by the explosive activity of lava coming up through water, in this case through the ancestral Snake River or its water-saturated floodplain. Such craters are very wide with a circular rim of glassy ash grains a couple hundred feet high. This is the same type of cone as Diamond Head in Hawaii.

A number of buttes stick up through the lava surfaces—such as Twin Buttes, on the center of the plains, and Big Southern Butte, nearer Craters-of-the-Moon. Some of these are probably old eroded volcanoes; such has been suggested for Big Southern Butte, a rhyolite mass a thousand feet high.

Along the southeast side of the plains, between the mountains and the Snake River, are low foothills of rhyolitic lavas and ash flows. Continuing studies on these rocks suggest that large craters, or calderas, several miles in diameter, were the source areas for this material; the calderas are now almost completely buried under the basalts of the plain. The rim of one of these calderas may be present where the Snake River flows northward out of Swan Valley onto the lava plains. Another may be present under the Teton River where the dam failed in 1976. A dam should never have been built on this rhyolite ash flow tuff.

Special Features

One of the very economically important factors relating to the Snake River Plains is the behavior of surface water. Many rivers coming out of the mountains of central Idaho flow out a short distance onto the lava plains, and then their waters disappear. We have the Lost River and the Little Lost River, for example. Rivers also flow out of the Centennial Mountains to the north into this area of disappearing rivers. All this water moves along underground several hundred feet below the surface through porous zones between lava flows. The top of a lava flow is extremely irregular, full of cracks and openings of all kinds. When another flow comes onto this top, the zone of high porosity is buried and becomes an ideal place for water to move in large quantity. So in this great thickness of basalt lava flows are many zones through which water can move.

This water moves steadily along underground and eventually comes out into the Snake River Canyon, west of Twin Falls, at a place called Thousand Springs. Here water cascades out of the cliff wall from hundreds of openings between lava flows in tremendous quantity. The springs are not as visible as they used to be, as much water is taken directly into pipes to be used for irrigation. The lost water of the rivers has moved 50 to 150 miles underground to reappear far downstream in a lower part of the plains.

In an increasing number of places on the plains, wells are drilled a few hundred feet deep to tap this underground water. The water is then used for irrigation to bring desert areas of soil-covered lava into production. The supply of water is great and, so far, the amount being used is a small portion of the amount underground. This is probably the largest underground water reserve in the United States.

The Island Park caldera at the northeastern end of the Snake River lava plains is associated in origin with the rhyolite ash flows and lavas in Yellowstone National

Park. However, the caldera lies outside the Yellowstone area and perhaps relates more closely to the lava plains. For example, similar calderas are buried to the southwest all along the margin of the plains, progressively older calderas as one goes further southwest. So this caldera may represent a typical structure in the gradual development of the lava plains.

The Island Park caldera is a semicircular ring of hills rising above the plain's surface. The ring material is rhyolite welded ash flow, one to two million years old. The eastern half of the caldera has been buried completely beneath much younger lava flows coming out of Yellowstone Park. The floor of the western half of this giant caldera is covered with flat basalt lavas of the same kind that occur on the Snake River Plains. The succession, therefore, seems to be thus: rhyolite lavas first, erupting very explosively and leaving extremely large calderas; much later fluid basalt lavas erupting very quietly, spreading out in flat layers over all the low country, filling in the great caldera.

Chapter 3

Trip Guides

Let's get out and see the mountains and their rocks! Yellowstone has a very special meaning for all those interested in rocks and fossils and the natural processes which have shaped the landscape, for the Park is foremost a geological park. An extraordinary sequence of natural events have produced in and around Yellowstone an exceptionally fine outdoor laboratory for studies of the Rockies and their origin.

This chapter locates and explains what you can see as you drive toward Yellowstone on any of the main highways coming from the north, east, south, or west; the logs start as one approaches a scenic mountain range. Thus, trip guides from the east start at the Big Horn Mountains; routes from the south start along the Wind River Range, from the north with the Madison and Gallatin valley highways; etc. Finally, as a climax, the many geologic wonders in Yellowstone and Teton National parks are detailed. However, some of the finest scenery and most exciting rocks and structures actually lie outside the Park in the several ranges of the Middle Rockies which surround the Yellowstone region.

Trips are arranged in logs, or routes, for driving into Yellowstone Park. See Figure 3.1 for locations of specific logs. Of course, you will drive out again, presumably on a different route! With a little practice a trip log can be followed in reverse. Just remember that left becomes right, "first view" becomes "last view," etc. To anticipate the need to use these logs in reverse, some remarks like "last view of the mountains" are intended to guide a first viewer coming home. Maps are included for all trip logs showing locations of geologic features and road junctions. These should be used in conjunction with highway maps. Topographic maps of the U.S. Geological Survey, especially the 1:250,000 scale series, can be very helpful in visualization of where you are and how mountains, valleys, and plateaus are arranged. See Appendix B for further details on what maps to get and where they are available.

On the assumption that most travelers don't like to check the odometer continually, specific mileage references are kept to a minimum. Sometimes, however, it helps to know that a special rock outcrop is 5 miles from a junction or main bridge crossing; thus, a suggestion to check your odometer is made occasionally. You can write your odometer readings in the margins of these pages at intersections or prominent places for easy reference. Direction to some features is most easily stated in terms of the hour hand of a clock, with 12 o'clock straight ahead, 9 o'clock to the left, 3

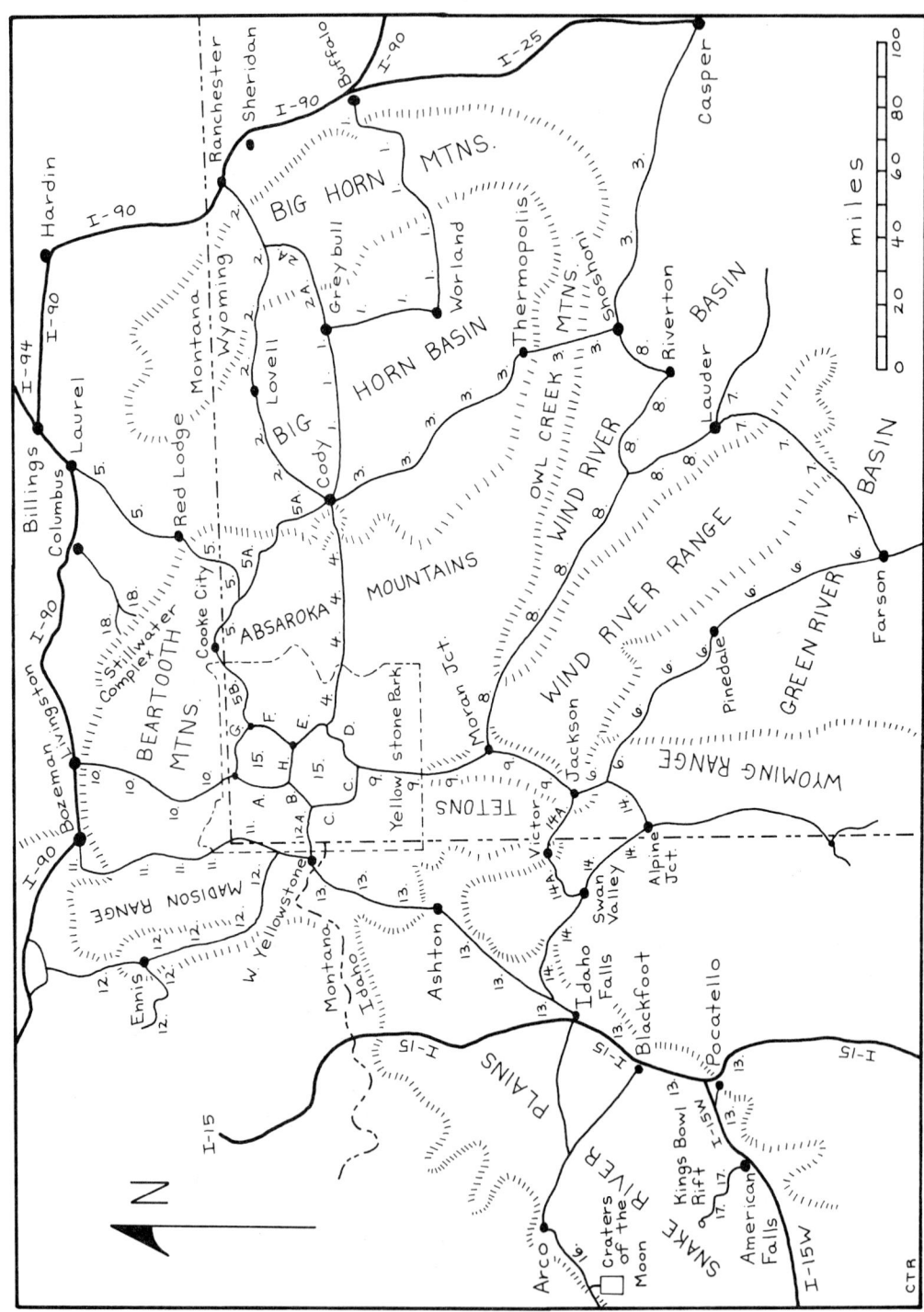

Figure 3.1. Map of the trip logs or routes described in this chapter.

o'clock to the right, and so on. Just imagine a clock face laid down flat in front of you with 12 o'clock directly ahead. Some locations on the maps in this guide are numbered thus, ②, and also in the text to help with location. Such points are not necessarily the most important places; they are just sites that seemed to need better location on the maps. Many other places are equally interesting stops but are clearly located by names or other marks on the maps.

Following a trip guide requires alertness and practice. Try to keep track of where you are in reference to points of interest, and keep your location on the various maps you may have. Appoint one of the passengers in your car as navigator! Read the log of your trip and study maps in advance to anticipate what can be seen to get the most out of your trip. Don't be too disturbed if you don't understand everything or if you miss some features. And remember that light conditions change with the weather and the time of day; thus some features that are very obvious on a clear morning may not show up in the afternoon or on a very cloudy day.

At many places a stop is suggested to look at the view or the rocks. This may mean a short walk as explained, or as is obvious. In some areas short hikes are suggested, especially in Yellowstone Park. In several places in Yellowstone little walk guides are available for a few cents, as at the canyon area or around Old Faithful. Also short side trips of 3 to 10 miles are included in the main log to places of unusually fine interest. Some longer side trips are given at the end of regular route logs, especially for those with more geological background. Longer hikes, up to all day, are suggested occasionally, especially in the parks.

Why rush? You are out for a vacation: see the scenery and other features of interest. Take time now; you may be sorry later that you missed a close view of Obsidian Cliff rocks, or the expression of a fault. Take this chance to know your Earth a little better.

Remember to check frequently with the charts of rock formations in Appendix A. What is the Madison limestone, the Chugwater red beds, or the Lava Creek Tuff of the Yellowstone group? Look these up in this appendix to keep your perspective of the geologic column. Check back to Chapter 1 for rock names, and so on, and refer to the Glossary for a brief explanation of geological terms which are not familiar to you.

ROUTES LEADING TO EAST ENTRANCE TO YELLOWSTONE PARK

The East entrance reached via Cody is perhaps the most widely used gateway to Yellowstone National Park. Visitors coming from the Black Hills on I-90 will usually cross the Big Horn Mountains by any one of three routes. Those coming from Cheyenne via Casper on I-25 may also opt to cross the Big Horns, or may come through the Wind River Canyon and thence to Cody. On I-94 via Billings it is also possible to come south to Cody. The most scenic routes, however, are those that cross the Big Horn Mountains.

Log 1: Buffalo to Worland to Cody,
U.S. 16, 180 miles
Map: Figure 3.2

Coming from the Black Hills on I-90 the route has been across the semidesert of the western high plains, the section known as the Powder River Basin. Since the town of Gillette, the rocks have all been sandstones and shales of the Fort Union Formation (early Tertiary in age). This formation contains some very important coal beds; the one being mined at Gillette is over 90 feet thick. Others are being mined north of Sheridan. At places, as seen on I-90 near Buffalo, some coal seams have burned in the past, ignited by grass fires. This has caused the immediately overlying shale beds to fuse together in red clinkery masses that look a little like rough, reddish lava.

Take the Buffalo exit on U.S. 16 and proceed through the town. Buffalo, elevation 4,645 feet, lies in the shallow valley of Clear Creek which has water for irrigation, and thus has green fields. This green valley is quite a contrast between the dry mountain foothills ahead and the barren bluffs of the Fort Union sandstone behind.

(Note odometer reading in the center of Buffalo.) About 2 miles from town the road ascends onto a terrace, and in another 3 or 4 miles the road starts the steep climb up the narrow valley of Clear Creek into the mountains. Very coarse bouldery gravels are exposed for the next few miles. These are glacial deposits.

① At 8 miles from town, the first rock outcrops are seen; these are nearly vertical beds of limestone and crushed red, green, and white sediments, probably all of Cambrian age. The main fault zone which borders the Big Horn Range at this side passes through here; thus, the vertical and crushed aspect of the rocks (see Map, Figure 3.2). In

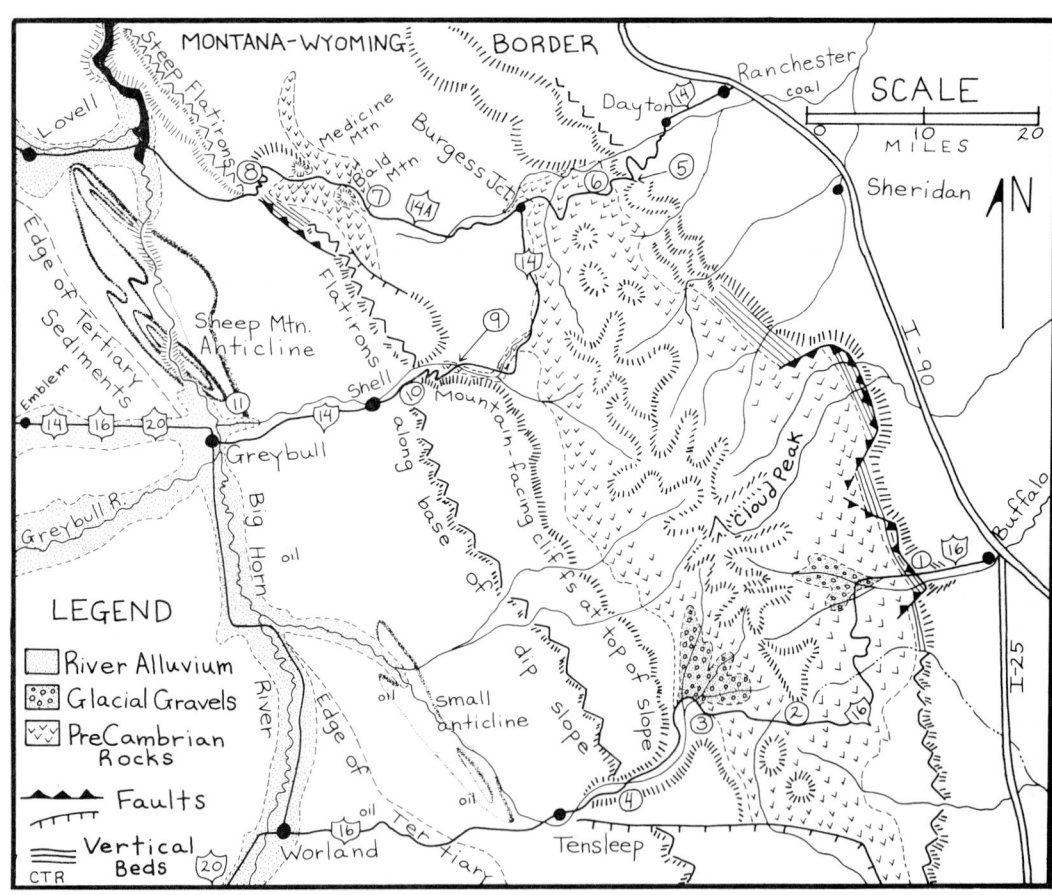

Figure 3.2. Map of trips across the Big Horn Mountains, Logs 1, 2, and 2A.

about half a mile, a large road cut of dark-colored gneiss indicates that the Precambrian has been reached.

In another mile or two the road comes up out of the narrow, steep part of the valley, and the first view ahead (west) may be had of the high snow-streaked central Big Horn Mountains. Cloud Peak, at 13,175 feet, is the peak to the right. The road now climbs more gently for the next dozen miles through open forest and grassy meadows with continuing views of the high mountains to the west and northwest (Photo 2.1). Some road cuts expose glacial gravels; other cuts and scattered rocky knolls are dark hornblende-rich gneisses.

The road emerges on a gently rolling upland or plateau surface, often in dense forest but with numerous outcrops of the dark gneisses. The road goes up and down with a relief of about 600 feet, but stays near an elevation of 8,000 feet for several miles. Gradually the road climbs again with more open grassy patches until it has covered another 15 miles.

② The gently sloping Powder River Pass at 9,666 foot elevation is reached approximately 36 miles from Buffalo. While the terrain is quite open and rocky, it is not above timberline. The peaks now in view rise only about 1,000 feet above the pass and have slopes covered with frost-shattered granite and gneiss slabs. Down from the pass on a very gentle grade for the next 6 miles are open meadows, scattered tree patches, and rocky knolls of granite and gneiss.

At 6 1/2 miles from the pass are the first small outcrops or ledges of nearly flat Cambrian sandstone (Flathead formation) along the edge of the road; these continue for about a mile.

③ A scenic viewpoint and Fire Fighters Monument at 8.3 miles from the pass overlook small Meadowlark Lake and a ski resort. This point is on the western edge of the upland Big Horn Plateau surface. About 2 miles to the west across the lake are low limestone scarps or cliffs.

For the next 6 miles the road drops down gently and swings around the lake in forests, but with road cuts in terminal moraine gravels containing large boulders. Finally the forests give way to mostly open grasslands, but the road cuts in moraine gravels continue for nearly 2 more miles. Along these same 2 miles large limestone cliffs may be seen ahead with giant fallen blocks at the bases of the cliffs.

A scenic parking place on the left (nearly 16 miles from the pass) affords a good view down into Tensleep Canyon, here still quite broad with high limestone cliffs set back from the valley and the road. The cliffs are cut in the Madison limestone, which is usually a cliff-former in the Middle Rockies.

The road drops down steeply with several switchbacks into an ever-narrower part of the canyon. The cliffs are near vertical and 1,000 feet high, exposing almost the entire thickness of the Madison limestone.

A junction to the left of Wyoming 435 is some 22 miles from the pass. (Check odometers here.) The canyon here is cut into the upper part of the Madison limestone with the Amsden limestone on top in the upper part of the cliff. The various sedimentary rocks are dipping gently to the southwest, the same direction that the road is trending. However, the dip of the rocks is a little more than the dip or grade of the road. Consequently, the formations are slowly going beneath the surface as one travels down the canyon.

④ A bridge over Tensleep Creek is 1.4 miles from the last junction. Here at road level is the Amsden limestone with many caves in it. Above the Amsden limestone is a 200–300-foot vertical cliff of Tensleep sandstone on each side of the canyon, seen straight ahead down the valley where the canyon turns abruptly to the right (see Photo 3.1). The Madison limestone is now below the surface due to its westward dip.

For the next 2 1/2 miles the canyon is cut into this Tensleep sandstone. The sandstone is massive or thick bedded but with large-scale, well-developed cross-bedding. This is the locality where this sandstone was first carefully studied and named. The sandstone formation dips at a low angle to the west and so finally dips beneath the surface, and the canyon ends immediately! (This is 4 miles from the Wyo. 435 junction.)

The view now opens up with outcrops of the red Chugwater formation, and a large mesa of this red sandstone to the right. This terrain continues for 4 miles to the small town of Tensleep on the eastern edge of the Big Horn Basin at 4,200 feet elevation, more than a mile in elevation below the Powder River Pass. The lowlands here have green irrigated fields. About a mile beyond the

Photo 3.1. Cliffs of the Tensleep sandstone formation, a very thick bedded, resistant quartz sandstone. Cliff about 200 ft. thick.

town, the road climbs up some low hills of steeply dipping sandstones out of the irrigated valley.

For the next 12 miles the road crosses sage-covered, semiarid hills of Cretaceous sandstone and shale, sometimes with steep dips, sometimes flat-lying. Then for another 4 miles the road passes through a small oil field with scattered pumping wells. The rocks look the same but the sandstones are lower Tertiary in age (Fort Union formation).

Low badlands in the colorful Willwood formation characterize the next 5 miles. And for another 5 miles the road is on a flat alluvium-covered surface, which is part of the wide floodplain of the Bighorn River.

The city of Worland is located on the west side of the Bighorn River on the floodplain which is over 5 miles wide at this point. Here route U.S. 16 joins U.S. 20. Turn right, northward, with both 16 and 20. It is now about 40 miles to Greybull, also in the Bighorn Valley. The route from Worland to Greybull is entirely on alluvium in the floodplain of this river. Much of this plain is irrigated and in crops or hay. However, due to the presence of the Burlington Railroad and nearby oil fields some machinery mars the already dull scenery. The trip is quite featureless, and in summer it can be very hot. Halfway from Worland to Greybull, at the town of Manderson, the road crosses the Bighorn River from the east side to the west and continues north on that side of the floodplain. Just south of Manderson the road runs close on the right to low river bluffs cut into Tertiary sedimentary rocks (Fort Union formation).

⑪ Just north of Greybull lies the southern end of the Sheep Mountain anticline. This is the largest anticline in the Big Horn Basin, and its ridge rises 2,000 feet above the basin surface. North of town and across the Bighorn River, red beds of the Chugwater form a prominent hogback. Then the main mountain rises to an even summit level. The Bighorn River has cut a canyon diagonally through the ridge (see Map, Fig. 3.2), and the railroad follows the river through this canyon. There is no auto road. It may be possible to get to the southern end of the canyon mouth on a dirt road that parallels the railroad.

In Greybull route U.S. 14 from the east joins 16 and 20. Proceed straight through town and curve left with all three routes to proceed some 50 miles west to Cody. This is a flat, essentially featureless trip across the Big Horn Basin. The first 20 miles is through farmland irrigated with water brought in by canal from the Greybull River. The next 25 miles (see Map, Fig. 3.8) is semidesert with sparse sagebrush typical of the central Big Horn Basin. Rocks, when visible, are sandstones and shales of the Willwood formation.

As the route approaches Cody, the flat, but notched, profile of Rattlesnake Mountain becomes apparent. The notch, to the left side, is the canyon of the Shoshone River cut through an anticlinal uplift. Behind this mountain and to the southwest (at 10 o'clock) are the Absaroka Mountains. To the northeast (about 2 o'clock) is an odd-shaped, isolated knob known as Heart Mountain. Behind this on the skyline is the Beartooth Plateau, usually snow-covered in early summer.

Log 2: Sheridan to Lovell to Cody, U.S. 14 and 14 Alt., 154 miles
Map: Figure 3.2

The northern crossing of the Big Horn Mountains really starts at Ranchester, but Sheridan is the ideal place to spend the night and get ready for a mountain trip in the morning. Therefore, this trip log starts at Sheridan. Coming west on I-90 from the Black Hills, proceed past the Buffalo exit and come north along the front of the mountains to Sheridan.

If the weather over the mountains is impossible or dangerous for driving, the traveler may continue north on I-90 into Montana to Billings, from where a return to either Cody, Wyoming, or Red Lodge, Montana, will allow the continuation of a trip to Yellowstone Park. On doing this, the route passes Custer Battlefield National Monument in Montana about 75 miles north of Sheridan, where the rocks are Cretaceous sandstones.

Leaving Sheridan, get onto I-90 northbound and proceed to the Ranchester exit to U.S. 14 westbound. This route passes rocks of the Fort Union formation which contains several coal seams. Mining activity and development may be noted at a distance to the right of the road. Also, a number of reddish clinker beds are visible, formed where coal has burned underground and the shales have fused to clinkery masses.

From Ranchester to Dayton, the road travels the valley of the Tongue River. Check odometer at the bridge across the Little Tongue River in Dayton. In about a half mile the view ahead of the mountain front will also give a view up the Tongue River Canyon. The high part of the mountain front is made up of Madison limestone. Just below the top, the reddish slopes are cut in the Amsden formation.

For about 5 miles the road climbs through various sandstones and shales of Mesozoic age over treeless slopes. As the route goes up, it crosses rocks of older and older age. The rocks are dipping to the east but at a greater angle than the angle of the slope to the road (see Figure 3.3). Therefore, the trip up is going down in the section of rocks!

At about 6 miles from Dayton, the road cuts expose more rocks, and trees are now present. Many types of sedimentary rocks

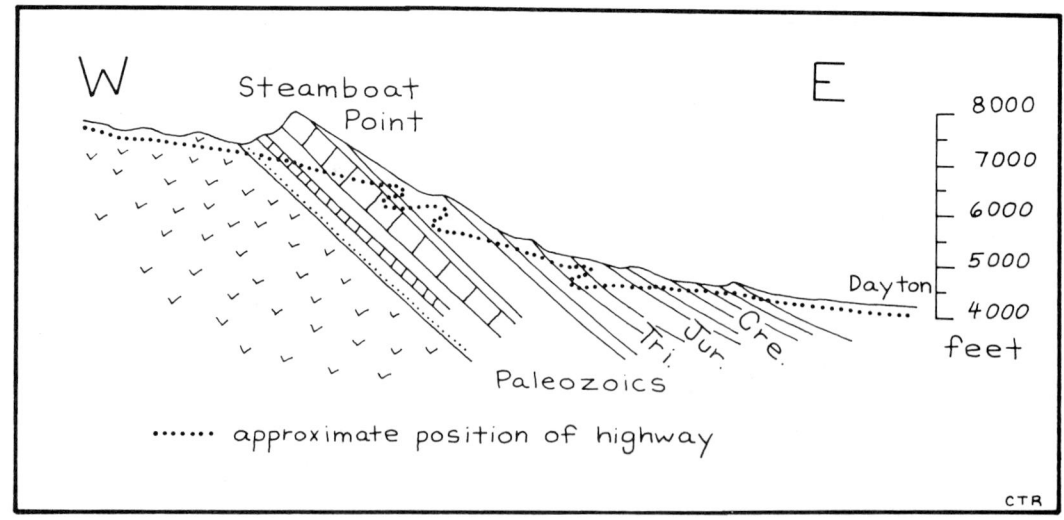

Figure 3.3. Cross section along Log 2 (U.S. 14) going up the eastern slope of the Big Horn Mountains from Dayton, Wyoming. The position of the highway and its switchbacks is shown diagrammatically relative to rock formations.

are well exposed along the road, and stops can be made to study rock types. For the next 4 miles, as the road switchbacks and dips into valleys, it zigzags back and forth through the various upper Paleozoic formations—Tensleep, Amsden, and Madison—so that the same rocks are seen several times.

(5) Sand Turn Observation Point is 10 miles from Dayton. This is a fine large parking area on the left from which a panoramic view is obtained to the east out across the plains and down to the road below, and south across the valley of the Little Tongue River to the mountain front to the south. The rocks across the road are the Amsden sandstone on top of the Madison limestone.

Walk around the curve of the road at this observation area and look down into the valley of the Little Tongue. Two landslides are visible. To the left and directly across the valley, much rock has crumbled away and fallen down to dam the creek, making a small muddy lake directly below. Further up stream and to the right, seen best if you walk or drive 1/2 mile around the corner and on up the road, is a different type of landslide, called Fallen City, where great house-sized blocks of dolomite have tumbled down as the Bighorn formation has cracked and slumped (Photo 3.2).

The next three miles present almost continuous rock exposure as the route turns

Photo 3.2. Fallen City landslide as seen from near the Sand Turn Observation Point. The rocks involved are massive blocks of the Bighorn dolomite.

back into the valley of Little Tongue Creek. From Sand Turn there is about a mile of Madison limestone, nearly a mile of Devonian limestones and shales (here looking almost flat, since the route is at right angles to the dip), and then a half mile of the Bighorn dolomite. Now the road comes out on a grassy surface of the Cambrian sediments; a view up to the right or back shows the impressive top of Steamboat Point, a great cliff of Bighorn dolomite dipping to the east and down the mountains (Photo 3.3).

The road almost immediately goes into a curve through a rockcut and here Precambrian granite gneisses are exposed with thin basalt dikes and numerous joints, an ideal place for detail study except for the danger of passing cars.

⑥ Drive about a half mile up and around until you face Steamboat Point. This is an ideal place to stop and see the geography and geologic relationships. Steamboat Point stands up very prominently with the Bighorn cliff above a grassy slope which contains a few rock ledges. This is the posi-

Photo 3.3. Steamboat Point, a large hogback of Bighorn dolomite dipping back down the mountains to the east.

tion of the various Cambrian rocks. At the bottom of this slope, just below where you are standing, is the Cambrian-Precambrian contact. To the north (left as one faces the Point) is the canyon of the main Tongue River, with most of the Paleozoic rock section exposed on its far side. The great cliff about halfway down the canyon side is the Bighorn dolomite. The upper part of the far wall in the trees is Madison limestone.

For the next 13 miles the route is on a rolling upland or plateau surface on Precambrian gneisses and granites and is largely forested. A few distant vistas both right and left show flat-lying Cambrian and Bighorn sedimentary rocks.

Burgess Junction is the road fork approximately 28 miles from Dayton. This Trip Guide goes straight ahead (right) on U.S. 14 Alternate. The route to the left, U.S. 14, goes down Shell Canyon and is logged later as Log 2A.

The route is across open grassy meadows into the broad upland valley of the North Tongue River. Rounded granite outcrops are scattered in the fields for the first 2 1/2 miles. The distant hills on both sides of this broad valley show cliffs of the Bighorn dolomite.

For the next 10-12 miles the route is up the Tongue River valley. The valley quickly becomes narrower and the Cambrian limestone and overlying Bighorn dolomite cliffs become closer. There is no more granite in the valley. Finally, the road reaches the head of the now small creek at gentle Baldy Pass and then a bridge over the head of Beaver Creek, with a limited view of the Big Horn Basin to the left.

⑦ In about a mile the road comes out on an open view spot; a sign says "Observation Point—Scenic View of Big Horn Basin." About 20 miles to the southwest out in the Big Horn Basin, the ridge of the Sheep Mountain anticline may be seen. Little Bald Mountain, immediately above the road to the right, and Bald Mountain, about 3 1/2 miles on ahead to the northwest, are both composed of Cambrian limestones and shales. This observation sight itself is on a pebbly limestone and is 9,530 feet in elevation.

Continuing on the road, almost immediately granite outcrops will be seen. In 5 1/2 miles a large "Scenic Parking Area" lies off to the right. The flat area is composed of Precambrian granite, but all the smooth hills rising above are Cambrian sediments. Bald Mountain is only a mile away across the road. It is 10,040 feet above sea level and about 800 feet above the parking area. Medicine Mountain is about 2 1/2 miles to the west with a radar installation on top. This mountain is also just over 10,000 feet high, and the top is composed of the Bighorn dolomite. To the north and northeast, away from the road, the view is into valleys and low mountains of the central part of the northern Big Horn Range.

Two miles ahead a road to the right leads to the radar facility and the Medicine Wheel, about 3 miles each. This is a dirt road, but safe if dry. The Medicine Wheel consists of a roughly circular pattern of stones laid out on the surface of the ground, about 78 feet in diameter. A central rock cairn forms the "hub" of the wheel, while radial lines of stones from this cairn to the peripheral circle form the "spokes." Six additional cairns are located near the periphery. Some of the cairns line up to show the position of sunrise and sunset at the summer solstice, June 21st. Others may have been laid out to indicate the position of certain stars. This wheel was apparently built by Shoshone Indians about 200 years ago. It may mark the place where

92   *Trip Guides*

the Shoshone first danced the Sun Dance. It's an interesting trip if one doesn't mind a fairly primitive road.

The road now starts down gently and for 3 1/2 miles runs along with reddish granite outcrops and road cuts. This is a new section of road. The old road was above, and it traveled across Cambrian shales which caused continuing landslide problems every spring.

Now another viewpoint turnoff to the left is well worth making. An excellent view of Sheep Mountain in the Big Horn Basin is obtained here, showing very clearly the canyon through the anticline cut by the Big Horn River. This parking area is on Precambrian granites although they are not well exposed, due to soil and slump covering. Up the mountainside above here the overlying Paleozoic sediments are flat-lying. Below the parking site down the mountain the same Paleozoic sediments dip vertically! (See Figure 3.4.)

In another 2 miles the road crosses Five Springs Creek in a sharp switchback curve and starts steeply downhill. In the next 7 miles the road will drop over 3,000 feet! Drive in low gear. The road is on landslide deposits.

Watch, in another 3 miles, for the Big Horn National Forest boundary sign and check your odometer. Here is another good view ahead of Sheep Mountain and its gap.

⑧ In about 0.8 to 0.9 miles the road comes out on the mountain edge just above a very sharp switchback. There is limited parking on the left. Here is the upper, and best, view of the mountain front structure and the famous Five Springs Fault. Across the valley Paleozoic limestones are standing in vertical position. The small cave is in the Madison. On to the right, down the mountains, are

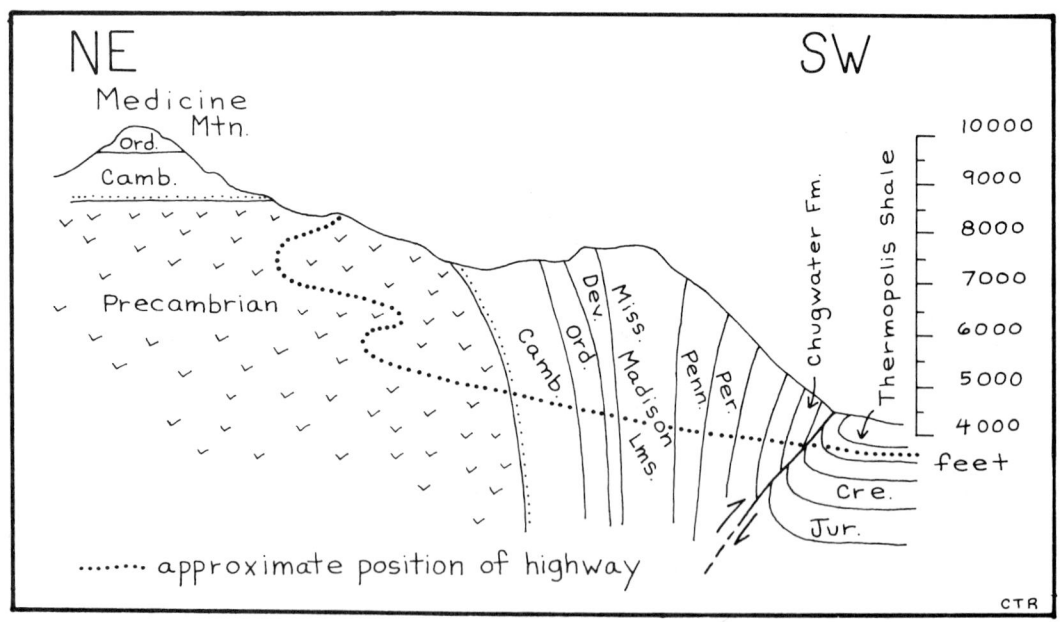

Figure 3.4. Generalized cross section of the west side of the Big Horn Mountains near route 14A. Upper position of the highway on left is at the scenic turnoff beyond Medicine Mountain.

other formations through the red Chugwater. These beds are in thrust fault contact with black Thermopolis shales (see Photo 3.4 and Figure 3.4).

The road makes a sharp reverse curve and in less than a mile is back to stream level. A road to the left goes to the Five Springs Falls Campground. The rock here is Precambrian granite.

Three quarters of a mile further down, and shortly after crossing a cattleguard, the road is opposite and nearest to the cave in the Madison limestone (Photo 3.5). At the next switchback is a lower and final view of the structure and fault across the canyon.

The road is soon off the mountains and continues down a more gentle slope now in the Big Horn Basin. To the right is a view of

Photo 3.4. Vertical Paleozoic formations on the west side of the Big Horn Mountains as seen from U.S. 14A, Log 2. On the left are cliffs of Bighorn dolomite, in the center the Devonian rocks, and the large cliffs on the right are the Madison limestone. To the far right on the more gentle slopes is the position of the Five Springs thrust fault (compare to Figure 3.4).

Photo 3.5. Cave in vertical beds of the Madison limestone as seen across Five Springs Creek valley from U.S. 14A, Log 2.

steeply dipping triangular-shaped flatirons along the mountain front. To the left for a few miles is a long ridge formed by the black Thermopolis shale formation. In 14 miles the Big Horn Lake or Reservoir is reached. Just before the bridge, a road to the right goes to a boat launching site and campground. This gives access to boating on Big other formations through the red Chugwater. These beds are in thrust fault contact with black Thermopolis shales (see Photo 3.4 and Figure 3.4).

The road makes a sharp reverse curve and in less than a mile is back to stream level. A road to the left goes to the Five Springs Falls Campground. The rock here is Precambrian granite.

Three quarters of a mile further down, and shortly after crossing a cattleguard, the road is opposite and nearest to the cave in the Madison limestone (Photo 3.5). At the next switchback is a lower and final view of the structure and fault across the canyon.

The road is soon off the mountains and continues down a more gentle slope now in the Big Horn Basin. To the right is a view of

Photo 3.4. Vertical Paleozoic formations on the west side of the Big Horn Mountains as seen from U.S. 14A, Log 2. On the left are cliffs of Bighorn dolomite, in the center the Devonian rocks, and the large cliffs on the right are the Madison limestone. To the far right on the more gentle slopes is the position of the Five Springs thrust fault (compare to Figure 3.4).

Photo 3.5. Cave in vertical beds of the Madison limestone as seen across Five Springs Creek valley from U.S. 14A, Log 2.

steeply dipping triangular-shaped flatirons along the mountain front. To the left for a few miles is a long ridge formed by the black Thermopolis shale formation. In 14 miles the Big Horn Lake or Reservoir is reached. Just before the bridge, a road to the right goes to a boat launching site and campground. This gives access to boating on Big

Horn Lake, which goes through the Big Horn Canyon across the northern end of the range to the Yellowtail Dam in Montana.

Cross Big Horn Lake on bridge and causeway, and in another mile cross the Burlington Railroad: Check odometer here. To the right at 3 or 4 o'clock is a good view across the lake of a monoclinal fold on the east side of the Big Horn uplift. Chugwater red beds are exposed at the base of the fold, and then the Tensleep sandstone curves up and flattens out on top. Behind the car—driver, don't look without a stop—the dipping beds are eroded into triangular flatirons along the front.

For the next few miles the dipping beds on the east side of the Little Sheep Mountain anticline will be seen to the left (at 10 or 11 o'clock). The Chugwater red beds will be easily recognized with a very steep dip.

At 4.9 to 5.0 miles from the railroad crossing, just after making a final curve before straight road again, the road crosses the extension of the axis or trend of this anticline. Actually, the view is not as good as it was a mile earlier to the left. To the right at about 10 o'clock is a good view of two fault blocks in the Pryor Mountains, each dipping gently to the west. The irrigated valley immediately to the right is that of the Shoshone River.

In 4 miles U.S. 310 merges from the left and both routes now enter the small city of Lovell. Proceed through town, cross the Shoshone River with outcrops of Cretaceous sandstones, and turn left with U.S. 14 Alternate.

In about 3 miles the route crosses the Byron anticline and oil field; and in another 3.5 miles, the Garland anticline and oil field! Oil has been produced since 1905 from four different horizons, currently from the Madison limestone 4,000 to 5,000 feet below the surface. Any rocks seen at the surface are Cretaceous shales or sandstones.

At the town of Garland, turn left toward Powell. Along most of this route water from the Shoshone River is available from canals for irrigation. Powell is the center of rich farmland based on this water.

From Powell to Cody, some 24 miles, many views of Heart Mountain jutting up sharply will be obtained to the right. Across the Shoshone River to the left are extensive badlands, eroded in the colorful Willwood formation of Eocene age. The high group of hills cut out of the Willwood, that rise more than 1,000 feet above the river, is known as the McCullough Peaks. Two major gravel-covered terraces are well developed along this section of the river. From Powell to the bridge over the Shoshone River the route is on the upper Powell Terrace. After the bridge, the road is on the lower Cody Terrace. Both terraces are former stream cut levels; in fact, they are remnants of gravel-covered floodplains formed during the glacial period. As the route approaches Cody the high ridge of Rattlesnake Mountain, with its sharp gap on the left, will dominate the skyline ahead. To the left and in the background are the Absaroka Mountains. The nearest mass of this range, about 20 miles away to the southwest, is Carter Mountain.

The flat-topped mountains far to the right behind Heart Mountain form the Beartooth Plateau.

Side Trip to Elk Basin Oil Field

For those who have strong geologic orientation, a trip north from Powell to the anticline at Elk Basin is recommended. Turn right on the main street of Powell from U.S. 14 Alt. and continue due north (see Map,

Figure 3.8). The paved road proceeds through the irrigated farmland for 6 or 7 miles and then climbs 500 feet up onto the arid and barren Polecat Bench. This bench is a long gravel-capped mesa 20 miles long by 2 to 5 miles wide. It is believed to be a remnant of a former course and floodplains of the Shoshone River, before the action of stream piracy by a tributary of the Big Horn River. The surface of Polecat Bench slopes to the northeast at the constant rate of 25 feet to the mile—essentially the same slope as present streams in the Big Horn Basin.

After 10 miles on the bench, the driver comes to the south end of the Elk Basin anticline. Shales in the uplifted middle of the anticline have been eroded more rapidly than the surrounding sandstones. So the center of the anticline is a lowland surrounded by 200- to 300-foot-high hogback ridges of various Cretaceous sandstones. Many geology field course groups map here, and after the students learn the various formations, they can readily locate a dozen or so faults which cut across the anticline. The exposed part of the structure is 5 or 6 miles from north northwest to south southeast and crosses the Wyoming-Montana state line.

Some 300 producing oil and gas wells make this field one of the top producers in Wyoming. Much of the oil comes from the Tensleep and Madison formations at 5,000 to 7,000 feet below the present surface.

A return by paved road retraces the trip to Powell. It is also possible to drive north on a dirt road along Silvertip Gulch some 12 miles into Montana. Turn left on the first road after the last ridge on the left. Then it is 2 miles to the paved road, Mont. 308. Left again, and cross the Clarks Fork River, about 1 1/2 miles to Belfrey, then right to Red Lodge.

Log 2A: Burgess Junction to Greybull, U.S. 14, 44 miles
Map: Figure 3.2 (Sheridan to Cody, 142 miles)

An alternate route from Sheridan to Cody is to stay with U.S. 14 all the way. This trip starts off, as Log 2, from Sheridan up onto the Big Horn Mountains to Burgess Junction, some 48 miles from Sheridan. At this junction, turn left with U.S. 14.

The road traverses a broad, flat grassy upland with occasional granite outcrops and forests set well back from the road. About two miles to the right is a tree-covered ridge, or series of low mountains, composed of Cambrian limestones and capped by Bighorn dolomite. After 10 miles the very gentle Granite Pass at 8,950 feet is reached. Check odometer. The route now starts downward almost imperceptibly for a couple miles.

The grade steepens as the road enters the shallow valley of Granite Creek. Granite gneisses are visible in the stream bed, but the road is in slump deposits of Cambrian shale debris. The road approaches the valley of Shell Creek at about right angles; the creek is reached 9 miles from the pass. Ahead, the forested side of Shell Creek Valley has about 2,000 feet of various Paleozoic formations. On this same forested slope is a striking swath of downed trees from top to bottom. This is the effect of a small tornado a few years ago.

The road switchbacks to the right and is now on the side of Shell Creek. The route enters an extensive area of landslides and slump topography, which has involved almost the entire 1,000 feet of Cambrian sediments, but especially the shales in the lower part of the Cambrian. Eight main landslides, visible here, were activated by road rebuilding in 1965 and were not stabilized for 6 or 8 years. Water was such a great problem that a permanent 12-inch, 200-foot deep pumping well was installed in 1971. The road passes through the base of these landslides for the next 2 or 3 miles (see Photo 3.6). To the left in the creek bottom, granite is exposed beneath the slump deposits.

⑨ Almost 12 miles from Granite Pass, the road crosses a bridge over Shell Creek, and within a few hundred feet a large parking area called "Shell Creek Overlook" lies off to the right; it is maintained by the Forest Service. Here is a box canyon and falls with vertical granite walls, 100 feet deep on the upstream side, more than 200 feet deep on the downstream side below the falls. The Forest Service maintains walkways with railings and observation platforms to allow visitors access to fine views. In the high part of the area, the Precambrian granite is overlain by the Cambrian Flathead sandstone. The contact of the two is fully exposed. A finger can be placed on a contact that represents a time break in earth history of almost 2

Photo 3.6. Landslide scar and debris along north side of Shell Creek valley on U.S. 14, Log 2A.

billion years! The granite was formed some 2 1/2 billion years ago, was metamorphosed to granite gneiss, and was then partly eroded. An old land surface was covered by a sea as the land slowly sank. The waves of this Cambrian sea washed away all the soil, leaving a smooth rock surface on which beach sands were deposited; these sands continued to accumulate as the sea became deeper. The old beach sands are now the Flathead sandstone. In some places cross-bedding can be seen. Perhaps this represents dune sands along the old beach.

Across Shell Creek Canyon and high above are some projecting rocks which have been named Copemans Tomb. The top cliff here is a sheer wall of Madison limestone, and a lower cliff is the Bighorn dolomite. Similar rocks may be seen to the left, along the mountain tops.

The road runs precariously along the valley side, several hundred feet above the ever-deepening Shell Canyon. Granite can be seen in the canyon bottom, and 2 or 3 tributary streams enter from the far side with sharply cut granite canyons. A few thousand feet above on the opposite side a sharp drape fold (Photo 3.7) in the massive limestone cliffs comes more clearly into view. Here the gently dipping sedimentary rocks on the top

Photo 3.7. A fold in the upper Paleozoic limestones near the west side of the Big Horn Range. This is the upper part of a large monocline (see Figure 1.1) where the beds are draped over the uplifted block of the Big Horn Mountains.

of the Big Horn Range start to plunge steeply off the mountain front to the west.

About 4.5 miles from the Overlook parking site, the road makes the first of a few tight switchbacks and drops steeply to river level in less than a mile. In less than half a mile the canyon narrows abruptly with cliffs of the Bighorn dolomite. In another half mile cliffs of the Madison limestone box in the canyon. These rocks are all dipping westward at more than the slope of the stream bed, and therefore, each successive formation dips beneath the surface just as at the mouth of Tensleep Canyon. In still another half mile, reddish-orange cliffs are part of the Amsden formation. In a few tenths of a mile is a bridge over Shell Creek with low cliffs of Tensleep sandstone just ahead on the right.

⑩ Just one half mile beyond the bridge the canyon has ended; there is a wide gravel area on the right of the road just across from cottages in cottonwood trees on the left. Stop here, get out and walk up to the right to look along the mountain front to the north. Rock layers look flat on top but dip steeply down a 2,000-foot mountain front, where erosion has carved spectacular triangular flatirons (Photo 2.2). At the foot of the mountains and in the immediate foreground, the Chugwater red beds form hills of flat-lying beds in a red wilderness! South of the highway across the creek, the mountain folding is such that the dip-slope is uniformly gentle, and no corresponding flatirons have been developed.

Just a half mile further down the road much red Chugwater is present on both sides, especially a rock pillar to the left. Now the Big Horn Basin opens up and in about 4 miles the tiny town of Shell is reached, elevation 4,210 feet.

A mile beyond town is another excellent view of the mountains to the right rear, with the flat layers on top and the steep beds on the front itself. Just ahead on the left are some colorful shale and sandstone beds. This is the Morrison formation famous for dinosaur bones. Dr. Barnun Brown, of the American Museum of Natural History in New York, collected some of that museum's fine dinosaur skeletons just 13 miles north of here.

The rocks are fairly dull and drab for the 13 miles into Greybull from here; they are Cretaceous shales and sandstones of many different formations.

⑪ About 3 miles before Greybull and 11 miles from the town of Shell, the route crosses the axis of the Sheep Mountain anticline which lies to the right and north of Greybull. The mountain rises at about 10 o'clock with steeply dipping red Chugwater beds on its right side. (See more on this in the Log to route 1 under ⑪ .)

In Greybull the road joins routes U.S. 16 and 20 in the center of town. Turn right and refer to the guide from Greybull to Cody in Log 1.

Log 3: Shoshoni to Thermopolis to Cody, U.S. 20 and Wyoming 120, 86 miles
Map: Figure 3.5

Visitors coming from the east or southeast (Cheyenne) by way of Casper, Wyoming, will be on U.S. routes 20 and 26 into Shoshoni. Route 26 goes west to Jackson Hole; route 20 turns north into the Big Horn Basin and to Cody.

In Shoshoni turn right with U.S. 20 and proceed northward directly toward the Owl Creek Mountains. Check odometer. For many miles from Casper westward the route has been over semiarid uninteresting flat or slightly hilly basin country. The next 12 miles are more of the same. The rocks here belong to the Tertiary Willwood formation and weather into low badlands.

100 Trip Guides

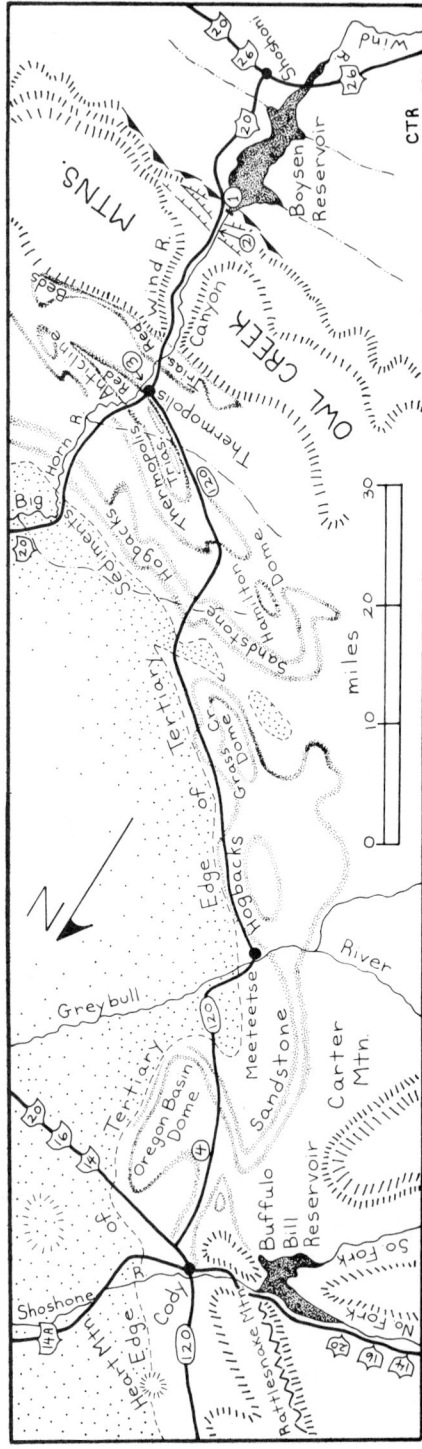

Figure 3.5. Map of area along the route of Log 3 across the Owl Creek Mountains and up the west side of the Big Horn Basin.

Mostly, the road is on a flat plain with a view of the Boysen Reservoir to the left after a few miles. The mountain front ahead is a fault scarp with steep south-dipping sedimentary rocks. The mountains appear to have been shoved or thrust to the south onto the Wind River Basin crustal block (see Fig. 2.3).

The road now begins to curve to the right, probably crossing the first fault. The actual fault is often covered by talus and alluvium just in front of the mountain. Red beds are exposed at 13 miles and granite at 13.6 miles.

① "Points of Interest" parking on left at Boysen Reservoir just above the dam, 14 miles from Shoshoni. Cambrian sedimentary rocks are exposed in the roadcut here and across the reservoir with several small faults visible in both areas. Also, a small Precambrian gneiss area is visible across the lake to the left. The entire Paleozoic section up to the Madison limestone is visible on the high mountains (Boysen Peak) across the dam on the skyline.

Drive for one mile past the dam passing road cuts in Cambrian sediments, shales, and thin limestones, and several small faults. There is parking space on the left below the dam. Across the river valley are Precambrian gneisses and overlying Cambrian formations cut by several small faults. For the next mile and a half there are more views of Cambrian rocks and small faults across the river.

② Historical marker of the Original Boysen Dam and a picnic and campsite entrance are on the left. Just ahead the road enters a tunnel in a "wall" of dark Precambrian rocks cut by lighter colored granite bodies. This wall is the final fault along which the center of the Owl Creek Range is uplifted (see Figure 2.3). The route for the next 2 miles leads through three small tunnels, and the rocks are all Precambrian: grayish gneisses with some layers of very dark gneisses, several whitish and pink pegmatite dikes or lenses, and a small granite mass.

Just less than 2 miles from the first tunnel, the contact or unconformity between the Precambrian rocks and the Flathead sandstone is visible along the right of the road. Here is a time break in earth history of almost 2 billion years: that is, time from the formation of the Precambrian gneisses and granites and the later deposition of sand from the Cambrian seas. Small cross bedding is present in some of the sandstone which shows wave or wind action along the ancient beach.

For the next 10 miles in the Wind River Canyon all the sedimentary rocks of the Paleozoic (see table, Appendix A.2) are present and quite well exposed. These rocks are dipping very gently, perhaps 5°, to the north in the direction that the river is flowing. At the time of this writing signs were posted on each formation by the Wyoming Geological Association. The route is over Cambrian formations for almost 6 miles; then the great solid 300- to 400-foot cliff of the Bighorn dolomite; and the 1,000-foot Madison limestone cliffs in another two miles. The very last cliffs as the canyon ends are Tensleep sandstone with a little Phosphoria limestone on top by some picnic tables.

The canyon ends abruptly, and you are in the Big Horn Basin! Ahead are bright red hogbacks of the Chugwater sandstones and siltstones. The road crosses the river and shortly passes through a major road cut in these red beds. The valley widens ahead and includes the town of Thermopolis. Incidentally, the river is known as the Wind River to the south and through the canyon, but as it flows into the Big Horn

Basin it is called the Big Horn River from here to the north.

Route U.S. 20 passes through town and follows the Big Horn River to Worland and Greybull. This is a dull route and the longest way to Cody. Wyoming 120 turns left in the center of Thermopolis; it is a good paved road and a short cut to Cody; also, it is more geologically interesting!

③ Hot Springs State Park, on the east side of Thermopolis across the river, is worth a short side visit. Active hot spring terraces are arranged along the river bank and are accessible by road and walking trails. These hot springs produce a daily flow of 18,000,000 gallons of water at about 135° F. The State Park has large, pleasant picnic grounds in a cottonwood grove and free hot water baths and swimming pools. The latter have a slight odor of hydrogen sulfide, but one soon gets accustomed to that!

Leave Thermopolis on Wyo. 120 and climb gently uphill and later down across Owl Creek following the southwest side of the Thermopolis anticline for at least 9 miles. (Road to left goes to Hamilton Dome oil field.) Various Cretaceous sandstones and shales are seen; most are dipping steeply toward the road, with occasional outcrops of steep Chugwater red beds near center of the anticline, with local faulting at one place.

For another 11 miles a less obvious extension of the anticlinal structure continues to the right of the route to the top of a hill 20 miles from Thermopolis. Now it is 7 miles to the Grass Creek oil field road to the left, and the route is over rolling semiarid country in Cretaceous shales and sandstones trending in various directions as the route crosses several folded structures. The many sandstone hogback ridges and shale valleys ahead for the many miles to Cody are parts of anticline and syncline folds in the Cretaceous formations. This part of the Big Horn Basin looks almost identical, from the air, to the valley and ridge terrain north of Sheep Mountain, as illustrated on Photo 2.3 in the previous chapter. You are driving along valleys and across ridges just like those in this picture!

From the Grass Creek road to Meeteetse is over 26 miles. The route approximately parallels sandstone ridges or hogbacks all dipping to the right. Sometimes the ridge is to the right of the road, sometimes to the left. In addition to sandstones, many shale outcrops are seen as well as a few small coal outcrops. Coming down the two-mile long hill into Meeteetse the view across the Greybull River valley shows Carter Mountain on the horizon. This mountain, up to 12,378 feet high, is composed of Absaroka volcanic rocks. Flat-lying layers of lava flows can be seen near the top if the light is right.

In Meeteetse the road junction to the left (Wyo. 290) allows access to the Southern Absaroka Mountains via the Wood River valley. The real high country, however, can only be reached with 4-wheel drive vehicles.

Leaving Meeteetse, the road follows the irrigated floodplain of the Greybull River for 7 miles, and then turns left back up into the semiarid hills of Cretaceous sandstones and shales. At 11 miles from town the route starts downhill toward and ever closer to a steep ridge of sandstone on the right dipping toward the road.

The road finally passes through a gap in this sandstone ridge, or hogback, near an historical marker, "Halfway House Stage Stop." Now the road runs uphill with the ridge on the left; the rocks dip away from the road. The hogback ridge is about 600 feet high along this section.

④ The top of the hill, just beyond Oregon Basin oil field road to the right, affords a view to the north. Ahead is the city of Cody in the lowland, with the jutting peak of Heart Mountain beyond. Heart Mountain, 8,123 feet high, is composed of Paleozoic limestones resting on much younger Tertiary sediments. It is a remnant of an unusual type of gravity fault. To the left at about 11 o'clock is Cedar Mountain, the south end of the Rattlesnake Mountain anticlinal structure. Beyond, on the far skyline, is the Beartooth Plateau.

Oregon Basin oil field can be seen to the right. The main oil-producing field lies 3 to 5 miles to the right, and the field extends about 10 miles north to south. It is a major producer in the Big Horn Basin.

The junction of Wyo. 120 with U.S. routes 14, 16, and 20 is 12 miles beyond this view point. The road travels a flat sandy plain. Along the middle stretch of this section, low ridges, some 2 miles to the left, are east-dipping sandstones on the east side of the Horse Center anticline, which is an offset, southern extension of the Rattlesnake-Cedar Mountain anticline. The latter is the high mountain ahead at about 10 o'clock. Just across from the junction is the Cody airfield. To the immediate left is a shallow, muddy alkali lake. At the junction turn left, and proceed two miles into Cody. The road is on a flat upper surface known as the Powell terrace. In town the road goes down a steep hill, exposing stream gravels in a road cut, onto the Cody terrace level 60 feet lower. The center of Cody is built on this level.

Log 4: Cody to East Entrance to Lake Junction, U.S. 14 and 20, 78 miles
Map: Figure 3.6

Cody was founded in the mid-1980s by Col. William "Buffalo Bill" Cody and friends. In 1902, the town was incorporated and Col. Cody opened his famous "Hotel in the Rockies," the Irma Hotel, which is still standing. In the same year Buffalo Bill also induced the Burlington Railroad to build a spur into the new town. A few years later he persuaded his friend, President Teddy Roosevelt, to establish the Bureau of Reclamation and to build the Shoshone Dam and Reservoir. Later renamed the Buffalo Bill Dam and Reservoir, it was completed in 1910. At the west end of Cody's main street, Sheridan Avenue, stands a statue to Col. Cody. Immediately to the left of this is the Buffalo Bill Historical Center, including the Whitney Gallery of Western Art, the Plains Indian Museum, and the Buffalo Bill Museum.

The main part of Cody is built on the so-called Cody terrace, a Pleistocene river floodplain level. The industrial plants and railroad north of town across the Shoshone River are on this same level. A lower terrace level, down in the canyon of the present river, is used primarily for dumping. This lowest level is the youngest. Above the main town is a higher terrace, the Powell terrace. This level, 60 feet above the town, is the oldest terrace. That is, it was formed when the river was at this level in mid Pleistocene time. Some of the finer homes are up there.

On the trip to Yellowstone, check the odometer as the road turns by the museums. In 0.8 miles the road crosses a small tributary creek and valley in which Cretaceous sandstones form a cliff below the road. The road then returns to the Cody terrace level. Ahead is the gap of the Shoshone Canyon with Cedar Mountain on the left and Rattlesnake Mountain on the right. Red Butte, eroded from the Chugwater formation, is far to the right just in front of the mountain. At 1.8 mile a road to the left and uphill at a Y junction is the South Fork road (Wyo. 291). This road may be followed for 40 miles up the South Fork of the Shoshone River into the impressive mountain scenery of the southern Absaroka Range. The moun-

104 Trip Guides

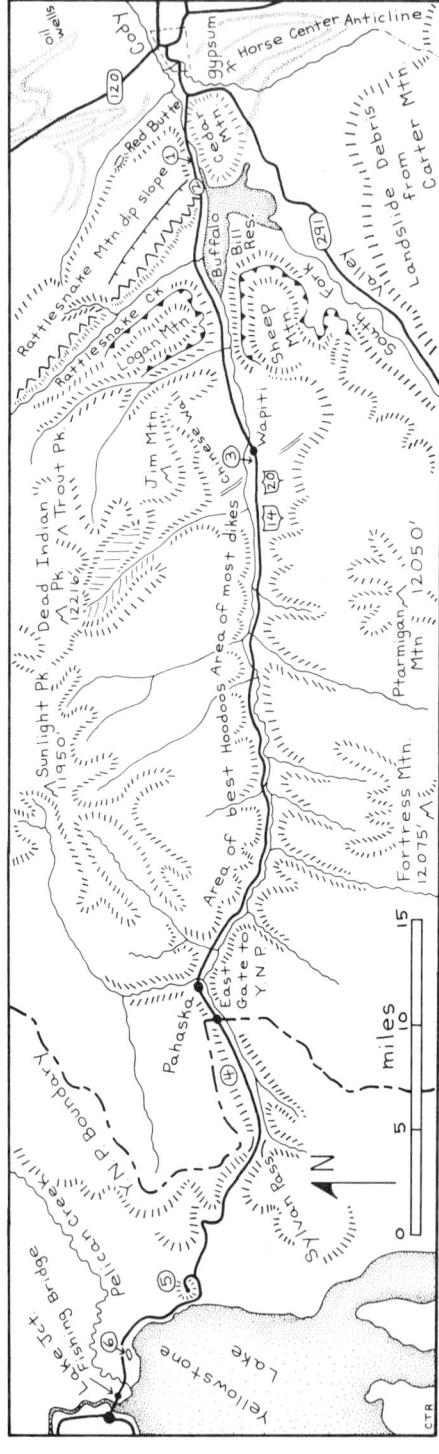

Figure 3.6. Map of the strip of the Absaroka Mountains from Cody via the East entrance into Yellowstone Park.

tains contain a thick section of the Eocene andesitic volcanic rocks of the Absaroka Volcanic Field.

About 3 miles from the museums, as the road curves right, turn into a parking area on the right. Here one looks directly down into the inner canyon of the Shoshone River, approximately 120 feet below. Immediately below are light-colored and drab rocks of the Tensleep and Phosphoria formations. Down the canyon about half a mile the red beds of the Chugwater can be seen. This inner canyon runs through Cody and beyond. In a 7-mile airline distance (the river follows many meanders) downstream all the formations of the Mesozoic are completely exposed, although access is difficult due to the steepness of these inner cliffs. On the Cody terrace level near this parking site are many travertine hot spring deposits, several of which contain local sulphur deposits. Sulphur was mined here before World War I. One of these deposits is across the road and back a little. Locally this site is called "Colter's Hell," as John Colter, mountain man and early explorer, was the first white man to cross the Shoshone River. The faint odor of hydrogen sulfide can be noted if the wind is right. In the canyon about a half mile down are the de Maris Hot Springs which still bring up a little sulphur.

The road now enters the Shoshone Canyon with canyon walls rapidly getting higher. The first cliffs are Madison limestone. Over the next 3 miles the canyon is cut through the entire Paleozoic section, all of which is dipping back down the valley to the east at about 15°. Landslide and talus deposits cover some of the formations, especially on the left side.

① At 6 miles from the museum just before entering a tunnel, the basal Flathead sandstone is seen lying on the eroded Precambrian granite surface. Here is the best place in the region to see and study this great unconformity. Use a small parking area to the left just before the tunnel. This unconformity represents 2 billion years of geologic time. The granites were originally formed about 2.6 billion years ago; much erosion continued for 2 billion years. Then ancestral North America sank slowly beneath the advancing Cambrian seas about 600 million years ago. At this place, pebbly sandstone lies on 2 or 3 inches of weathered granite, an old soil zone, and above many feet of finer-grained sandstone. This kind of contact is one of the keys to geologic understanding of the earth's history. Take a moment to look at it! (see Photo 3.8)

② Enter a nearly mile-long tunnel and come out at a major parking lot on the left just above the Buffalo Bill Dam. You are still in the canyon, but it is flooded by the narrow part of the reservoir. A walkway along the base of the cliff and through a small tunnel of the original road takes you to the dam where you may walk across its top. This dam is 325 feet high and less than that wide. Downstream is a narrow canyon in granites, schists, and small pegmatites. Along the walkway and tunnel from the parking lot is a horizontal dike of basalt, also of Precambrian age.

Here is the center of what is called the Rattlesnake Mountain anticline. Paleozoic sedimentary rocks are arched up over Precambrian rocks in an asymmetrical anticline; but in the brittle Precambrian granites, a fault block has been pushed up (see Figure 3.7), forcing the sediments to stretch and tear as they were draped up over the slowing rising block. The wall of rock from which the tunnel emerges is the remains of the fault face or scarp. Look along this line across the reservoir and up to the skyline. Note that the sedimentary rocks are almost flat on top but very steep down to the right. Some forma-

Photo 3.8. Contact of Cambrian Flathead sandstone layers (above) with the older Precambrian granite gneisses (light-colored). This is a typical unconformity. The actual contact can be seen in many places at the base of the sandstone beds if one walks up to the rock face. This is a roadcut just downstream from the Buffalo Bill Dam.

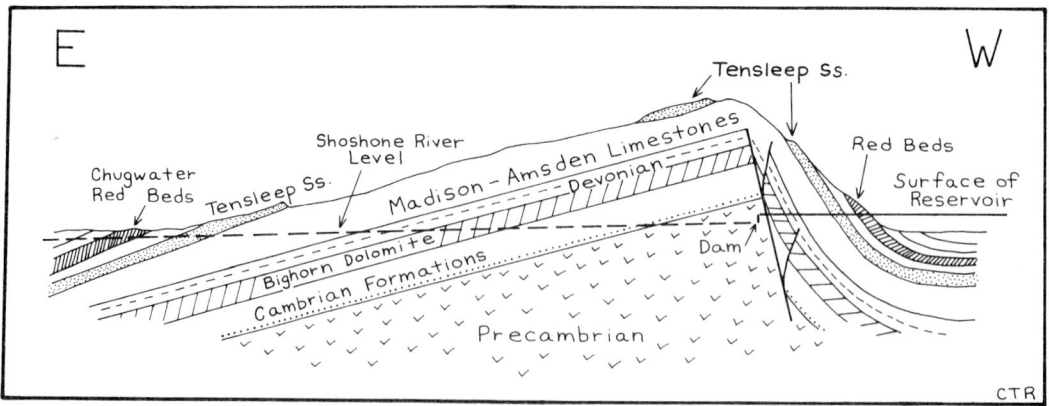

Figure 3.7. Generalized cross section of Rattlesnake Mountain anticline. The level of the Shoshone River in the canyon through the mountain uplift is indicated.

tions are missing in the gully down to the lake; others are much thinned out. Compare this view with the diagrammatic cross-section of Figure 3.7.

On the rock face across the road from the dam parking lot, several small faults can be seen. The base of the massive cliff, the Bighorn dolomite, is a fault which dips away from the granite about 30°. Below this fault contact are Cambrian shales and thin-bedded limestones which are folded and broken (faulted) as can be seen if one walks over and looks closely. As the main block of Precambrian granite slowly moved up, the various sedimentary layers against the steep fault side not only had to stretch, but were squeezed and broken into many small pieces and slices.

Continue 0.7 miles to where the lake widens out; this is the real end of the canyon. A large parking lot on the lake side is opposite fresh outcrops of the Tensleep sandstone on the right. Immediately across the narrow part of the reservoir these same sandstone beds are seen dipping steeply all the way down the right side of Cedar Mountain. Just left, in the middle of the mountain, the biggest steeply dipping beds are those of the Madison limestone. Note that some beds appear nearly flat-lying on top and slightly farther left (Photo 3.9).

Across the wider part of the reservoir to the south (left) and on the skyline, is Carter Mountain, the eastern-most exposure of the Absaroka volcanic rocks. Across the reservoir more to the right (west), is Sheep Moun-

Photo 3.9. Cedar Mountain, the south side of the Rattlesnake Mt. anticline, as seen a couple miles west of the Buffalo Bill Dam. Note gentle dips on the left and very steep dips on the right and into the foreground.

tain with its light-colored Paleozoic limestone cliffs overlying Mesozoic sandstones. This is one of the largest blocks of the amazing Heart Mountain gravity fault, along which mountain-sized blocks moved horizontally for several miles! (Photo 3.10) A sheet of rocks, starting near the northeast entrance to Yellowstone Park and extending out into the Big Horn Basin at Heart Mountain, was involved. (See more on this fault in Log 5A.)

The route now runs along the reservoir and beyond for 12 miles, with views at first to the right up Rattlesnake Creek of the well developed triangular flatirons in the vertical Madison limestone beds on the west side of Rattlesnake Mountain. Then near the head of the reservoir, there are views of Sheep Mountain across the lake to the left, and Logan Mountain to the right, both of which are Madison limestone blocks of the Heart Mountain gravity fault complex. Shortly

Photo 3.10. Sheep Mountain from the air with the Buffalo Bill Reservoir in the foreground. The big cliffs with dark vegetation on top are Madison limestone, a large flat block of the Heart Mountain gravity fault; the rocks below the cliffs and under the block are Mesozoic sediments. Carter Mountain is in the background across the South Fork valley. This mountain mass is composed of the Absaroka volcanics.

beyond the lake are the first close views of the brownish volcanic rocks of the Absaroka Range on either side, but especially well exposed on the right in cliffs and pinnacles.

③ Check odometers at the bridge over the North Fork of the Shoshone River; almost immediately on the right is the Wapiti lodge and post office. In just 1.5 miles on the right is a parking area and historical sign, "Absaroka Volcanic Field." Across the valley in the foothills are light gray and yellowish sandstones of the Willwood formation. Above them are the Eocene andesitic volcanic rocks. The first high mountain with many flat layers of lava flows is Jim Mountain (Photo 3.11). To the left and farther back is the great mass and higher flows of Dead Indian Peak, 12,216 feet. Across the valley in the lowlands but upstream a little, is a vertical wall locally called the Chinese Wall, which is a dike traceable for many miles back into the mountains. It continues across the road to the left side of the valley.

In another 3 miles the valley narrows. For the next 26 miles to Pahaska Tepee the road winds back and forth between valley spurs

Photo 3.11. Jim Mountain from highway U.S. 20 at the historical sign "Absaroka Volcanic Field." The light-colored sedimentary rocks in the right foreground are Willwood formation. Next above is a thick section of Absaroka volcanic breccias; the upper third of the mountain is composed of about one dozen dark-colored lava flows.

from either side; there is hardly a straight place in the highway. This valley is a typical water-cut V-shaped valley, becoming more canyonlike upstream. It is obvious that glaciers did *not* play a part in its formation. The rocks are the Absaroka volcanics consisting of alternating sandy layers and more bouldery layers. These are the so-called "alluvial facies" of the volcanic accumulation. Ash and larger fragments thrown out during explosive eruptions have become wet during rains and then been moved downslope by streams and mudflows. Thus, the original volcanic material has been modified and redeposited by the action of water after the volcanic activity. The original volcanic fragments have become better sorted and layered by the stream and mudflow activity. This detail can be studied almost anywhere in this valley, but is quite accessible for close observation at Chimney Rock, well up the valley (Photo 3.12).

During the first 10 miles of this section watch for dikes, igneous magma squeezed into near vertical cracks. Many will be seen, on the right side of the valley especially. However, a few are exposed in the roadcuts on the left, but you will pass them before you realize what they are if you drive too fast.

Also along these 26 miles, but best developed during the last half of the trip, are vertical spires or pillars weathered out of the rocks. This is "hoodoo" weathering and is typical in flat-lying layers with near vertical cracks or joints (Photo 3.13). Many of these sharply pointed cliffs and pinnacles have been given picturesque names: such as, Elephant Head, Chimney Rock, and the Holy City.

Pahaska Tepee is the site of a hunting lodge built and used by Buffalo Bill Cody. The old building still stands. New buildings include the restaurant and souvenir shop, which represent the last such facility before the entrance to Yellowstone. Here the road crosses the North Fork of the Shoshone River and begins the 10-mile climb up a tributary valley to Sylvan Pass. At Pahaska the elevation is near 6,800 feet; at Sylvan Pass, 8,541 feet.

④ The actual East Entrance Gate is reached 2.3 miles from Pahaska. From there on, the road climbs steadily up the valley side. For several miles there are high roadcut cliffs in dark-colored basalt, which is the exposure of very thick lava flows of the Eocene period. Some of these flows are over 100 feet thick. Between each flow are thin beds of fragmental or pyroclastic volcanic rock, mostly covered by soil and forest. A few thick dikes, 20 to 100 feet thick, of light-colored igneous rocks, diorite in composition, cut through these basalt flows. These dikes are so thick and irregular that they are not as obvious as the thinner andesite dikes seen down the valley. Many good parking places have been constructed along this section; it is easy to stop and see the basalts and diorites.

At Sylvan Pass a great cliff towers on the left, held up by diorite dikes. Immense talus slopes are present on both sides of the road. As the road starts down out of this gap, a small roadcut in whitish diorite is on the right. Soon little Eleanor Lake, and then larger Sylvan Lake appear on the left. The road winds down through forests with only scattered and insignificant outcrops of brownish volcanic rocks.

⑤ Ten miles from the Pass, a road to the right climbs a half mile to a view point on Lake Butte. From the top a panoramic view is unfolded of the Yellowstone Plateau and Yellowstone Lake. All of the low flat terrain is part of the Yellowstone Caldera, a great volcanic depression 30 miles across which was formed only 600,000 years ago! On a

Photo 3.12. Chimney Rock, a succession of water and mud flow deposited volcanic sands and gravels.

Photo 3.13. The Holy City, an example of hoodoo weathering so well developed along the Cody road to Yellowstone.

clear day the Teton Mountains can be seen to the southwest, more than 50 miles away.

The road reaches the lake a mile beyond this turnoff and then follows along the shore another 9 miles to Lake Junction, a mile beyond the campgrounds and stores at Fishing Bridge. About 4 miles after reaching the lake, the road passes along a sandy beach which has been built as waves have washed up gravels and sand from the lake. A small part of the lake was cut off by this sandbar development. Today this is the low sandy area to the right.

⑥ Just over a mile from this beach the road curves left around a small lake known as Squaw Lake. This round lake fills a shallow crater formed by a hydrothermal explosion; that is, an explosion of superheated steam and water from a few hundred to a thousand feet below the surface. This might be likened to a super gigantic geyser explosion. The explosion probably threw sand, debris, and water as much as a mile into the air. Geologists have suggested that this probably occurred as the last ice was melting, perhaps only 10,000 years ago.

ROUTES LEADING TO NORTHEAST ENTRANCE TO YELLOWSTONE PARK

The northeast entrance to Yellowstone National Park is reached via the Red Lodge-Cooke City highway across the eastern Beartooth Plateau. Those coming from the east across eastern Montana on I-94, or from Wyoming on I-90, will pass through Billings and continue to Laurel. The northeast entrance may also be reached via the Dead Indian Hill secondary road up the Clarks Fork Valley to the Cooke City highway.

Log 5: Laurel to Red Lodge to Cooke City, U.S. 212, 125 miles
Map: Figure 3.8

Use the Laurel exit from I-90 to U.S. 212 and proceed south past an oil refinery, then cross the Yellowstone River and continue southward on a level irrigated plain. At a main intersection, in a few miles, stay right on U.S. 212. (U.S. 310 to the left allows access to the Big Horn Basin towns including Cody.) This road will now enter the broad valley of Rock Creek, still through irrigated fields. Low bluffs, composed of Cretaceous sandstones, are visible for the next several miles at a distance from the road.

From Laurel views of the Beartooth Mountains to the south and southwest will become more and more distinct. To the east may be seen the Pryor Mountains, a northward extension of the Big Horn Mountain uplift. The upper part of the Beartooth Mountains will have some snow at all times of the year, but will be heavily snow-covered in June and July. As the traveler gets closer to Red Lodge, the even crestline of the Beartooth Plateau will become more obvious. Near to and at Red Lodge, the sides of the valley rise to flat bench levels on either side; just over 100 feet high on the west (right), but over 250 feet on the east. These benches are remnants of the gravel-covered valley bottoms formed during the melting stages of the Pleistocene ice advances (see p. 45). The differences in level of these two benches means that each was associated with a different ice advance.

Red Lodge was settled originally as a coal mining town. Although all mining ceased long ago, traces of this mining can be seen on both sides of town, such as the old coal dump on the west bench, near the rodeo grounds and airstrip. This dump has a red-

114 Trip Guides

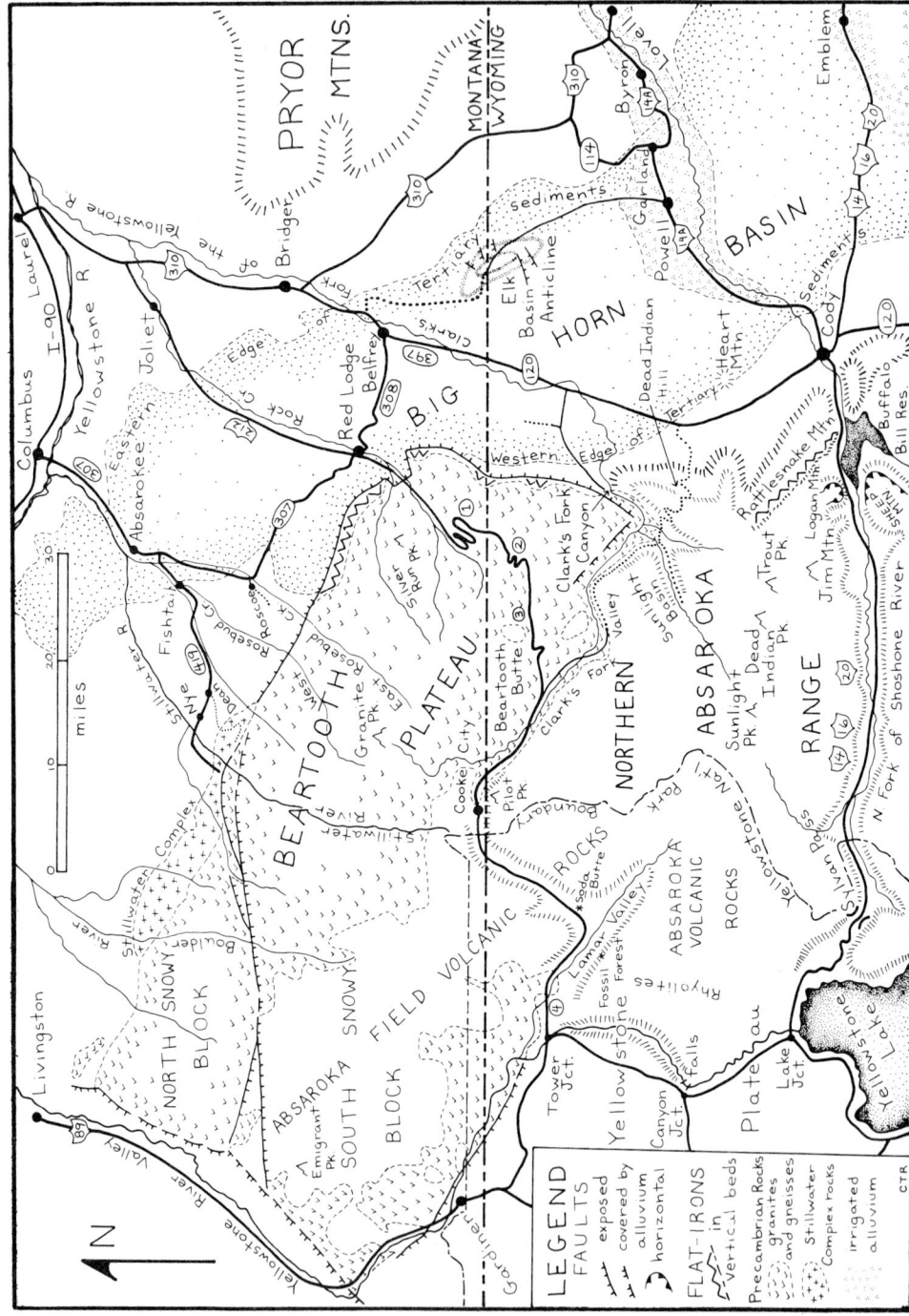

Figure 3.8. Map of the Beartooth Mountains, the Big Horn Basin, and the northern Absaroka Range primarily to show the route of Logs 5, 5A, and 5B, but also showing the position of Log 4, the western end of Logs 1 and 2, the side trip to Elk Basin and various connecting roads in the Big Horn Basin.

dish color, produced years ago when coal fragments in the dump burned slowly and baked the clays. This is the same color change that takes place when light brown clay bricks are fired and come out red; the red color is due to oxidized iron or hematite.

Just before reaching Red Lodge and just after the town, high vertical limestone cliffs can be seen along the mountain front, both east and west a mile or two away. These same faulted and vertical sedimentary rock structures are set back into the range along two cross faults immediately ahead (south). Due to the valleys of Rock Creek and its west branch, these outcrops do not stand up as prominently as the cliffs on either side.

Read odometers at the south edge of Red Lodge, say at the zoo, and proceed southward toward the mountains on U.S. 212. At 4 miles a pinnacle of limestone stands up on the right. This is the Madison limestone formation and is the most visible part of the vertical sedimentary rocks along the eroded zone of the mountain front.

The road now enters the Rock Creek valley, which is a broad, U-shaped, ice-gouged valley. Talus, moraine, and alluvial fan gravels cover both sides of the forested valley for the next several miles with a relief of about 3,000 feet. The first rather poor outcrops of actual Precambrian gneisses occur on the right at about 7 miles. At 10 miles, the road crosses Rock Creek and then parallels it closely for another 2 1/2 miles. To the right across the creek the low gravely hills are terminal moraine of the last ice advance. At 12 1/2 miles, where a road turns right to Forest Service campgrounds, the main road is on the top part of this terminal moraine. The space down to the campgrounds and on up the valley was occupied by former ice, the actual end of the glacier some 10,000 years ago. Perhaps you can visualize yourself as a caveman or woman, standing on a barren rocky moraine at the edge of a great tongue of ice extending on up the valley for many miles.

The road now climbs up the valley side for the next 6 miles, past three major switchbacks. Many outcrops of granite and gneiss, much broken rock and talus, and some outcrops of the younger porphyry dikes and sill-like masses are along the road during this climb.

① (21 miles from Red Lodge) There is a large paved parking area called Rock Creek Vista Point where you may park. An easy 800-foot walk, level and paved, leads to a railing-enclosed observation point, from where a wonderful view of the glaciated Rock Creek valley is obtained (Photo 3.14). The U-shaped canyon drops 2,000 feet below the observer. Across the canyon the irregular, but relatively gently sloping, Beartooth Plateau surface, above timberline, runs on up above 12,000 feet in several mountain peaks. The mass to the right is Silver Run Peak at 12,610 feet. A road can be seen climbing the opposite side of Rock Creek valley swinging around the head of a small tributary hanging valley. This is a four-wheel drive vehicle road that was built during World War II to gain access to a few small chromite deposits which produced a few thousand tons of ore. The dumps for one of these can still be seen across the canyon. The view behind this observation point, to the east, is into Wyoming Creek where some spectacular talus slopes can be seen.

Upward another 2 miles a paved parking area is present on the right, just before the road actually leaves the canyon side to go onto the plateau surface. This is at the head of Quad Creek, immediately below. For those interested in seeing the details of the Precambrian metamorphic rocks, this is the best place to park and walk a half mile, or as much as 2 miles. The rock exposed in the

Photo 3.14. Rock Creek valley from Rock Creek Vista Point. This wide U-shaped glaciated valley is typical of many canyons in the Beartooth Mountains.

roadcut across from the parking place is an old, somewhat metamorphosed, gabbro, a dark-colored igneous rock of altered pyroxene and plagioclase. The dark gabbro is cut by a few narrow, light-colored veins or dikes of granite pegmatite composed of coarse quartz, pinkish microcline feldspar, and a little mica. Along the contacts of some dikes are small "books" of altered and weathered biotite mica.

A walk down the road for about a mile allows the inspection of many rock types. At first are weather-stained granites, then granite gneisses, hornblende and mica gneisses and schists, and finally, at the sharp curve in the road around the cliff to the right, a great cliff of shattered massive white quartzite. Further on beyond this curve are more gneisses, a basalt dike, and finally, some amphibolites (hornblende-rich rocks). All these rocks along the road are very old, dated at over 2.6 billion years.

Shortly beyond here, the steep but grassy tundralike surface extends down to the highway surface, so that it is possible to climb sharply upward to some small dumps on the local skyline. This is the edge of the High Line Claims, where approximately 24,000 tons of chrome ore were mined in late 1941 and early 1942. The same dumps can be reached by an old road on top of the plateau surface that leaves the highway, just up from where your car is parked.

In these old pits the chief rock is a mass of serpentine, intruded into the amphibolites, which had a vein of chromite, now mined out. The serpentine occurs in a variety of textures and colors, from very light green to almost black, and contains specks of a few other minerals, such as chrome-green tremolite. The serpentine in the main pit is intruded by a porphyry dike about 30 feet wide which comes to an abrupt termination in the pit. The large crystals of orthoclase feldspar in this dike make the latter a spectacular rock. However, this rock has weathered quite rapidly, so that many of the feldspar crystals have weathered out over the past 35 years and may be found as individual crystals at various places in the dumps and pit bottom. It takes a painstaking search to find these now, as hundreds of students and mineral collectors have collected before you!

Continuing toward Cooke City, the road almost immediately runs onto the plateau surface, above timberline, with tundra vegetation and a gently rolling topography with a relief of about 1,000 feet. The highway crosses into Wyoming in about 2 more miles and soon gradually climbs along the upper edge of a cirque basin drained by a stream tributary to Rock Creek. Here, below the road, are the Twin Lakes, two cirque lakes in ice-gouged rock basins (Photo 3.15). The road now climbs around above the headwall of this cirque to the East Summit at 10,920 feet, about 28 miles from Red Lodge.

The road now descends gently along the plateau surface, down about 400 feet in 1.2 miles. Here to the left, is another cirque basin with Gardner Lake 600 feet below the road. The road ascends to the west summit at 10,941 feet via a few small, sharp switchbacks.

② (32 miles from Red Lodge) There is a parking area at the summit to the right. This point offers excellent views to the southwest of the Absaroka Range. By walking back down the main road perhaps 0.3 miles, a spectacular view is obtained into a U-shaped valley which is a tributary to Rock Creek (Photo 2.7). You are in effect standing on a cirque headwall and looking down some 2,000 feet into the head of a typical ice-carved valley.

The rock here at the summit is highly shattered by frost action and shows a patterned ground effect typical of Arctic tundra in permafrost areas. The so-called "patterns" are polygonal areas of rock fragments surrounding areas of soil, from 4 to 10 feet across, separated by small fractures in the ground.

Before leaving the summit again read your odometer, and then head down the switchbacks, past ice-smoothed outcrops of granite with some darker gneiss, for 4 1/2 miles, back into scattered timber. As the road comes around the last switchback and straightens out, a long wide gravel-covered area at the right side of the road can serve as an unofficial parking area for many cars. Park at the farthest end of this gravel shoulder. Walk across the road to the left and up a slight rise to the edge of a small quarry; road building material was obtained here. This is in a basic dike of the type so common in the Beartooth Precambrian area. This particular rock can be called coarse-grained basalt or fine-grained gabbro. The dike is perhaps 70 feet wide. It was intruded

Photo 3.15. Lower Twin Lake still covered with ice in late June. The outlet of this lake drains down a hanging valley into Rock Creek Canyon, right center. Beyond the canyon, note the rolling plateau surface starting at about 10,000 ft. and rising gently to the summit peaks over 12,000 ft.

as a magma into a crack in the granite. Along the edges, the basalt liquid was quickly chilled and solidified as very fine-grained basalt. In the center of the dike cooling was slower, and larger crystals were able to form; thus, the coarser-grained rock in the center is best called gabbro.

Walk around this locality, on both sides of the dike and away from the road, and note that the dike extends to the east at least 1/2 mile. Across the highway an extension of the dike can be seen over a mile away to the west (Photo 2.8). This dike has been traced for several miles across the plateau in a northwest-southeast direction. It is typical of the larger dikes in the range.

The road soon passes Long Lake and others and swings around into a broad, open, grassy valley looking directly ahead at Beartooth Butte. At 8 miles from the summit, just before a small bridge over Little Bear Creek, there is a wide gravel shoulder on the right with space to park 5 or 6 cars. Here, just beside the road, is a small ledge of sandstone on the granites across the creek. This is the Flathead sandstone of Cambrian age. It is a beach sand deposited 600 million years ago along a shoreline on a flat landscape, developed after long erosion of the Precambrian granites and metamorphic rocks. Such a contact is called an unconformity. This sandstone is the oldest sedimentary rock under Beartooth Butte.

③ (11 miles from summit) You are now driving along the shore of Beartooth Lake with the famous view of Beartooth Butte (Photo 3.16) across the lake. Beartooth Butte is composed of 1,500 feet of sedimen-

Photo 3.16. Beartooth Butte with Beartooth Lake in the foreground. The rocks on the cliffs are the Bighorn dolomite and the Jefferson limestone (on top). The dark patch in the center is a lens of red siltstones deposited as a channel near sea level. Below the cliffs is an immense, grass-covered accummulation of landslide debris.

tary rocks of Cambrian, Ordovician and Devonian age. Lake level is about 9,000 feet; the top of the Butte at 10,514 feet. Beartooth Butte is an outlier of Paleozoic sedimentary rocks sitting on the gentle southwest slope of the Beartooth uplift block. Of special significance is the Beartooth Butte formation, the lens of red rock on the face of the Butte. This red rock is made up of shaly limestones and siltstones and appears to be the cross section of a stream channel deposit. Plant and fish fossils indicate a Lower Devonian age and deposition in fresh or brackish water in an estuary along the ancient Devonian seashore. The fish fossils include five species of primitive fish (ostracoderms). With few exceptions the fossils consist of detached body plates and scales, indicating that the soft parts had decayed before fossilization.

Those who wish a rugged climb may start from here by crossing the bridge over the outlet of the lake and then following the shore to the far side; then up! There is no trail except along the lake. Fossil fish fragments may be found in the red rock in the talus just below the cliffs. Specimens by now are quite rare. These same talus slopes can also be reached, perhaps easier, from the top of Clay Butte.

After another 1.4 miles, a gravel road turns off to the right to the Clay Butte Forest Service fire lookout tower. If this road is open, it is well worth the 3-mile drive to the observation tower. The road may be closed permanently by the Forest Service, however. The view from the fire tower of the Clarks Fork valley and the Beartooth Range is really spectacular. If the road is not open, one can hike up, or proceed another mile down the main road to a scenic turnoff on the right, where about the same view is obtained although from a lower vantage point. The view is across the Clarks Fork valley showing a ledge of white limestone in the forest, traceable for many miles up and down the valley (Photo 2.9). This is a 100-foot high cliff of the Pilgrim limestone, which dips gently under the volcanic rocks and away from the observer from the same cliff in Beartooth Butte. Above this continuous limestone ledge are several areas of younger limestones which are blocks of the Heart Mountain detachment fault (described on p. 125). Above all, the brown volcanic rocks of the Absaroka Range extend to the highest peaks on the southern and western horizon. Prominent to the west in this range are two very sharp peaks, Pilot and Index. Pilot Peak is a glacial horn carved by ice from flat-lying basalt lava flows.

Clay Butte is composed of shales and thin limestones of Cambrian age. This material has suffered considerable slumping, causing small landslides on the west side of the butte. The road to its summit crosses this slide material and is difficult to maintain.

The road now descends around a few more switchbacks into the forests in the Clarks Fork valley past several cascading creeks. The roadcuts are either in Precambrian granite gneisses or glacial gravel deposits (moraines). At about 20 miles from the summit, a paved road turns off to the left towards Cody, Wyoming. This road is not paved all the way (see Log 5A).

Now the main highway soon reaches stream level with many views of Pilot and Index peaks (Photo 3.17); the road is running directly toward those peaks. After crossing the Clarks Fork River, the road gets so close below these mountains that their tops are no longer visible. Now watch for Fox Creek (28 miles from the summit) for a view ahead high on the valley wall, which shows clearly the light-colored limestones overlain along a level contact by the brown volcanic rocks. This contact is the so-called "plane of tec-

Photo 3.17. Pilot Peak and Index (right) rising above the Clarks Fork River. These peaks are ice carved from vent facies volcanic rocks of the Absaroka series. The steep part of Pilot is carved from flat basalt lava flows.

tonic denudation" described by Dr. Pierce in his discussion of the Heart Mountain detachment fault (p. 126).

In another few miles the Montana state line will be crossed. Then, on the left for the next mile, there are several extensive piles of coarse, brown talus blocks of igneous rock (andesites). These are from a thick sill intruded into Cambrian sediments exposed on the cliffs above the road.

The road crosses a low, forested pass from the valley of the Clarks Fork to the headwaters of Soda Butte Creek, and then descends rapidly to Cooke City at 35 miles from the summit.

Cooke City is located in the broad, deep U-shaped valley of Soda Butte Creek. A major glacier from the Beartooth Plateau wore away the divide from the Clarks Fork valley to move west and then south into Yellowstone Park. On the south side (left) of the valley, on the face of Republic Mountain, the ledge of Pilgrim limestone is continuous from the Clarks Fork area. Here it is about 700 feet above the town and has a big scar where it has been quarried out by workings of the Republic Mine. Silver and lead ores were mined here on a small scale for several years earlier in this century.

Cooke City was discovered in 1869, and its ores in the 1870s, but this was still Crow Indian country. Chief Joseph and a large band of his people passed through here in 1877 in full retreat from the U.S. Army. In the 1880s Cooke City became a roaring mining town and flourished until about the turn of the century. There was another small burst of activity during World War I. Since then, however, activity has been limited to the Republic Mine and the McLaren Mine at Daisy Pass. The latter mine was discovered in the 1930s and was an active producer of gold for about 17 years. Altogether, $4,000,000 worth of gold, copper, silver, and lead has been mined here in a hundred years.

Side Trips from Cooke City

Two interesting side trips from Cooke City require 4-wheel drive vehicles, horses, or just plain hiking! They are the McLaren Mine and Grasshopper Glacier.

McLaren Mine: Retrace the highway back toward Red Lodge for 0.7 miles, and turn left on a steep, rough road that is posted "not maintained." It climbs some 2,000 feet in 5 miles, up through the basin of Miller Creek to Daisy Pass. This basin is a cirque once filled by a small glacier, tributary to the larger Soda Butte Glacier. Here are many abandoned prospect pits and small mines. The climb starts up in Precambrian gneisses, and then goes across soil and forest-covered slopes to the pass. At the head of Miller Basin stands Crown Butte, composed of Cambrian limestones cut by a thin dike. To the right as the road climbs, is Henderson Mountain, a laccolith of monzonite porphyry with a few patches of metamorphosed limestone on top, especially noteable at the pass. The view from Daisy Pass is into the headwaters of the Stillwater River. Most obvious are the yellowish and rusty-weathered dumps and workings of the McLaren gold mine, about a half mile away. Mining was successful from about 1934 to 1951, the ore being smelted near Cooke City. The Kennecott Copper Company has done extensive stripping and trenching here in the past dozen years and is reported to have purchased the entire property including much of Miller Basin. This suggests that the company must believe that a large amount of gold-copper ore is present under the Daisy Pass area, which is worth holding as a reserve for the distant future. The ores are all associated with the igneous intrusive mass under Henderson Mountain and came from one of the magma chambers under the Cooke City volcanoes about 45 million years ago. The ores contain the minerals pyrite and chalcopyrite in hard baked (metamorphosed) Cambrian sedimentary rocks. Gold occurs in microscopic grains.

Grasshopper Glacier: Retrace the highway from Cooke City back toward Red Lodge for 2 miles, turn left on a dirt road for a couple of miles to an old cabin and wreck of a smelter just across Fisher Creek. Cars must be left here and further access is by 4-wheel drive or foot past Round, Long, Star, and Goose lakes. This trail leads past outcrops of Precambrian gneisses and basalt dikes. From Goose Lake at 9,800 feet, a foot trail leads around the right side of the lake up to a pass at 10,700 feet next to Iceberg Peak. At the divide, one is on the edge of Grasshopper Glacier. This is a small cliff glacier in a north-facing cirque (Photo 3.18). As a glacier, it is rather disappointing, but it does have thousands of disintegrated grasshoppers frozen in its ice. These have been dated by carbon-14 by the U.S. Geological Survey at about 300 years old. Apparently a horde

Photo 3.18. Grasshopper Glacier in a picture taken in the mid 1950s. The ice has melted back some since then. The dark bands are the grasshopper remains with many dust particles.

of grasshoppers on the plains were blown up and brought down in a snowstorm to be frozen into the ice. This is best seen in August, as earlier in summer the previous winter's snow may cover the ice. Refer to the Cooke City, Montana-Wyoming quadrangle topographic map for full location and directions. Inquire locally in Cooke City as to conditions, and plan to spend a full day no matter how you travel.

Log 5A: Cody via Dead Indian Hill to Cooke City, Wyoming 120 and 296, 84 miles Map: Figure 3.9

This route is suggested mainly for geologists who want to see the features of the Heart Mountain gravity fault and some of the details of an intrusive center in the Absaroka volcanics at White Mountain. The route involves about 40 miles of gravel road, sometimes slippery in wet weather, and steep grades down Dead Indian Hill to the west. The trip is through very scenic mountain country with several Forest Service campgrounds and is passable, with care, with any car.

Leave Cody on Wyo. 120 at the junction with U.S. 14A, and drive down to the bridge

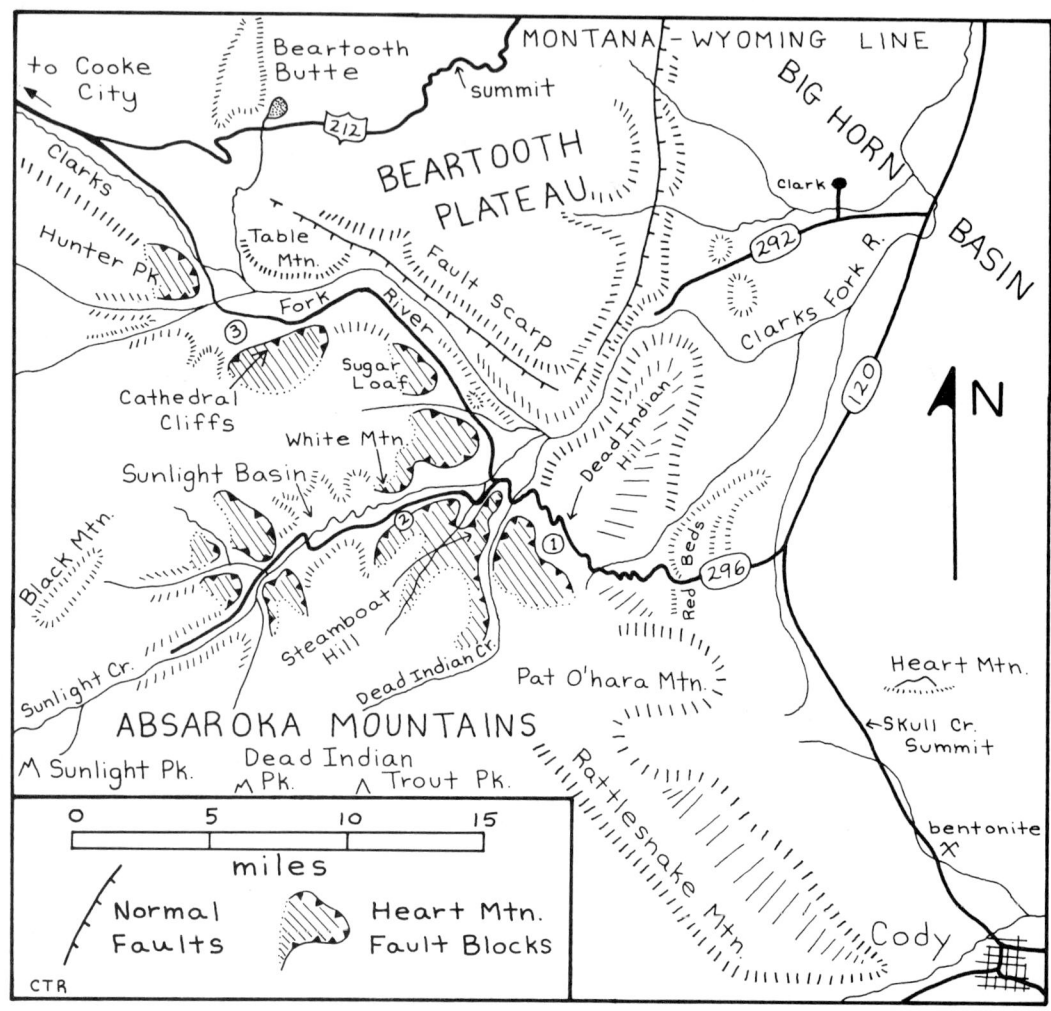

Figure 3.9. Map of the Sunlight Basin—Clarks Fork Valley trip, Log 5A, over Dead Indian Hill from Cody.

over the Shoshone River past exposures of coarse river gravels along the edge of the Cody terrace. Now ascend to the north onto the Powell terrace in about a mile. Views ahead reveal Heart Mountain.

At 4.8 miles from Cody, small abandoned pits occur to the right about 1,000 feet across the shallow valley of Cottonwood Creek. These are outcrops of bentonite in the Mowry shale of Cretaceous age. Bentonite is an altered volcanic ash, now a type of clay that swells many times its dry volume when put into water. If you walk over to these pits, watch out for rattlesnakes!

Skull Creek summit is reached 10 1/2 miles from Cody. A fine panorama opens up down and ahead with the Beartooth Plateau on the skyline. Pat O'Hara Mountain lies to the left and Heart Mountain to the right. Ahead some 3 miles a small syncline is apparent near the road. All the rocks near the road are various Cretaceous sandstones or shales.

Watch for a road to the left at 17 1/2 miles from Cody with the sign "Sunlight Basin Road" and "to Cooke City." This is Wyo. 296, although that number may not appear on the sign. This is the start of gravel roads.

Note: This turnoff from Wyo. 120 may also be reached by driving south from Belfrey, Montana, on Mont. 397 which becomes Wyo. 120 at the state line. It is approximately 30 1/2 miles from Belfrey to the Sunlight Basin junction.

The road rises gently up a dry valley for about 6 miles past 3 or 4 gentle grass-covered hogbacks of Cretaceous formations, until a white rock appears in a cut immediately at the right of the road. This is gypsum, a calcium sulfate mineral, in the Gypsum Springs formation. Just around the sharp turn to the right, and below this gypsum, will be the start of a thick section of red siltstones and sandstones of the Chugwater formation. The road climbs along the base of this bright red cliff for a half mile and then turns left, to start a series of switchbacks up a long dipslope eroded on the Phosphoria limestone, which is visible in road cuts.

It is 4 miles to the summit of this climb from the gypsum outcrop. The road levels off on the side of a narrow canyon cut largely in the Tensleep sandstone. The highway department has had continuing landslide problems on this section of road.

The road goes down and then up twice in the next 4 1/2 miles, before arriving at the actual summit of Dead Indian Hill at 8,000 feet. Here is a historical monument referring to the passage across this pass of the Nez Perce Indians in 1877 under Chief Joseph during their retreat before the U.S. Cavalry.

① Just over the summit is a parking area and viewing stand on the left. This is one of the great visual and geologic panoramas of the West with views to the left of the Absaroka Range and to the right of the Beartooth Plateau. More specifically, from left to right, we see on the skyline Trout and Dead Indian peaks, over 12,000 feet; and with considerably more snow than the others, Sunlight Peak. In the middle distance is Sunlight Valley, recognized by the white talus of White Mountain (Photo 3.19). Then we look down below to several mountains which are blocks in the Heart Mountain fault, where two rivers flow into the Clarks Fork of the Yellowstone in its deep canyon cut into granites. And to the right of this, the Beartooth Plateau rises steeply along a bounding fault. Immediately across the road from this stop is an exposure of the Tensleep sandstone.

A 2,000-foot descent along 7 miles of switchbacks brings one down to Dead Indian Creek. On the way down are increasingly closer views ahead of Steamboat Hill and Point. The upper part is a typical Heart Mountain fault block broken into several units. Note that the bedding is not continuous across the upper part. These several blocks rest on very gently dipping Cambrian formations that are not broken. These beds project to the right as the "prow" of the steamboat!

In broad outline, the Heart Mountain fault is a nearly horizontal "gravity thrust," whose overriding sheet broke loose along a bedding plane and moved on a surface of not over a 2° slope, finally riding across a former land surface. The present remnants of the Heart Mountain sheet include more than 50 separate blocks, which range in size from a few hundred feet to five miles across and up to 3,000 feet thick. They are scattered over a triangular area 30 miles wide and 60 miles long, trending east-southeast from near the Northeast Gate to Yellowstone out onto the Big Horn Basin. In the vicinity of

Photo 3.19. View from the summit of Dead Indian Hill to Dead Indian Creek valley in the foreground and Sunlight Valley beyond; the white slopes in the latter valley are talus of White Mountain. All the foreground and center hills are Heart Mountain fault blocks; center right is Steamboat hill, one of the most broken of these blocks. High Absaroka Range in left background.

Dead Indian Hill, the bedding plane fault changes to a transgressive or cross-cutting fault where the moving blocks cut across younger rocks as the latter dip under the Big Horn Basin.

In the western part of the fault area, from Dead Indian Hill to Cooke City, the various fault blocks are covered by younger Absaroka volcanic rocks. This suggests that the cause of this very unusual gravity-type fault was somehow associated with the start of widespread volcanic activity. Further discussion of the Heart Mountain problem is beyond the scope of the present guidebook, and the reader is referred to one or more of the many articles by Dr. William Pierce, of the U.S. Geological Survey, who has studied this fault for the past 25 years.

From the Dead Indian Creek crossing, the road swings around the prow of Steamboat Point and in two miles comes to a road fork. The right fork continues to Cooke City,

while straight ahead leads up into Sunlight Basin. A trip up this road is strongly recommended for at least a few miles.

Sunlight Basin Road: From the junction the road soon swings left then right over Elk Creek, and starts a long gradual two-mile climb up a wide grass-covered surface. This is a rather smooth terminal moraine which fills Sunlight Valley at the foot of White Mountain. About 10% of the pebbles and boulders in this moraine are Precambrian rock fragments; rocks of this age do not occur up Sunlight Creek. For this and other reasons, it has been assumed that this moraine was deposited by a glacier which moved up from the Clarks Fork valley. Sunlight Valley was dammed by this ice, and a lake formed upstream. The lake was completely filled in with stream deposits to form the present flat-bottomed area known as Sunlight Basin, seen from the top of the moraine.

② At the top of the moraine not only is there a fine view of Sunlight Basin but also of White Mountain, across the valley to the right (Photo 3.20). White Mountain is an old

Photo 3.20. White Mountain as seen across Sunlight Basin. The whitish rock is marble formed by volcanic heat which metamorphosed the Paleozoic limestones in the center of this old volcano. Note small, dark, irregular dikes, especially on the right. The rock spire on the right is volcanic material of the old volcanic cone.

volcano which has been moved horizontally as one of the Heart Mountain fault blocks. The white rocks are heat changed or metamorphosed Paleozoic limestones, now marble. The sharp spire is a mass of metamorphosed volcanic rock; the actual core of the volcano is behind the mountain and out of sight from the road. The entire mountain is cut by many dikes, some of which are clearly visible from this location. It is possible to drive to the base of the mountain in a high-clearance vehicle by driving through the Wyoming Fish and Game Commission's camp; the entrance road to the camp is ahead less than a mile, to the right.

It is possible to drive up Sunlight Valley another 10 miles or so on a dirt road; not recommended if wet. Beyond the wide valley of Sunlight Basin the road is along the base of Madison limestone cliffs of Little Bald Ridge. Here, also, are terminal moraine deposits of the glacier that came down Sunlight Creek. Above the limestone cliffs, the valley again widens and becomes a typical U-shaped glaciated valley cut in brown volcanic rocks.

Cooke City Road: The road goes down through Cambrian shales (slippery when wet) and in less than half a mile crosses Sunlight Creek. At this bridge on the right is a cliff of the Flathead sandstone.

For several miles the road now approaches the Clarks Fork Canyon. In 4 or 5 miles a small flat butte on the right, called Antelope Mesa, has a 100-foot sheer cliff in the Pilgrim limestone. Just past this butte, the road is on the edge of the canyon. The front of the Beartooth Plateau rises abruptly some 4,000 feet; this is a fault scarp. The rocks in the canyon and on the fault scarp are both Precambrian gneisses.

The road is located just above the Flathead sandstone, and above on the left, but hidden by forest, is Sugarloaf Mountain, another Heart Mountain fault block. After crossing Reef Creek, the route comes out in more open country in front of Cathedral Cliffs.

③ Somewhere in the open after reaching the new paved road is a good place to pause and look about. Cathedral Cliffs are over 2,000 feet high and eroded from a Heart Mountain fault block. Near the base and in the trees, a long continuous cliff of the Pilgrim limestone is visible below the fault plane. Above this the bedding and rock succession is quite erratic, due to the breaking of the block as it slid horizontally. The biggest cliffs on the right are Madison limestone, and a number of dark igneous dikes can be seen cutting vertically through the limestone. The top of the mountain is composed of the volcanic rocks which originally covered all the fault blocks.

In the foreground are ice-smoothed and polished knolls of granite gneiss. Far to the west, almost straight ahead on the road, is the high mass of Hurricane Mesa, 11,064 feet, a major volcanic intrusive center. To the right of the road and to the north, are flattish beds of Cambrian limestones forming Table Mountain. Behind this rises Beartooth Butte and the Beartooth Range.

This last stop should have been only about a mile before the road to the left to the Crandall Ranger Station, and then almost immediately, the bridge over Crandall Creek. In another mile and a half, cross the Clarks Fork River bridge.

The road now follows the Clarks Fork River for 6 1/2 miles to the road junction with U.S. 212, the Red Lodge-Cooke City highway. Along this section are granite outcrops on the right. Across the river to the left the hills are composed of volcanic rocks lying on the continuous ledge of the Pilgrim limestone. Hunter Peak, shortly after crossing the Clarks Fork, is a Heart Mountain fault block.

At the junction with U.S. 212 turn left and go 14 miles to Cooke City. Refer to Log 5.

*Log 5B: Cooke City via Northeast Entrance to Tower Junction, 33 miles
Map: Figure 3.8*

Looking westward down the valley of Soda Butte Creek, steep mountains rise on both sides and ahead. These mountains are composed of the Absaroka volcanic rocks sitting on the nearly flat Cambrian sediments. The Pilgrim limestone is just visible, usually in the trees. In the nearer mountains these volcanic rocks exhibit the characteristics of vent facies: that is, small lava flows are interbedded with pyroclastic rocks and all dip from a central region. For the 3 miles from Cooke City to the town of Silver Gate the valley has been eroded right through the middle of an old, complex, major volcano, as indicated by dip of these vent facies volcanic rocks.

The actual northeast gate to Yellowstone Park is just over 4 miles from Cooke City (check odometers here). About 100 yards before the actual gate, through an opening in the trees, the breakaway fault of the Heart Mountain gravity fault system may be seen across Soda Butte Valley. A complete section of Paleozoic formations up into the Madison limestone is present to the right, while volcanic rocks lie on Cambrian sediments only to the left. This is not very obvious except to actual geologists.

Within a half mile the road comes out of the forests with a clear view ahead. The mountains on either side have a treeless cliff exposure of a thousand feet or more of sedimentary rocks, especially the yellowish Devonian formations. These rocks have not been disturbed by any kind of faulting. Immediately ahead is Barronette Peak with its thick layers of brown volcanic rocks. This layering is in contrast to the attitude of the volcanic materials above Cooke City and Silver Gate. The Barronette rocks have been eroded from the outer slopes of the old volcano, and represent the so-called alluvial facies of stream and mud flow deposited volcanic fragmentary materials.

On down the valley high mountains of volcanic rocks rise about 4,000 feet above the valley to as much as 10,900 feet. Ahead in a couple of miles and to the left is the Thunderer. The top part of this mountain has obvious steplike layers of lava flows.

From 7.5 to 8 miles from the northeast gate the road passes several rock exposures on the right composed of fragments of all sizes up to 5 feet or so. These are volcanic mud flow deposits, a mixture of fragments of many sizes without any distinct layering. Most of the actual rocks are different kinds of andesites. To the left is the small and narrow Ice Box Canyon.

In another mile the valley has widened considerably to a gravel-covered floodplain with the Pebble Creek campground off to the right. Soon the valley narrows again, due to the presence on the right of a large prehistoric tree-covered landslide. This extends for nearly a mile. As the valley widens for the second time, look back and up to the right and see the indentation or valley in the mountain wall from where all this slide material came.

At 12 1/2 miles from the Park entrance is The Soda Butte, a small geyser cone, beside the road on the left. While this geyser is now extinct, faint odors of hydrogen sulfide may be detected. The geyser deposit is travertine (calcium carbonate), because the hot waters came up through thick limestones below; just ahead are limestone outcrops on the right under the thick volcanic rocks.

In 2 more miles Soda Butte Creek joins the Lamar River. This junction may be seen close at the left of the road. The route now enters the wide Lamar valley which was carved by a glacier coming down from the Absaroka Range far up to the left (southeast).

Watch for a geology exhibit sign and small parking area to the left, "Fossil Forests," where the Park Service has a story about these fossil trees. Across the Lamar valley at this locality, a mile away on the cliff side of the mountains, is the place where a geologist, Professor Erling Dorf of Princeton University, has found 28 fossil forests each buried one above another in 2,000 feet of volcanic ash and mudflow deposits (Photo 3.21).

The route follows along the side of the wide Lamar valley for 6 miles and then enters a narrow part of the valley, where the river has cut a small canyon about a mile long through Precambrian granite gneisses.

④ A half mile after this narrow section, the road crosses the Lamar River. In about a mile a long parking strip is on the left. From here look up to the left onto Specimen Ridge, a long slope in grass to the left, and cliffs in trees to the right. In those cliffs are several excellent fossil trees standing in place in the volcanic rocks (Photo 3.22). A climb

Photo 3.21. The Fossil Forest site on the 2,000-foot high slopes of Amethyst Mountain in a view across the Lamar River valley from the "Fossil Forest" exhibit on the main road. The 28 different fossil forest levels are best exposed along the ridge up the center of the picture. Note the broad alluvial fan in front of the mountain and behind the trees in the foreground.

Photo 3.22. Two large fossil trees standing in place and weathered out of the surrounding volcanic breccias on Specimen Ridge. The trees are composed today of grey to brown silica, a flintlike form of quartz.

of about 1,400 feet up the grassy slope to the ridge top and then along a trail on the ridge to the right into the forest, leads to the fossil trees. Check with the Park Rangers for guided hikes to this locality if you want to see these fossil trees.

The road continues again in a wide valley now covered with terminal moraine deposits. Small hills and depressions in the deposits are typical along with many large granite boulders left by the ice. These boulders are known as glacial erratics. Watch on the right for a geology exhibit about these glacial deposits.

Visible at this parking area and ahead to the right is a small flat-topped hill or butte with talus of dark-brown rock. This is Junction Butte which is capped by a flat area of basalt lava. The lava has been dated at more than 2 million years old. A few other remnants of this basalt have been found across the Yellowstone valley to the north and up near Tower Falls. Here is the evidence for a lava flow on a floodplain near the junction of the ancestral Yellowstone and Lamar rivers. This old floodplain must have been at the level of the flow remnant now on Junction Butte, some 400 feet above the present river levels.

Shortly the road goes down into the present Yellowstone valley and crosses that river on a high bridge. In another mile, Tower Junction is reached.

ROUTES LEADING TO SOUTH ENTRANCE TO YELLOWSTONE PARK

Visitors from the east traveling on I-80 may cross southern Wyoming to Rock Springs and there turn north via Pinedale to Jackson, or they may detour around the Wind River Range for different sightseeing, by turning at Farson to Lander and later arrive in Jackson Hole via Togwotee Pass. Other routes across central Wyoming may lead through Shoshoni or Lander, or over Togwotee Pass to the middle of Jackson Hole. All these routes mean a visit to Teton National Park before Yellowstone Park.

Log 6: Farson via Pinedale to Jackson, U.S. 187, 136 miles
Map: Figure 3.10

Leave highway I-80 at Rock Springs and turn north on U.S. 187. Continue northward to the small town of Farson, where a road junction to the right, via Wyo. 38, leads to Lander (see Log 7). Continue straight ahead, that is, left, on 187 to Pinedale. Farson to Pinedale is a trip of 61 miles across the flat plains of the northern Green River Basin. The scenery at close hand is very monotonous, a few small badlands or valleys from time to time, but mostly a sagebrush-covered grazing country. Ahead, and slightly to the right on the skyline, are the Wind River Mountains. A long, high range, whose top peaks usually contain some snow, even in summer.

① As the traveler reaches the south edge of Pinedale, he should take a 2 1/2-mile side trip to the right on the road to Fremont Lake. This road will climb up on a terrace above town and then up over a terminal moraine, composed of coarse boulders and gravel. This is a fine example of a well-developed terminal moraine. Two and a half miles from Pinedale, the road comes to a scenic parking area with a fine view of Fremont Lake stretching up into the Wind River Mountains. Here are views of exceptionally high lateral moraine ridges on either side of the lake stretching upward against the mountain front (Photo 3.23). The terminal moraine here is about a mile and a half wide. It has parallel ridges, each of which represents a stand of the ice front for a few years' time.

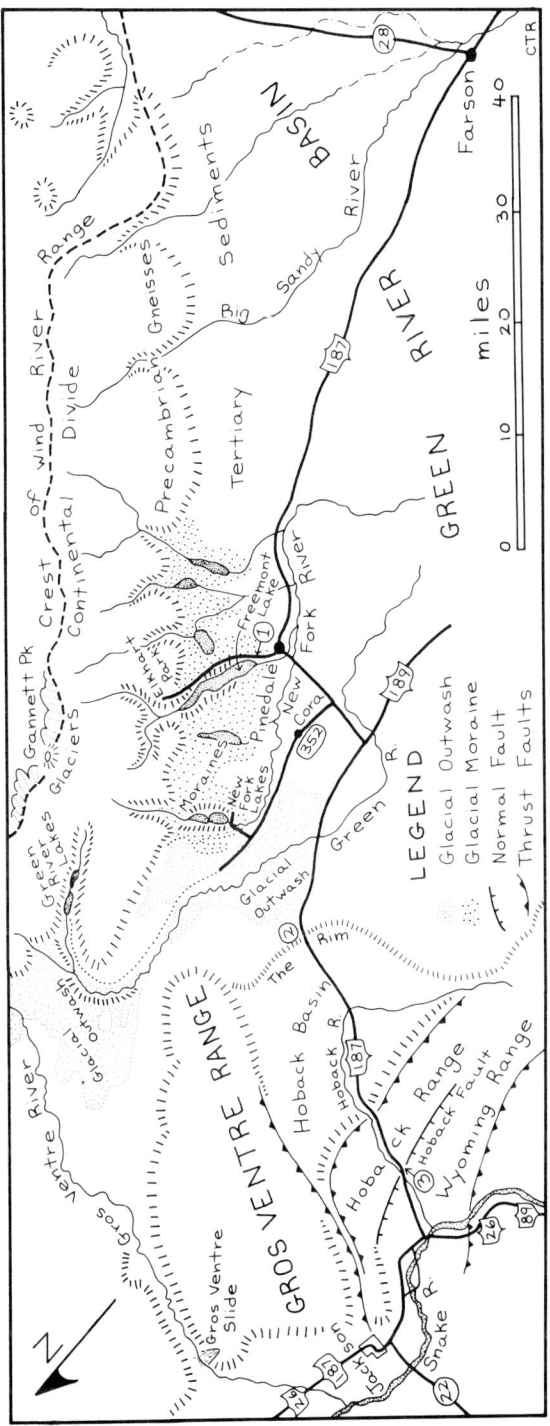

Figure 3.10. Map of route, Log 6, from Farson through Pinedale to Jackson along the southwest flank of the Wind River Range.

Photo 3.23. Freemont Lake and its terminal moraine from the viewpoint just out of Pinedale, Wyoming. Note the four terminal or recessional moraine ridges in front of the lake. The high land on the right and left of the lake are immense lateral moraines. The Wind River Mountains rise in the background.

These ridges are covered by irregular rows of boulders and gravel materials. (NOTE: The road continues another 12 or 13 miles up into the edge of the mountains, and is a good trip. However, this and another side trip from Pinedale will be described at the end of this log.)

Pinedale is a small town, elevation 7,175 feet, which is the jumping-off place for backpacking in the Wind River Range. Leaving Pinedale on U.S. 187, the last view back of the Wind River Mountains will be obtained in about six miles. The road then goes across a very low, gentle hill, then descends to the floodplain of the Green River. Here are irrigated fields stretching for a mile or two across the Green River to the left.

Eleven miles from Pinedale is a junction with U.S. 189 to the left; both routes continue ahead. In another 10 miles, the road will cross the Green River and then trend away from the farmland and the floodplain. For another 10 miles the route is across gently rolling plains, covered with sagebrush and grass.

② Finally, 31 miles from Pinedale, the route arrives at The Rim, where the road starts downhill abruptly. This rim is the divide at an elevation of 7,921 feet between waters flowing southward into the Green River–Colorado system, and waters down the hill ahead flowing into the Snake River–Columbia system. As one starts down the hill large outcrops of sandstone and conglomerate are exposed on the right for about one mile. This is the Pass Peak conglomerate of early Tertiary age. The material of this conglomerate was formed by the rapid erosion of the slowly rising Hoback and Gros Ventre ranges at the end of the Rocky Mountain uplift period.

Descending the hill from The Rim, there are excellent views ahead of various mountain ranges. More or less directly ahead is the Hoback Range. Off to the right, the Gros Ventre Range is an impressive group of high mountain peaks. Rather sharply to the left, the Wyoming Range is visible on the far horizon.

The route downhill is into the Hoback Basin, an area of hills and valleys. It is a small area of moderate relief surrounded by mountains on two sides and The Rim on the third. The basin is drained by the Hoback River, the first bridge across which will be reached about 10 miles from the rim summit.

Beyond this crossing, the various mountain ranges are continuingly visible, with the Hoback Range directly ahead, the Gros Ventre Range to the right at 9 or 10 o'clock, and the Wyoming Range rather far to the left and slightly back. Some 7 or 8 miles from the Hoback River bridge, the route will enter the Hoback Canyon, and all distant views will be shut out. This canyon extends for the next 11 miles with cliffs of various sedimentary formations, both Paleozoic and Mesozoic rocks. The structures are very complicated. The route crosses two or three thrust faults where Paleozoic rocks are pushed over Mesozoic rocks. The traveler will see steep dips, and obviously folded rocks in the roadcuts. The biggest cliffs are in the Madison limestone and Tensleep sandstone.

③ The route emerges from the Hoback Canyon at a bridge across the Hoback River, after passing some extremely high cliffs in the Madison limestone with excellent talus slopes at their base. The main cliffs are to the right across the river, before the bridge. This, the west side of the Hoback Range, is bounded by the Hoback Normal Fault, along which the Hoback Range was uplifted vertically in late Tertiary time. This normal fault is much younger than the thrust faults which were the cause of the complex structures in the Hoback Range.

About a mile beyond this canyon mouth, on a wide terrace a half mile to the left is the University of Michigan Geology Field Camp, a group of buildings out in the sun.

Just over 3 miles from the canyon mouth, large cliffs of coarse conglomerate and sandstone will be passed on the right. These are late Tertiary deposits and are known as the Camp Davis formation, named for the University of Michigan Field Camp.

The route continues on down the Hoback valley with hills on either side to Hoback Junction, where U.S. 26 and 89 turn off to the left. The Hoback River joins the Snake River at this point.

The route continues to the right along the Snake River for about a mile and a half, and then crosses the river. The route is on the west side of the Snake River for about 3 miles. The old road was on the right, or east, side of the Snake River and may be seen across the valley. The road had to be relocated because of landslide problems, and some of these landslides can be seen along the old road. The slides developed in some very slippery Cretaceous shales. The road was finally relocated after several hundred thousand dollars had been spent to clear the road every year after these continuing slides and earthflows.

Shortly after the second Snake River bridge, with the road back on the right side of the river, the valley to the left becomes several miles wide; this is the south end of Jackson Hole. The Snake River swings far over to the west side of the Hole, and the main road stays to the east, or right, along the face of the north end of the Hoback Range. This part of Jackson Hole is well irrigated and is good farmland. The route enters the city of Jackson in about 6 miles.

The elevation at Jackson is approximately 6,200 feet.

Side Trips from Pinedale

Fremont Lake and Skyline Drive: The Skyline drive via Fremont Lake turns off on U.S. 187 on the south side of Pinedale, as previously mentioned. A drive of 2 1/2 miles brings one to the top of the terminal moraine at the end of the lake, with a grand view of the lake and the mountains beyond. The terminal moraine here is a broad irregular ridge of gravel and boulders. It stands about 150 feet above lake level and is actually a compound ridge of roughly parallel ridges, each of which is a terminal or recessional moraine.

Continuing from the view point on top of the moraine, at a road junction in about 0.8 miles, the Skyline drive goes to the right. The left hand road goes down to lake level, cottages, and campgrounds. Continue on the right road along the moraines, and gradually come up and follow the top of a lateral moraine. This, too, is a compound series of gravel ridges, where boulders and gravel were deposited along the edge of the ice tongue and pushed up into parallel ridges as the ice expanded and melted alternately with weather changes.

There is a scenic overlook, to the right in about 5 miles, to see Half Moon Lake, which is another lake held in by a terminal moraine system.

At 9 miles from the top of the moraine there are scenic overlooks to the left. It is necessary to park and walk 100 feet to get this view down on Fremont Lake from the top of the lateral moraine. One sees a narrow part of the lake where a peninsula of granite outcrops projects out partway across the lake. The granite knobs are ice-smoothed and represent part of the rock bottom on which the ice was moving.

From the shape of the valley and the height of the lateral moraine ridges, it can be calculated that the Fremont Lake glacier tongue was 2 miles wide and over 1,500 feet thick extending several miles out beyond the front of the mountains.

Just before and beyond this overlook, to the right, are some high hills of Precambrian granites which form the outer edge of the Wind River Mountains proper. Here the lateral moraines are plastered against the granites, and then are built on out over the basin towards Pinedale.

A second scenic overlook at 12 miles is at the upper end of the lake, and affords a view up Pine Creek and other canyons in the high country of the Wind River Range, where U-shaped valleys are carved into the Precambrian granites.

The road continues to Elkhart Park, a small grassy basin in the forest, with a campground and ranger guard station. This is the starting place for hiking trails into the Wind River Range. At this point the road is 2,000 feet above lake level and about 9,400 feet in elevation.

On the return trip back down the lateral moraine along the Skyline drive, there are excellent views out across the Green River Basin to the Wyoming Range on the far western horizon, more or less straight ahead.

Green River Lakes: A very interesting side trip for geologists from Pinedale is a 110-mile round trip to the head of the Green River. It is partly on rough gravel roads, but is well worth it for the scenery and geologic interest. Starting at Pinedale, proceed 6 miles west along U.S. 187, then take a right turn on Wyo. 352 and in 4 miles pass the very small community of Cora.

The road will now continue on outwash plains for another 10 miles with moraine ridges off to the right, at a distance at first, and finally, quite close.

A junction to the right leads to the New Fork Lakes. Take a 3-mile trip to the outlet of these lakes. The road starts up a terminal moraine immediately, and will then cross 4 or 5 recessional moraine ridges of coarse bouldery material before it comes to the outlet of the New Fork Lakes. Here a long double lake reaches back into the mountains, in a valley once occupied by a long glacier extending out from the mountains onto the surface of the Green River Basin. Both sides of the lake are held in by high lateral moraine ridges; the end of the lake is dammed by the 4 or 5 terminal moraines across which one has just driven.

Continuing back on the main road, pavement ends in approximately 4 1/2 miles. After a gentle hill past outcrops of sedimentary rock, the route is down onto the Green River's mile-wide floodplain, and past summer homes and ranches. This wide floodplain continues for about 4 miles, and then the valley is considerably narrower with outcrops on both sides of the valley of sandstones and shales, with some red beds.

Nearly 12 miles from the end of the pavement the road passes a sign, "Kendall Warm Springs." Springs of warm water issue from the side of the valley to the right and have deposited a small travertine terrace into the Green River on the left. A very rare species of tiny fish is found in these warm waters—about 85°F.

The road continues along the right side of the Green River in a wider valley again for about 15 miles, swinging sharply around to the right and finally making a total bend of about 120°. This wide valley is obviously a glaciated valley with patches of moraine at first. Finally, around the big bend to the right are long, parallel, lateral moraine ridges (or terraces) extending up against the mountain front more than 1,000 feet above the valley floor (Photo 3.24).

Photo 3.24. Lateral moraine ridges in the Green River valley just below the Green River lakes. The youngest ridge across the river in the center has many dark-colored boulders. A couple of older lateral moraines form the ridges that rise to the skyline in the center of the picture, rising more than 1,000 feet above the valley floor.

At 52 miles from Pinedale, one reaches a parking lot and campground less than half a mile from the outlet of the lower Green River Lake at approximately 7,900 feet. Here is a spectacular view up the lake into the mountains. In the middle is striking Square Top Mountain (Photo 3.25), carved out of Precambrian granite, elevation 11,679 feet. On either side of the lake, and considerably closer, are mountains with steeply dipping Paleozoic rocks, folded and faulted during the Rocky Mountain uplift period. Closer to the campground are steeply dipping Mesozoic rocks which trend down the mountain side, almost to the valley floor. The lateral moraines, which are plastered up against the mountains across the Green River valley, partially cover these Mesozoic outcrops. This very geologically interesting area is the start of many hiking trails into the Wind River Range.

Log 7: Farson to Lander, Wyoming 28, 77 miles (plus!)
Map: Figure 3.11

This route goes around the south end of the Wind River Range, starting at Farson, which is about midway between Rock

Photo 3.25. Lower Green River Lake with Square Top Mountain on the right as seen from the campground at the outlet of the lake. The great mountain mass to the left of the lake is composed of tilted and folded Paleozoic sedimentary rocks while Square Top has been carved from Precambrian granite gneisses.

Trip Guides 139

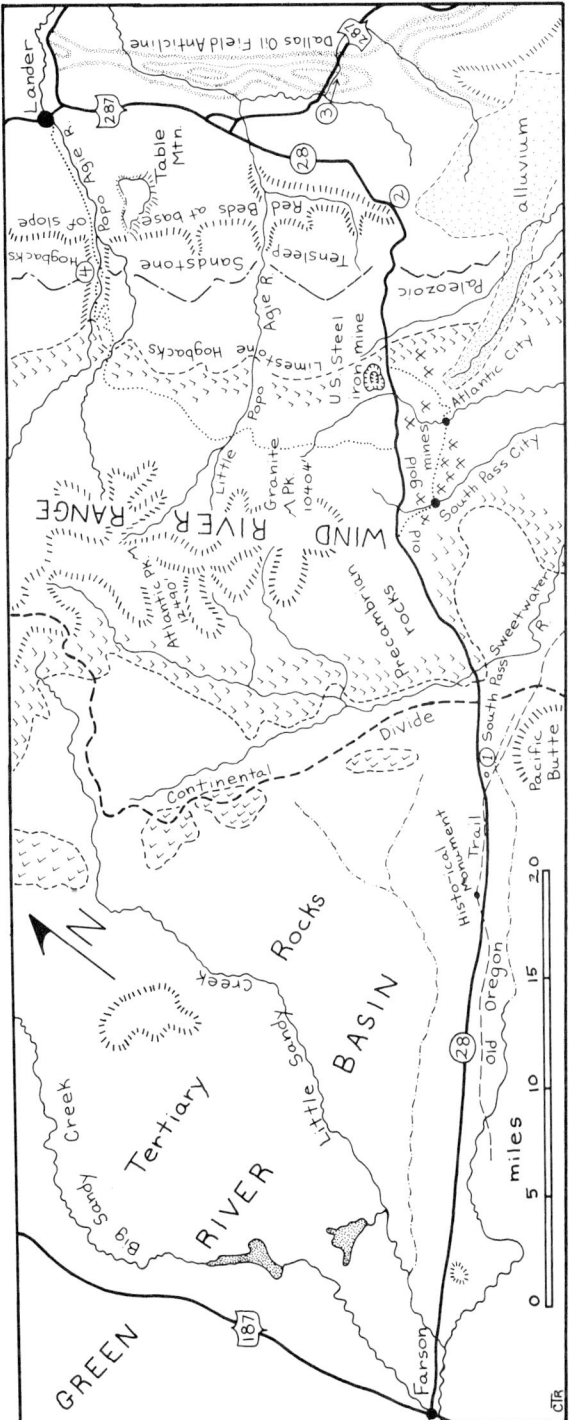

Figure 3.11. Map of the Green River Basin and the southern end of the Wind River Range along Wyo. 28 on the route of Log 7.

Springs and Pinedale. Turn right on Wyo. 28, off U.S. 187.

In about 6 1/2 miles pass low buttes with outcrops of shaly sandstones, a part of the Tertiary sedimentary fill in the Green River Basin. About 22 miles from Farson, a low escarpment of Tertiary sediments can be seen ahead to the right.

An historical marker, "Oregon Trail," 28 miles from Farson, is a short distance to the left from the main highway. Here, actual wagon wheel ruts of the old Oregon Trail can be seen in the sagebrush-covered surface. This is a worthwhile historical stop.

① About 5 miles further another historical marker, "South Pass Viewpoint," lies 0.3 miles to the right. From this point one can look out over the Oregon Trail where it crossed South Pass. There is no mountain climbing at this pass! Pacific Butte rises to the right of the Pass, and Pacific Spring forms a green place in the valley. Today, a railroad goes through here to the iron mine at Atlantic City. The south end of the Wind River Range is to the left across the main road.

In another 5 miles the road itself will have crossed a very low divide (at about 7,500 feet) and down perhaps 50 feet to the Sweetwater River bridge. This river flows eastward into the North Platte River of the Missouri system. The gentle slope the road has come up from Farson, drains into the Green River of the Colorado system.

Looking upstream from the bridge over the Sweetwater River, one may see outcrops of Precambrian rocks. However, it's almost 4 miles from here before Precambrian rock outcrops will become numerous on both sides of the road. These outcrops are granite gneisses with other darker-colored gneisses.

About 10 miles from the Sweetwater bridge a road turns off to the right, marked "South Pass City." This leads past several old abandoned gold mines and the old buildings of South Pass City and Atlantic City, now historic sites. After about 11 miles the road comes back to the main paved road. This is an interesting historical detour, but drive carefully on these gravel roads.

While many men followed the Oregon Trail just south of here to the California gold rush, it was not until 1865 that gold was finally found at what became South Pass City. A gold rush developed here in 1867 and within two years, more than 2,000 people lived in these towns. The gold has long since given out, and the population was once down to less than fifty people, but now both South Pass City and Atlantic City are being rebuilt as historic sites by the Wyoming Recreation Commission. The rocks here are brown, iron-stained, gold-bearing schists, dark-colored gneisses, and a small amount of granite.

Where the detour road from Atlantic City returns to the paved Wyo. 28 highway, lies the open-pit iron mine operated by U.S. Steel, discovered in more recent time. This can be seen at several places from Wyo. 28 as a large open pit, terraced into the side of Iron Mountain. The iron ore is Precambrian in age and occurs in low grade, iron-rich, slaty rock, called "taconite." The iron mineral is magnetite, and is separated from the crushed rock by a magnetic technique. At the separation plant the crushed magnetite powder is mixed with a little clay as a binder and is roasted into pellets; the pellets are shipped 76 miles by rail to Geneva, Utah, for smelting. A mile beyond the magnetite deposit, limestone cappings will be seen on the hills ahead, and the first actual outcrop of Paleozoic rock will be passed 2 1/2 miles from the Atlantic City junction. The road will then pass through gently dipping Paleozoic formations for a few miles.

② About 8 miles from the Atlantic City junction, the road comes past a steep valley down on the left, exposing the gently dipping, bright red beds of the Chugwater formation. The road swings around the head of this valley for a few miles with continuing views down this rather spectacular red canyon, locally known as the "Red Grade." The road swings left and starts downhill beneath outcrops of the pinkish Nugget sandstone of Jurassic age. On downhill rather steeply, the route passes a number of hogbacks of Mesozoic rocks to a junction with U.S. 287.

Straight ahead the road leads to Lander in 9 miles, but we urge the visitor to make a detour and turn right on 287 for perhaps 7 miles. This will take one across the center of the Dallas oil field anticline, a rather well-exposed anticlinal structure.

③ From the junction it is about 5 miles to a bridge across Twin Creek on U.S. 287. Here outcrops on both sides of the road are dipping to the southwest, that is, back in the direction from which one is coming. Within half a mile, the Chugwater red beds are flat-lying. This is the actual center of the anticline; notice an oil well to the right. In another half mile the Chugwater red beds are reversed, that is, they are dipping to the northeast, or in the direction one is driving. In another mile or so, the Nugget sandstone hogback, a pinkish or orange-colored sandstone is dipping to the east, and finally, by another bridge over Twin Creek, gray Cretaceous shales are also dipping in that direction; one has completely crossed the anticline! Now turn around and proceed back on U.S. 287 to the junction with Wyo. 28.

On the drive into Lander a flat-topped mountain on the left is visible for several miles. This is Table Mountain, and is an erosional remnant of an old gently dipping "pediment" surface, cut in middle Tertiary time by streams coming out into the Wind River Basin from the higher mountains. Since middle Tertiary time, erosion has removed most of the original surface along the edge of the Wind River Basin, and just this one remnant is preserved. The rest of the surface has been eroded to the lower present surface of the basin. Geologists call a broad sloping erosion surface at the foot of mountains in a semiarid region, a "pediment." Such surfaces have a covering of stream gravels; this is true at Table Mountain.

Side Trip to Sinks Canyon

An interesting side trip from Lander up the canyon of the middle fork of the Popo Agie River allows a visit to an underground section of the river. Start from Main Street at 9th and proceed southwestward on 9th toward the mountains. For the first 5 miles the route is over flat farmlands in a wide valley with low Cretaceous sandstone hogback ridges. Then the zone of the Triassic red beds is reached, and gently dipping red sandstones occur on either side of the main valley. To the left, the red beds extend up almost 1,000 feet where they are covered above by the gravels that cap Table Mountain. Ahead is the long high dip-slope of the Paleozoic rocks sloping on up toward the higher mountains.

In another mile the road has entered a very narrow canyon cut in this dip-slope. The first narrow part of the canyon is cut into the Tensleep sandstone, and some of the usual cross bedding can be seen in these rocks. As the canyon widens a strong contrast exists between the north-facing slope (left) which is forest covered and the drier south-facing slope which is brush covered; more direct sunlight means a drying effect and not enough water for forests.

④ Now the canyon is cut into the thick Madison limestone. Groundwaters have dissolved some of the limestone to produce caves and underground passages, such that the Popo Agie River runs underground for almost half a mile. On the right at a parking area and sign, "The Rise of the Sinks," is the place where the river comes out from underground. The waters come up quietly in a series of springs in a small elongate pool before flowing down as a normal river again. Half a mile further up the valley are "The Sinks," with parking on the left by a small museum. A short walk allows a view of the river rushing down rapids into a large underground cavern and disappearing into the Madison limestone.

This is close to the end of pavement, but a good gravel road continues up the canyon past dipping beds of Devonian rocks, the Bighorn dolomite, and Cambrian formations. About 2 1/2 miles from "The Sinks" the road crosses the river and switchbacks to climb the other side of the canyon. Here are exposed Precambrian granites of three kinds. The road climbs over 1,500 feet in the next 5 miles in a series of tight switchbacks, with spectacular views of the geology across the canyon—all the Paleozoic formations dipping about 10° towards the basin and away from the mountainside. From the top at Switchback Overlook the view is breathtaking with the high snowcapped peaks at the crest of the Wind River Range behind the great limestone hogbacks in the foreground.

The road actually continues all the way over to Wyo. 28 near the U.S. Steel Iron Mine for a total of 37 miles. From the switchback summit the grades are more gradual up and down across the small valleys. The highest point is about 9,500 feet above sea level, crossing the Blue Ridge in the granites. The route is through spruce and fir forests, past small lakes and many outcrops of granite and glacial moraine gravels.

Log 8: Lander (or Shoshoni) via Togwotee Pass to Jackson Hole, U.S. 26 and 287, 130 miles
Map: Figure 3.12

This log will serve those travelers coming from Farson on Log 7 to Lander, or from Rawlins on U.S. 287 to Lander, or those coming west across Wyoming from Casper on U.S. 26 past Shoshoni who will join this log 32 miles north of Lander.

Start in the center of Lander and drive northeast along the flank of the Wind River Mountains. To the left, a very well-developed Paleozoic dip-slope or hogback is obvious. The lower part is grass covered, but the upper part to the skyline is tree covered. In the background the high, snow-covered crest of the Wind River Range shows occasionally. Closer at hand, within a few miles of the road, low hogbacks of Mesozoic sandstone are visible from time to time. This situation continues for at least the first 16 miles. Then the road crosses a wide river valley near Fort Washakie.

Twenty-five miles from Lander oil wells of the Winkleman Dome Oil Field are seen on the right side of the road with steeply dipping Cretaceous sandstones. The Paleozoic hogbacks are still visible on the left on the mountain front.

The road has been traveling on a high flat terrace, dropping at times to a lower terrace. Finally, about 30 miles from Lander, the road goes down to the level of the Wind River, and in 2 miles reaches the junction with U.S. 26, on the right, from Riverton and Shoshoni. This junction is 56 miles from Shoshoni. The latter route has come across the monotonous Wind River Basin on Tertiary sediments and Quaternary alluvial gravels.

Check odometers at the junction. In 4 miles the road crosses terminal moraines from Bull Lake Creek. This material is coarse, bouldery gravel, heterogeneous as to the size of boulders (Photo 3.26).

Ahead for the next 6 or 7 miles, and across the Wind River to the right, an unusual butte may be observed, standing on the otherwise relatively flat surface of the Wind River Basin; this is Crowheart Butte. It is an erosional remnant of Eocene sediments which

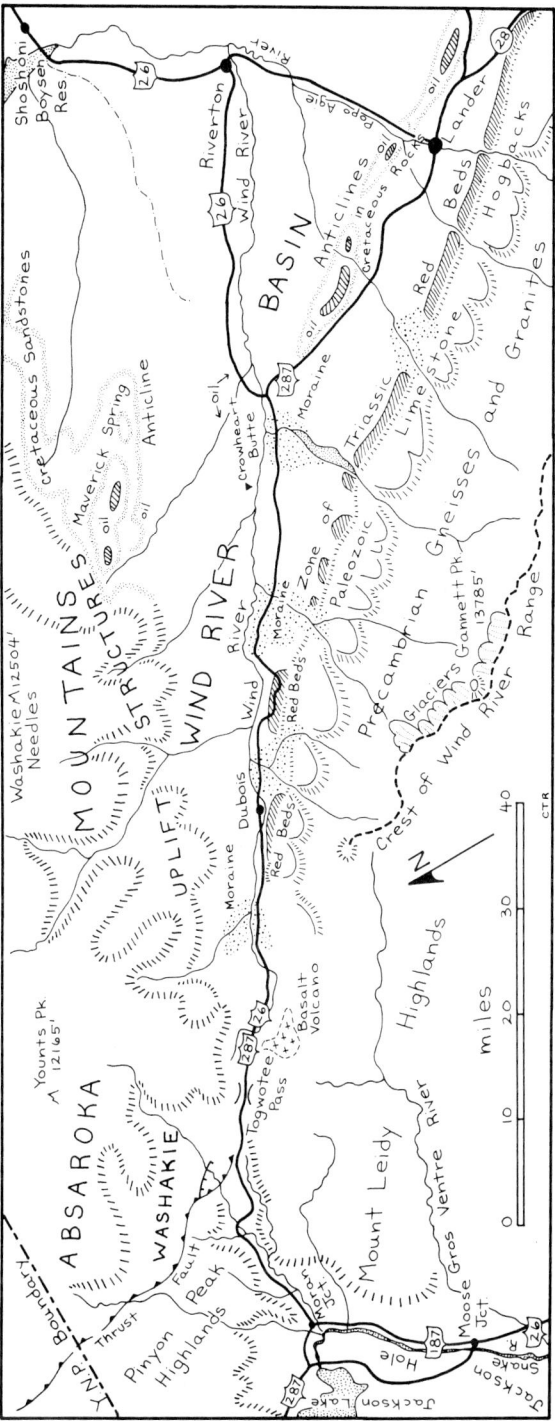

Figure 3.12. Map of eastern Wind River Basin and the northern Wind River Range along the route of Log 8 to Jackson Hole.

Photo 3.26. Outcrop of terminal moraine material; typical boulder, gravel and clay mixture known as boulder clay or *till*.

once filled in this basin to a much greater depth than at present.

For about 27 miles from the last junction, the road runs largely on a gravel-capped terrace. The road occasionally dips down across small stream valleys, but soon returns to this high terrace level. Cliffs and occasional badlands across the Wind River to the right are all cut from the Eocene sedimentary materials.

In another mile the road goes down to the level of the Wind River past steeply dipping Cretaceous rocks and enters a fairly narrow canyon. Triassic red beds and variously colored Jurassic sediments are present on both sides of the road. Note several small faults at various places. This continues for 3 to 4 miles until the valley gradually widens and the rocks become talus covered.

The route now enters about a 10 mile stretch of variable but wider valley character to Dubois. Throughout this 10-mile stretch, the cliffs to the right are composed of the Eocene Willwood formation. These sedimentary rocks are flat-lying, and are often banded red and white; they are sandstones, siltstones, and shales.

Near the middle of this stretch another area of coarse, bouldery, terminal moraine will be passed, visible especially on the left of the road. This material was brought down by glaciers from the high Wind River Mountains.

Enter Dubois, the last town before the route crosses the pass into Jackson Hole. Reset odometers.

About 1 mile from town, outcrops of the Triassic red beds are on the left. Behind them, the Paleozoic dip slope on the mountains is still visible, and on the right, the Willwood sediments.

Shortly, the valley widens with badlands carved from the Willwood sediments continuing on the right. Behind these and ahead to the right, the high part of the Absaroka Range will now become more and more prominent. The valley itself, has a floodplain about a half mile wide. The rocks on the left are Mesozoic formations with dips toward the road. The scenery changes moderately; the valley widens and narrows, but, in general, about the same kinds of rocks are seen for 15 miles from Dubois to the Shoshone Forest boundary. To this point, most of the nearby terrain has been sagebrush covered; now trees become more and more abundant.

In 2 miles, ahead on the left at about 11 o'clock, a high flat-topped, tree-covered ridge of dark-colored basaltic lava flows becomes more and more apparent. This area contains a hill with a reddish patch which looks like an old cinder cone; it is! These rocks are the remains of a late Tertiary basaltic volcano. It is in view for several miles.

The abrupt rise of the Absaroka volcanic ramparts becomes closer and closer on the right side of the road; its very irregular bedding is now visible. This is part of the so-called alluvial facies of the Absaroka volcanics (see page 35).

Togwotee Pass is reached at 31 miles from Dubois. The volcanic rock ramparts continue on the right for the next few miles with outcrops of very coarse, bouldery, volcanic material, probably volcanic mudflow deposits. Soon the topography becomes more subdued and tree-covered.

From 5 and on to 8 miles from the Pass, steeply dipping beds of Paleozoic limestones occur on the right. This is an area of older rocks faulted up along the southwest edge of the Washakie uplift structure. Paleozoic rocks on the right are thrust-faulted against Cretaceous rocks on the left. The latter are largely soil- and vegetation-covered.

Nine miles from the Pass the first view of the Teton Mountains is obtained, a spectacular sight on the skyline ahead. There is a parking site on the right.

It is now about 15 miles on down-slope past Cretaceous sandstone and shale outcrops, largely covered by landslide debris, partly forested, and partly sage-covered. The valley widens and one passes the Teton National Park entrance sign; then in 2 more miles one reaches Moran Junction. The road to the right continues to Yellowstone; the road to the left goes down the east side of Jackson Hole to the city of Jackson. Here we connect into Log 9.

Log 9: Jackson to South Entrance to West Thumb Junction, 80 miles
Map: Figure 3.13

The city of Jackson is built on an alluvial fan deposited from the mouth of Cache Creek to the southeast of the city. This creek drains out of the Gros Ventre Range.

Leave the city from the central square on combined U.S. highways 187, 89, and 26, northbound. Jackson is at an elevation of 6,209 feet above sea level.

The road passes along the side of East Gros Ventre Butte, which is a fault block bringing up Paleozoic rocks and is capped with some basalt lava. This stands to the left of the road for about 4 miles. On the right are the wide grassy meadows of Flat Creek.

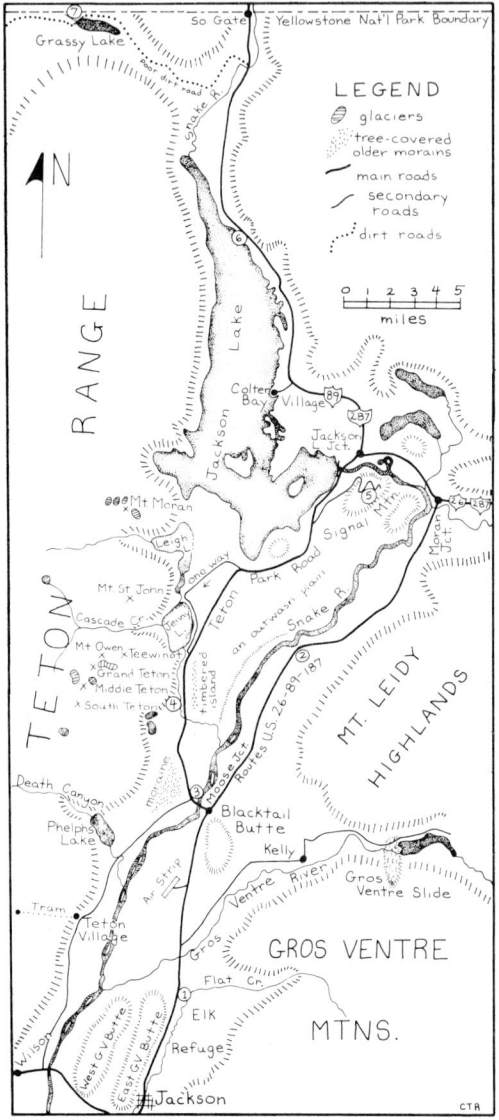

Figure 3.13. Map of Jackson Hole and the eastern side of the Teton Range showing the various routes in Teton National Park and to Yellowstone Park on Log 9.

① About 4 1/2 miles from town at a parking lot on the right, one may stop in front of a high fence at the Elk Refuge. During the summer one will usually see no elk, but in the winter thousands of elk feed in these meadows.

The road proceeds up a slight hill and soon comes out on the floor of Jackson Hole proper with the first view of the Teton Range ahead, slightly to the left. It is now 8 miles to Moose Junction.

However, in about 2 miles after a bridge over the Gros Ventre River, a road to the right leads to Kelly. Here begins a recommended side trip to see the Gros Ventre landslide of 1925. Following the Kelly road and the proper signs, it is about 12 miles each way to where the road is on this slide. The landslide took place when a slab of dipping Tensleep sandstone gave way suddenly, after saturating rains, and slid down on the underlying shaly sediments (Photo 2.21). The landslide dammed the river and produced Slide Lake as discussed on p. 70. Return to the main highway.

On to Moose Junction, the road passes across the flat, sage-covered surface of Jackson Hole, past the airstrip to the left. On the right is Blacktail Butte, another fault block mountain, partly buried by Tertiary sediments and standing about 1,000 feet above the surface of Jackson Hole.

At Moose Junction the main U.S. highway continues straight ahead 18 miles to Moran Junction. Along this road are about four "picture" parking areas to the left. Each one has a sign which identifies the mountains and features to be seen. This is true in all of Jackson Hole.

② At the Snake River viewpoint the river may be seen in one of its meanders. Two terrace levels are visible; the parking area is on the upper level. Both are outwash surfaces connected with the two most recent glacial episodes in Jackson Hole. The upper level is the oldest surface, while the lower level was cut out later and must be younger. The flat terrace surfaces are sagebrush- and grass-covered, but in the distance, especially off to the right, are low hilly areas which are tree-covered (Photo 3.27). In Jackson Hole, in general, outwash plains are formed of gravel deposited by melt water from glaciers. Thus, they have good drainage and become dry, so that only grass and sage will grow. The terminal moraine deposits, however, which are a mixture of boulders and clay will hold moisture and as a result, they are tree-covered. Therefore, you may assume that tree-covered surfaces in Jackson Hole are terminal or lateral moraines, and open grassy surfaces are outwash plains.

At Moran Junction turn left with routes 89 and 87 to continue on to Jackson Lake Junction and Yellowstone. The right fork at Moran Junction goes to Togwotee Pass, routes 26 and 287 (see Log 8).

Back at Moose Junction let's consider the left-hand fork. This is the Teton Park road to the Park Headquarters and the major Visitor's Center which crosses the Snake River almost immediately. The Visitor's

Photo 3.27. Mt. Moran, 12,605 ft., and the surface of Jackson Hole from the Snake River Overlook. The diorite dike is visible on top of Mt. Moran with Falling Ice Glacier below (see close-up air view of dike in Photo 2.20). Foreground shows Snake River (right) and several terrace levels. The main level is the glacial outwash terrace of the last major glacial period. The tree-covered ridge behind the terrace is a terminal moraine of this same glacial period.

Center has a museum which stresses man's history and early exploration in the Hole. Also here, near Headquarters, is the famous Chapel of the Transfiguration which is featured in so many illustrations.

Leaving Headquarters the route soon passes the Moose entrance station to Teton Park, and then proceeds northward along the foot of the mountains with a number of "picture" turnouts. Watch for one that gives a view of the Grand Teton and its glacier, the latter well up on the right-hand side of the main peak. Actually, one can see the terminal moraine of the Teton glacier (Photo 3.28). This is perhaps 4 miles from Moose Junction. At the same stop one can also see a thin, vertical, black dike cutting up through the base of the South Teton Mountain mass.

Eight miles from Moose Junction the road reaches Jenny Lake Junction. The left road at the junction goes to the outlet of the lake only, as a two-way road. To see most of Jenny Lake, therefore, it is necessary to drive 4 miles further north on the Teton Park road; that is, go straight ahead at Jenny Lake

Photo 3.28. Grand Teton, 13,766 ft., and the Teton Glacier (to right of peak). The terminal moraine of this glacier is most obvious.

Junction, and then turn left onto a one-way road which backtracks past Leigh Lake and then runs south along the edge of Jenny Lake. At first, one gets excellent views of Mt. Moran across grassy meadows; this view shows the black dike of diorite, 200-feet thick, which can be traced all the way from the top to the bottom of Mt. Moran, but which is readily visible only part way down. Mt. Moran rises 12,605 feet above sea level and is one of the great mountain masses of the Tetons.

This one-way road comes along the ridge bounding Jenny Lake. This is a narrow, forested, terminal moraine, formed when the glacier coming down Cascade Creek spread out on Jackson Hole as a semicircular bulge, perhaps a mile wide, and a half mile across. A terminal-lateral moraine system was built all around this ice bulge and now holds the Jenny Lake surface at 6,780 feet above sea level.

At the end of the one-way road, at the outlet of Jenny Lake, is the small ranger station where mountaineering trips must be registered. From here, also, hiking trails start around the lake and up Cascade Creek into the Teton Range. A boat service across the lake helps start the hikes!

Incidentally, many safe hiking trails for the non-mountaineer are maintained in several canyons; a few start near Leigh Lake. Another good hike goes up Death Canyon, across a lateral moraine, above Phelps Lake. This trail quickly gets up onto the rocks where good exposures of banded rocks and pegmatites may be seen. Ask a ranger where trails start, or get a trail guidebook.

The rocks of the central Teton Range are Precambrian gneisses, mostly light gray rocks of feldspar, quartz, and hornblende or black mica. Some of these gneisses are very highly banded, and the bands are intricately folded and contorted. Commonly, the gneisses are cut by pegmatites which vary from a foot or so to 10 or 20 feet in thickness. These pegmatites are coarse-grained rocks with masses of feldspar and quartz to several inches across, and with both black biotite mica and white muscovite mica, and small amounts of other minerals.

Now, returning to Jenny Lake Junction, proceed left, or north, on the route previously taken to the one-way Jenny Lake road, and at that junction, continue to the right on the main road. For a mile or two, the road passes through a terminal moraine belt near the side of Jackson Lake. This is hilly country with some abrupt depressions; the depressions are kettle holes. Two or three are visible on either side of the road. They were formed when masses of ice became stagnant and separated from the main glacier. Material was deposited around them, and perhaps, over them. Finally, the ice melted, leaving depressions in the deposits. Such hollows are anywhere from a hundred feet to a half mile across.

⑤ From the Jenny Lake one-way road junction, it is 4 or 5 miles to a road on the right which goes up Signal Mountain. This road is narrow, but paved, and climbs about 1,000 feet in 3 miles to an elevation of 7,731 feet at the summit. A spectacular view is obtained of Jackson Hole in every direction, and of the entire Teton Range. It is a special trip, not to be missed.

After descending Signal Mountain back to the main road it is 3 or 4 miles along Jackson Lake to the dam at the outlet. Jackson Lake has an average high-water elevation of 6,772 feet. A natural lake was here, held in by terminal moraines, but man has raised the level of the original lake with the dam. A short distance beyond the dam the road reaches Jackson Lake Junction. The right fork leads back to Moran Junction. Now continue to the left on routes 89 and 287 in order to reach Yellowstone.

The highway runs north through open forest, in 5 miles passing the entrance to Colter Bay Village, and then continues in forests for several miles.

⑥ The road finally comes out along the north shore of Jackson Lake with excellent views back down the lake along the front of the Teton Range. Here you are essentially looking southward along the Teton fault, and can see how abruptly the Teton Mountains rise above the flat level of Jackson Hole. The uplift, of course, was caused by Pliocene and Pleistocene fault displacement.

The trip from Colter Bay entrance to the actual south entrance to Yellowstone is 18 miles. However, about 2 1/2 miles before the south entrance is the Flagg Ranch, which is a big store, restaurant, and gas station, on the left of the road just after crossing the Snake River. On the right at this location, is a high mountain mass, rising 2,600 feet above the road, known as Huckleberry Mountain and composed of a thick section of the Yellowstone welded tuff.

At the south entrance, the road has reached an elevation of approximately 7,000 feet. It is now a 22-mile drive within Yellowstone Park to West Thumb Junction. For nearly 10 miles the entrance road climbs upgrade along the side of Lewis Canyon. The canyon, on the right, is cut in welded tuff from the youngest Yellowstone caldera. Note an imperfect vertical, columnar structure in the canyon walls. Above the canyon the river flows on the right, in grassy, swampy, meadows. From the bridge that crosses the Lewis River look back, left, to Lewis Falls. The rock here is obsidian-rich, flow rhyolite, one of the lava flows which filled in the Yellowstone caldera. Somewhere near here the road crosses the caldera rim, but the actual crossing is not obvious. The hills 2 or 3 miles to the right are carved from welded tuff outside the caldera, but on ahead the road is certainly on lava flows within the caldera.

In another mile the road runs along the shore of Lewis Lake, on the left, with an elevation of 7,779 feet. The beaches contain black sand which is disintegrated obsidian.

About 6 miles beyond the lake the route crosses the Continental Divide at a very low rise in the forests, hardly noticeable except for the sign. The elevation is approximately 8,000 feet.

In another 5 miles the road reaches West Thumb Junction on Yellowstone Lake, elevation 7,733. For the last 11 miles the route has been on the gentle surface of the Yellowstone Plateau. The West Thumb area will be described in the Yellowstone Loop road logs.

Side Trip to Grassy Lake Reservoir

⑦ An interesting trip for those who are geologically-minded, is a visit to a small quarry at the base of the Yellowstone welded tuff at Grassy Lake Reservoir. A road turns left just north of Flagg Ranch, as one proceeds north. This road is paved for a mile, and then becomes a very bad dirt road; beware in rainy weather. It is 9 miles through forests and meadows to Grassy Lake Reservoir, past some outcrops and cliffs of flow rhyolite and ash-flow tuff rhyolite.

Coming down a rough stretch to the dam of the reservoir, take a very narrow road to the left, just before the dam. This leads in about 100 yards to a small quarry, from which rock for the dam was obtained. Thus the same rock may be seen on the dam.

Here is the base of the so-called Lava Creek welded tuff, the unit of the Yellowstone tuff produced 600,000 years ago, by the last great ash-flow explosion. The actual base of this tuff is even with the quarry floor (Photo 3.29). The base has about 2 feet of almost pure, black glassy obsidian. The ash particles were so hot and fused together so completely that they formed a dense glass, which has cracked into short columns due to cooling and contraction. Above the 2 feet of actual glass, the rock is crystallized, forming a densely welded stony-looking ash-flow tuff.

While welded tuffs may be seen in many places along the highways in Yellowstone, it is not possible to see the actual glassy base of the welded tuff, without either a climb or a drive over bad roads, as at this place.

ROUTE TO NORTH ENTRANCE TO YELLOWSTONE PARK

*Log 10: Livingston to Gardiner
to Mammoth,
U.S. 89, 58 miles
Map: Figure 3.14*

Leave Livingston, elevation 4,487 feet, on U.S. 89, southbound; or, from the I-90 in-

Photo 3.29. Quarry near Grassy Lake Dam in the Lava Creek member of the Yellowstone Tuff. The lowest two feet is composed of beautiful black obsidian, even with the man's head. Above the glassy zone, the welded tuff is gray-colored, fine-grained and stony looking. The character of the rock changes at different levels due to differences in cooling and compaction but it is all rhyolite in composition.

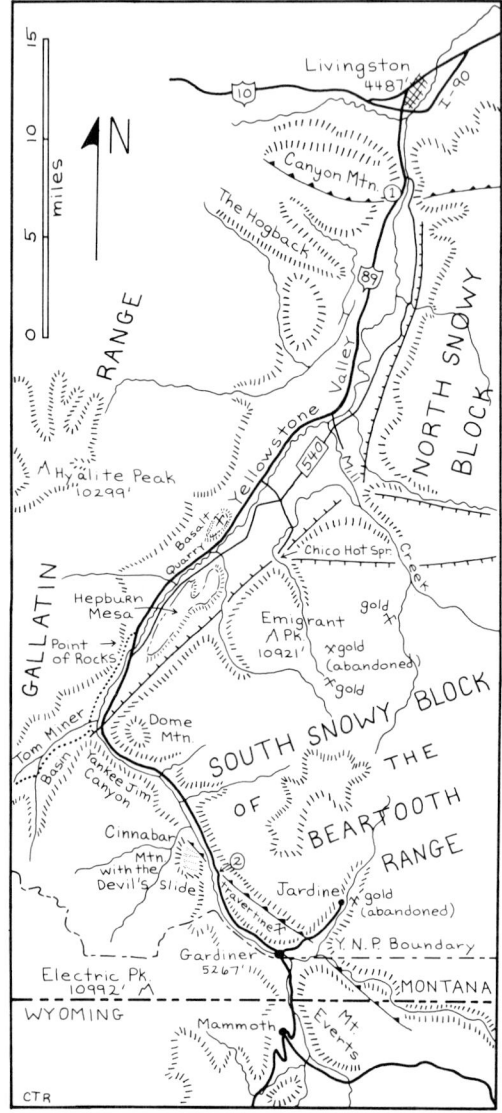

Figure 3.14. Map of the Yellowstone River valley from Livingston to Gardiner, Montana, along Log 10, between the Gallatin Range and the Snowy Blocks of the Beartooth Range.

terchange south of Livingston, exit south on 89. The road starts southward on the Yellowstone River floodplain, but within 2 miles of the I-90 junction, enters a lower Yellowstone River canyon, crossing the Canyon Mountain anticline. At first, north dips in Paleozoic rocks will be obvious as one is crossing the north side of this east-west trending anticline. Three miles from the interchange, Mont. 540 turns left and crosses the river.

① Four miles from the interchange are the scars of earthflows and slumps on the right hand side of the road, where Cambrian shales have caused trouble, and slumped in the past. This new road was constructed in 1965 and trouble began then, when the roadcut undermined old slumps in the Cambrian shales.

This is near the center of the Canyon Mountain anticline, which is thrust faulted, with dips nearly vertical. As you proceed from the earthflow site, notice that large blocks have rolled down from the mountain and are sitting out on the surfaces to the right of the road. These blocks of Paleozoic rocks are now sitting on Mesozoic rocks.

In 2 more miles one comes to the end of this canyon, and the wide Yellowstone Valley opens out before you, with an excellent view of the Beartooth Range ahead and slightly to the left. This is the North Snowy Block of the Beartooth Range, sometimes called the Snowy Mountains. The mountain range rises above the valley very abruptly along a normal fault scarp, the so-called Deep Creek fault system. Movement has occurred along this fault since the glacial period. This late Tertiary fault has cut across the original Rocky Mountain structures. The amount of uplift by the fault is estimated at 10,000 feet.

The route proceeds southward along the broad floodplain of the Yellowstone Valley. Since this is a down-faulted valley, it has a fill of Tertiary sediments, which are almost completely covered by river gravels and glacial materials. The road proceeds along a high terrace, associated with the older glaciation.

Glaciers came down all the valleys in the mountains to the left, depositing terminal moraines at the mountain front. Two different glaciations have been recognized, and most of the side canyons are choked by such material. Down near Mill Creek, the ice from a couple of valleys merged together to form a large fanlike glacier, which moved completely across the Yellowstone Valley. Terminal moraines occur at various places on terraces in the Yellowstone Valley, although this will not be obvious along the main highway.

About 22 miles from the starting point, a small road to the left crosses the valley. Check your odometer here, and watch for a dirt road on the right in 2 1/2 miles which goes up a short grade across the railroad, and into a basalt quarry. A mile-long remnant of a thick basalt flow caps a high terrace above the railroad. This basalt was quarried by the railroad to produce crushed rock for use as ballast along the right of way. In recent years the quarry has been used little, but it is possible to drive up the small gravel road across the tracks and then switchback into the quarry to study the basalt. It is coarse-grained basalt, and rather light-grey colored for basalt, with small light green olivine crystals. The quarry shows large columns in the rock, 3 or 4 feet in diameter, formed by contraction cracking as the flow cooled very slowly after deposition (Photo 3.30). The flow is 30 to 40 feet thick.

Across the main valley at this point, the Beartooth Mountain front is dominated by Emigrant Peak, 10,921 feet in elevation, which is part of an old eroded volcano, although the present peak's shape is not the original volcano.

Surrounding this mountain are numerous Tertiary intrusive and volcanic rocks of the Absaroka Volcanic Field. Around these intrusive rocks are many gold prospects and small abandoned mines. Some stream valleys were panned for gold years ago. In recent years some prospecting has occurred, but not enough gold has been found to justify any new mining activity.

Back to the main highway, continue southward and in a very few miles a long, low mesa, or high terrace, just across the river will be apparent for several miles; this is Hepburn Mesa. A thick basalt lava flow remnant forms the cap rock of this mesa. From its appearance one may think that more than one flow is present. The underlying very soft, easily-eroded sediments have been washed out allowing big pieces of the basalt to slump and slide part way down the sides of the mesa. These blocks give the illusion of more than one flow. The flow is an olivine basalt and is probably a part of the same flow seen back at the railroad quarry. It has been dated by radiogenic techniques at about 8 million years old.

Immediately under the thick basalt flow are stream gravel deposits, which in turn rest on an underlying white clay-rich, sedimentary material, probably lake beds of Late Miocene age. These are some of the sediments that fill the Yellowstone Valley Basin formed by down-faulting as the mountains rose to the east. Many years ago an unidentified mammal's tooth was found in these white beds.

At 33 miles from Livingston, the road crosses the Yellowstone River. Immediately to the right and for a mile or so before the bridge, are low but prominent hills along the river's edge called Point-of-Rocks; this is a group of small volcanic vent structures in the Eocene volcanic complex. A gravel road to the right about a mile before the Yellowstone bridge gives access to this area.

This same gravel road continues for a few miles on the right side of the Yellowstone River and leads up into Tom Miner Basin. This basin is surrounded on 3 sides by high mountains cut out of the Absaroka volcanic

Photo 3.30. Basalt quarry along the Northern Pacific railroad near Emigrant. The rock has broken along large columnar joints. This rock was used primarily for railroad ballast.

sequence. High up on several of these peaks and ridges are fossil trees, some still standing where originally buried. These are similar in type and age to the more famous fossil forests in Yellowstone itself. Specimens of agates have also been found in nodules and cavity fillings in the same volcanic rocks.

The main road half a mile after the Yellowstone bridge reaches a junction with the old road, now Mont. 540, back to the left. Check odometers.

In 2 miles, the road swings to the left and enters the mouth of Yankee Jim Canyon. Dome Mountain is the high mass on the left, rising about 3,000 feet above the river; its rocks have been ice-scoured up 2,000 feet. On turning into the canyon, the road crosses an extension of the normal fault along the mountain front to the north (see Map, Fig. 3.14). Across the river an alluvial fan is slightly offset by this fault, indicating that some movement has been quite recent. The uplift along this fault has pushed up the Precambrian rocks through which this canyon is cut.

The canyon is approximately 4 miles long and is carved in Precambrian gneisses and amphibolites. All the rocks are dark-colored, due to the presence of the mineral hornblende; small non-gem garnets are also present in some layers.

Near the middle of the canyon, the remains of a Late Pleistocene landslide deposit are present where rock broke and slid down Dome Mountain from the left. This slide formed a dam across the Yellowstone River, behind which a lake was backed upstream for over 14 miles. Today most of this landslide dam has been removed by the river, and the actual position of the slide material is not obvious except, perhaps, for extra large rapids in the river.

On up the river beyond the canyon, the valley widens a little, and volcanic rocks can be seen high up on the Precambrian gneisses. Many earthflow and slide tongues have come down from the high mountains, however, almost to water level on both sides of the river.

The small community of Corwin Springs is reached just over 11 miles from the last junction. About a half mile before this group of buildings, an archaeological site was studied a few years ago on the high banks above the Yellowstone River to the right of the road. Charcoal from an old fireplace or hearth was dated by Carbon 14 at 4,900 years. This site was associated with lakeshore silts, which suggests that the lake behind the landslide in the canyon was present when early man camped here. The site was studied and covered, so cannot be seen today.

At Corwin Springs a gravel road to the right crosses the Yellowstone River and can be followed all the way to Yellowstone Park past some old coke ovens at the abandoned Electric Coal field.

② The main highway stays on the left through Corwin, and passes a scenic parking area to the right in 2 miles. From here is a view of Cinnabar Mountain just across the river with its famous Devil's Slide (Photo 1.1). Here the Paleozoic and Mesozoic sections have been turned up to stand vertically with the Paleozoic to the right and the Mesozoic rocks continuing on to the left as one looks across the river. These beds have been pushed up by the uplift of the southwestern corner of the Beartooth Range along the Gardiner Fault. The Gardiner Fault must cross the river near here, and then trend along toward Gardiner behind the high benches on the right of the highway. The actual Devil's Slide is the smooth reddish zone which is the Chugwater red beds formation, here very thin. One of the high vertical walls just to the left of the slide is actually a sill of diorite, an intrusive igneous rock, which is about 10 feet thick (Photo 3.31).

The road continues along the left side of the Yellowstone valley for 7 miles, and then it crosses the river and enters Gardiner. Along this section, the road follows the base of a debris-covered slope with many blocks of basalt at the base. Another basalt flow caps the high bench or terrace above this slope. On the flows is an area of hot spring travertine deposits, which have been quarried for decoration and building stone.

Just before the bridge over the Yellowstone, a gravel road on the left climbs steeply up onto this bench with access to the old quarries, but it also continues 5 miles to the town of Jardine, the site of abandoned gold mines. The burned wreckage of the mill can still be seen on the left above the town. The gold occurred in quartz and pyrite veins in Precambrian schists.

The road through Gardiner turns left beyond the town through the original arch gate into the north entrance to Yellowstone Park. This was a busy entrance when the Northern Pacific passenger trains were running.

After entering this gate the road passes for a mile or so over a flat grassy surface, a high terrace level, and then turns to the right and

Photo 3.31. Great diorite sill in the Devil's Slide section on Cinnabar Mountain The sill stands as a vertical wall nearly 75-foot high where it has weathered out of parallel beds of fine sandstone and shale of Mesozoic age.

gradually enters a short canyon along the Gardner River. This canyon is cut in Cretaceous sandstones and shales where considerable landslide activity has been a problem along the highway, as can be seen.

About 2 1/2 miles from the entrance gate, one crosses the forty-fifth parallel of latitude, "halfway between the north pole and the equator!" according to the sign.

On uphill, Mount Everts rises steeply over 2,000 feet across the valley on the left. Here is a thick section of Cretaceous sandstone and shales with a sill of brownish igneous rock on the nearer end of the mountain. An ash flow caps the mountain on the far end, to be discussed in Log 15. The road passes the Mammoth campground and switchbacks above the latter to come out in Mammoth

Village. To the left are the Post Office and the Mammoth Museum; the Mammoth Hotel is ahead one block on the right.

ROUTES TO WEST ENTRANCE TO YELLOWSTONE PARK

Log 11: Bozeman to West Yellowstone,
U.S. 191, 90 miles
Map: Figure 3.15

This route starts at Bozeman, where one leaves I-90, coming from either east or west. Proceed on U.S. 191, westbound (the sign may say southbound). The road heads toward the west, but 8 miles from town turns south at the junction with Mont. 289.

Along this 8-mile stretch one is traveling in the wide basin occupied by Bozeman and other towns, known as the Gallatin Valley. It is bordered to the south by the imposing Gallatin Mountains and to the northeast by the Bridger Range. It is a down-faulted basin filled with several thousand feet of Tertiary sediments, partly covered by Quarternary stream gravels and alluvial fan deposits, built out from the mountain front.

Southward from the junction mentioned above, the route is along the floodplain of the Gallatin River and proceeds directly toward the mountain front. As the road approaches the mountains and crosses the Gallatin River, it enters a narrow, forested, V-shaped canyon. Dark-colored Precambrian gneisses, cut by pegmatite veins and dikes, outcrop on both sides of the road. This canyon is about 2 miles long.

① Now the valley widens as Spanish Creek enters from the right in a broad shallow valley. Just ahead, on the left, are large limestone cliffs. However, just before reaching these cliffs, one crosses the Squaw Creek reverse fault, where the Precambrian gneisses of the canyon have been uplifted and shoved southward against the limestones.

These first, high limestone cliffs are Madison limestone (Photo 3.32).

Limestones continue to be visible on the left, across the river, for the next 3 or 4 miles. These limestones are progressively older, until at Storm Castle Peak, the rock at the base of the mountain is Cambrian in age, and the Madison limestone is 2,000 feet up on top of this peak. A few sills of dark-colored igneous rocks are intruded horizontally into the lower limestone.

Opposite Storm Castle Peak, to the right, up Hell Roaring Creek, the Spanish Peaks may be seen at the head of the valley, rising to over 11,000 feet. These high peaks have been carved entirely out of Precambrian gneisses and granites.

After passing the mouth of Squaw Creek, on the left across the Gallatin River, the next high mountain is composed of Precambrian rock, although the contact of the Paleozoics may be seen running obliquely up the left side of the mountain, dipping steeply to the northeast. Now the Gallatin River runs in a deep canyon for many miles, cut in Precambrian rocks.

② A few miles beyond Squaw Creek, the highway crosses the Gallatin River. Then, in just 2 more miles, there is a water-smoothed rock, known as Kitchen Rock, of intricately banded and folded gneisses now beautifully exposed.

For the next 10 miles, the canyon continues in a sharp V-shaped canyon, indicating that it has not been occupied by a major glacier. However, piles of moraines are present at the mouth of most of the side valleys, indicating that glaciers came down

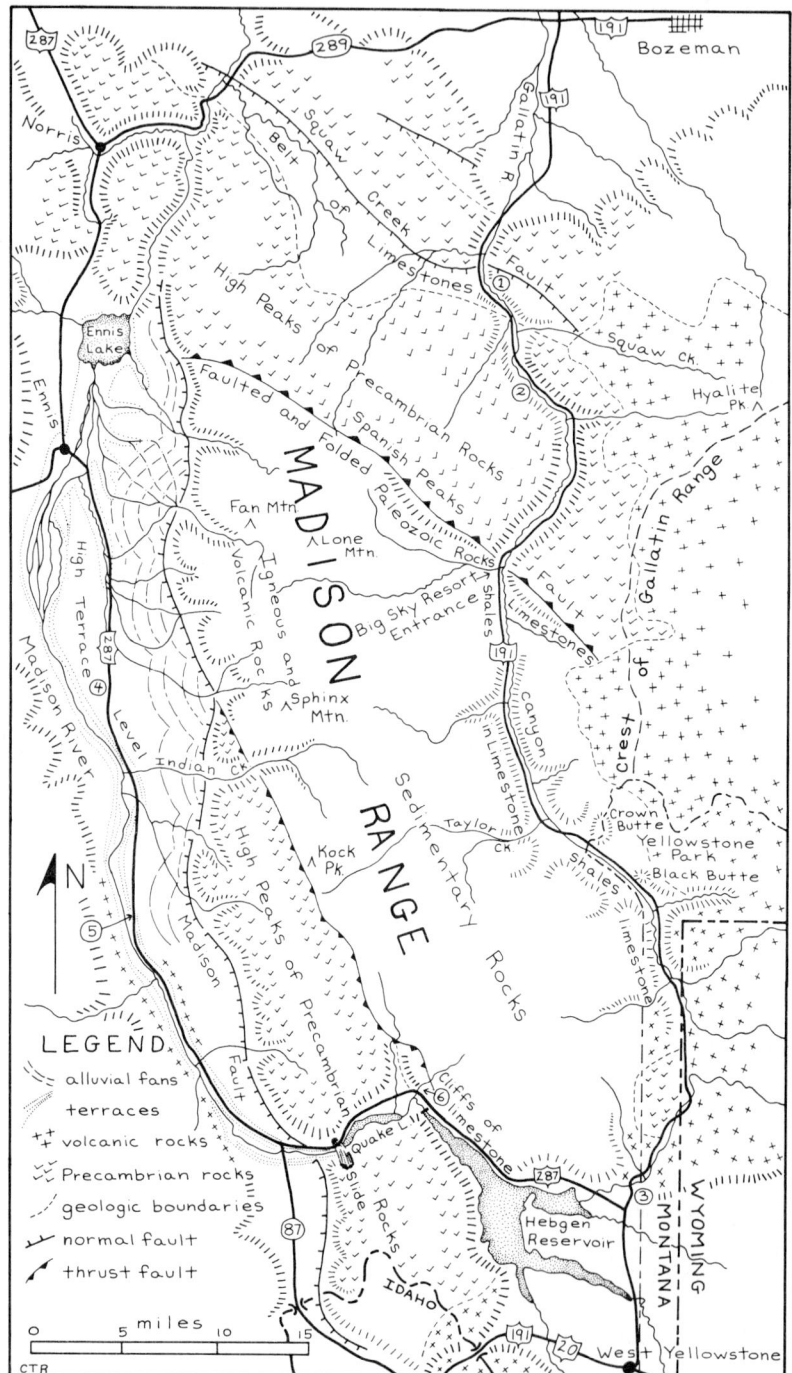

Figure 3.15. Map of the Madison Range and the western side of the Gallatin Mountains showing features along Logs 11 and 12 from Bozeman and Ennis to West Yellowstone.

Trip Guides 159

Photo 3.32. Madison limestone cliffs along the Gallatin River near Rock Haven Chapel. The talus slopes below the cliffs are partially stabilized by small trees.

from the higher mountains almost to the Gallatin River level. Also along this stretch of narrow canyon, is found evidence of small landslides which left scars on the mountain faces, and piles of debris in the valley.

As the highway again crosses the Gallatin River, look straight ahead up the valley perhaps 15 miles to Sphinx Mountain. This mountain is a very unusual 2,000-foot section of Tertiary conglomerates more fully described in Log 12.

In another mile, ridges of steeply dipping limestones are seen ahead, both right and left; these mark the Spanish Peak thrust fault. The northwest trending belt of Precambrian rocks just crossed has been pushed up to the southwest, and Paleozoic formations have been turned up on edge. The road soon crosses this fault and comes abreast of the vertical limestone beds, and then enters a wide valley section.

On the right is the entrance road to the Big Sky resort and the Soldiers' Chapel road, both along the west fork of the Gallatin River. Looking westward up this river, the sharp peak of Lone Mountain can be seen, perhaps 10 miles away. This 11,166-foot peak has been carved by glacial action. It is a land form known as a *glacial horn,* a small replica of the famous Matterhorn in Switzerland. It is carved out of intrusive igneous rock, hornblende andesite, perhaps of late Cretaceous age.

For the next 6 miles the valley is wide, having been carved from soft Mesozoic sediments. Looking back to the left, the long, high ridge of steeply dipping Paleozoic limestones along the Spanish Peaks Fault can be seen trending for several miles, diagonal to the Gallatin valley.

Now the Gallatin enters a narrow canyon in flat-lying limestones. At first, there are red limestones on the left, the Amsden formation; but soon, the canyon is cut entirely in the Madison limestone, with a depth well over 1,000 feet. This canyon continues for about 4 miles across the center of the Buck Creek anticline, which has brought up the older Madison limestone from under the Mesozoic rocks.

The valley widens again where the Buffalo Horn Creek comes in from the left. Note near the mouth of this creek the lobate tongue of an earthflow, a partially forested hilly area, where a mudflow-like slide has come down the Buffalo Horn Creek.

The Madison valley immediately enters another limestone canyon, cut again, into the Madison limestone. This is another smaller anticline.

Limestone cliffs continue on the left as the valley of Taylor Creek comes into view on the right. Looking up this creek a mile or two, one can see the end of a landslide into Taylor Creek valley. It is possible to drive on a side road up this creek for a mile or so and have a look at the old landslide deposit.

A mile beyond here, after crossing the Gallatin River, the valley widens out as the limestone cliffs end abruptly. A complex structure of folds and faults puts the Madison limestone against much younger Mesozoic rocks, and thus, the wide valley.

A few miles ahead on the left, at about 11 o'clock, a ridge, known as Crown Butte, has a long cliff near its summit, perhaps 800 feet above the river. This cliff is a remnant of the oldest (2 million years) Yellowstone welded tuff.

Some 2 1/2 miles from the last bridge one enters Yellowstone National Park. This is the small irregular, northwest projection of the Park, to the left of the road. On the right, the Gallatin River is the Park boundary for the next 3 or 4 miles.

The high mountains up behind Crown Butte, forming the skyline, are part of the Absaroka volcanics. They form the divide between the Gallatin River and Tom Miner

Basin, which drains into the Yellowstone River. Immediately ahead is Lava Butte, another exposure of the Yellowstone welded tuff. This rock has broken and slid down toward the road. The resistant, brittle welded tuff overlies soft Cretaceous shales. The shale weathers out; the welded tuff breaks off in blocks; and the mixture has formed a small-scale landslide down toward the road.

About a mile beyond this Lava Butte exposure there is a sharp, pyramid-shaped mountain, called Black Butte, an intrusive igneous body, associated with the Absaroka volcanics. It's actually one of several located in this vicinity. Very coarse slides, or talus deposits of blocks of this andesite have rolled down, almost to the road.

Five miles into the Park, the route crosses Specimen Creek on the left, with a view up this creek of Electric Peak, the highest mountain in Yellowstone Park. A trail leads up this creek valley into the volcanics, where numerous fossil forests may be seen.

The andesitic volcanic rocks lie on top of Madison limestone, and the Gallatin River has cut another small canyon in this limestone. Cliffs of Madison limestone are prominent for a mile or so, especially along the left side of the road, although this same rock is prevalent on the right but more tree-covered.

As the valley continues southward, the headwaters of the Gallatin turn left up into the mountains, and the route continues for a mile or two over a flat, swampy valley which has essentially no drainage. This area is actually the divide to Grayling Creek, which comes out of the mountains to the left and flows northward along the route of the main highway.

As the road runs gradually downhill into Grayling valley, the rocks exposed for 5 miles or so include Precambrian mica schist and the Yellowstone welded tuff. Driving through, it is difficult to tell which is which, but they can be easily distinguished if one stops and looks at the outcrops. There is probably more volcanic material than schist. As the valley of Grayling Creek becomes better developed and deeper, the outcrops of the grayish colored welded tuff become more prominent, especially on the right side of the road.

③ As the road crosses Grayling Creek in a left turn, up a small hill large outcrops of the welded tuff will be seen on the left at first, and a little further up on the right, extending to the top of the hill. This, again, is the oldest of the Yellowstone ash-flow welded tuffs. At the top of this small hill is a view southward of the West Yellowstone Basin, a broad partly forested plain. To the left is the flat tree-covered edge of Yellowstone Plateau; while to the right, across the basin, one can see the south end of the Madison Range.

On the way down this small hill, Hebgen Lake may be seen ahead, and slightly to the right. The road soon reaches the junction with U.S. 287 on the right from Ennis (see Log 12). One is now on the floor of the West Yellowstone Basin. Proceeding straight ahead it is 8 miles to West Yellowstone. The Madison River will be crossed a little more than halfway along this stretch.

Log 12: Ennis to West Yellowstone,
U.S. 287, 72 miles
Map: Figure 3.15

The traveler comes to Ennis from the north or northwest, either by U.S. 287 from the vicinity of Three Forks over a low pass from Norris, or across the Gravelly Range from Virginia City on Mont. 287, also over a relatively low pass. On either route, as one approaches Ennis there are excellent views of the Madison valley and the Madison Range beyond. Coming from Virginia City there is an excellent view area and parking place affording a fabulous panoramic view of the whole valley and mountain range with alluvial fans across the river. Sphinx Mountain, which is described in a sign at this parking area, is also visible from there.

Ennis is a small town on the edge of the Madison River floodplain, at an elevation slightly below 5,000 feet. Before passing through Ennis be certain to get a view across the valley to the east, from the somewhat higher ground above town, to see the alluvial fans, especially the Cedar Creek fan directly across the valley.

Leaving Ennis, southbound on U.S. 287, the road almost immediately crosses the Madison River and its floodplain. Here the Madison is a braided river: that is, it breaks up into many channels as it flows northward, building a delta into Ennis Lake.

The main road proceeds gradually uphill beyond the floodplain, along the valley of Bear Creek in a shallow valley cut into a high terrace. Notice the river gravels exposed along the edge of this terrace.

Finally, 7 miles from Ennis the road reaches the top of the highest terrace, known as the Cameron Terrace. This upper terrace was formed in late Pleistocene time in association with one of the earlier glacial episodes.

④ The road continues straight on the flat Cameron Terrace surface for 6 miles, passing the tiny community of Cameron. Along here are continuing views to the left of the Madison Range and its wide alluvial fans. The mountains are sharp, gray-colored peaks, eroded out of Cretaceous volcanic rocks. Further south the sharp, angular summit of Sphinx Mountain sitting all by itself will come more and more into view, especially beyond Cameron. Sphinx Mountain is a very unusual mass composed of coarse conglomerates and sandstones, 2,000 feet thick, of Tertiary age. These sit on top of Cretaceous volcanic rocks in a broad syncline, or downfold, in the mountain structure. No other exposures of this Sphinx Mountain conglomerate are known anywhere else in the Madison Range.

To the right, across the Madison valley, are the low nondescript hills of the Gravelly Range, mostly Precambrian rocks.

Fifteen miles from Ennis the route comes down off the high terrace to a lower terrace, and finally, still lower, to the crossing of Indian Creek valley. Then the road, in the next 3 miles, works its way back up to the high terrace level again. As you cross the edges of the various terraces, notice the coarse river gravels exposed by roadcuts, sometimes with boulders up to one foot in diameter. These are stream deposits left on the various terrace levels when each individual terrace was the floodplain of the ancestral Madison River. The higher terrace is oldest; successively lower terraces are younger; and the present river flows on the youngest level of all. The route continues on the high terrace for another 5 miles with excellent views to the left and ahead of the Madison Range.

⑤ Finally, the route drops off this high terrace to an intermediate terrace for two miles. As the route comes off this intermediate terrace there is a view, immediately across the Madison River to the right, of an outcrop of the Yellowstone welded tuff, in a steep cliff on the top of the highest terrace level. This has been cut by a fault, and the northward extension of the cliff is at a slightly lower level.

For the next 10 miles or so the road continues on the lowest terrace, or on the floodplain of the Madison River, in what seems to be a narrow valley. However, the wide area of alluvial fans is above the terrace edges on the left and out of sight. The main valley of the Madison is narrower here than it was at Ennis. At Ennis the valley is about 10 miles wide; here, the valley is only 4 miles wide.

Along this section, continuing outcrops of the Yellowstone welded tuff are visible on the right, although often almost completely obscured by forest. Actually, this same Yellowstone tuff occurs on the left side of the Madison River up above the road, between the road and the mountain front, but is not visible from the road which is down in the lower valley. At the end of this 10-mile stretch the big cliffs on the right become especially prominent. The cliffs are at least 200 feet high with vertical columnar jointing.

Now the road climbs out of this lower valley and again up to one of the higher terraces, and gradually approaches the mountain front on the left. Ahead, at about 1 or 2 o'clock to the south, is a wide valley extending to the horizon. This valley, known as the Missouri Flats, extends up to Raynolds Pass, at 6,834 feet, on the border between Montana and Idaho.

In the Madison valley on the right, at least 4 different terrace levels are visible (Photo 3.33). Soon the route reaches a junction to the right with Mont. 87, the road which goes on over Raynolds Pass.

Continue on U.S. 287 straight ahead, and enter the mouth of the Madison canyon in about 2 miles. The Madison River valley is choked with coarse boulders and gravel washed down from the great landslide which

Photo 3.33. Terraces in the Madison valley with the southern Madison Range in the background. The bridge of Mont. route 87 crosses the Madison River on the lowest terrace. Three higher terraces are visible beyond. The mountain front is along the Madison Fault.

blocks the Madison valley ahead. This great landslide becomes more and more obvious as one drives into the canyon.

After the road climbs up on the landslide debris, a road turns left to the Forest Service Visitor's Center and landslide view area. All the rocks involved in the great landslide are Precambrian rocks, including schist and dolomite marble, as explained in the Visitor's Center. This is a must for all travelers! Go up this road to the Visitor's Center building. Here displays tell the story of the terrifying landslide which occurred near midnight on August 17, 1959, at the time of the West Yellowstone earthquake, magnitude of 7.1 on the Richter scale. The quake caused relatively limited damage because this is not a populated area, but it did set off the tremendous landslide. Exhibits in the Visitor's Center and periodic lectures in summer months by Forest Service personnel tell the story of what happened. The great slide is immediately visible across the valley, and you are *on* the material which came down the mountain and back up the other side of the valley several hundred feet (Photo 2.11).

Up the valley is Earthquake Lake, formed behind the landslide dam. The level was originally 50 feet higher than at present. The dam was cut through by the Corp of Engineers to alleviate flooding danger downstream, thus lowering the level to its present position, but many trees had already been flooded and killed.

6   Beyond this Visitor's Center the road is along the left side of "Quake Lake." In about 5 1/2 miles a sign indicates the Cabin Creek fault scarp exposure to the left. Be certain to turn in here and see the actual fault, where the earth on one side went down 17 feet (Photo 3.34). This is what caused the earthquake. Here again, the Forest Service has excellent signs and photographs to tell you the story.

It is less than a half mile from the Cabin Creek turnoff to the Hebgen Dam; the reservoir level is 6,548 feet. The rocks across the reservoir to the right are Precambrian gneisses, but the rocks immediately to the left, behind Cabin Creek, are very steeply dipping Paleozoic limestones.

At the dam and along the highway for the next 10 miles are numerous Forest Service signs, indicating various features caused by the earthquake: such as, slumps, road destruction, partly wrecked houses, and scarps. This route is along the north shore of the Hebgen Lake reservoir.

Near the upper end of the reservoir the road comes into the West Yellowstone Basin. Ahead is a view of the Yellowstone Plateau, rising to a flat, tree-covered skyline on the eastern horizon. In a few miles, the route reaches the junction with U.S. 191 on the left (see Log 11).

During the 1959 earthquake the Red Canyon fault scarp, one of those along which movement occurred, cut across the highway, approximately at this intersection, with an 8-foot scarp. One car drove off this 8-foot cliff and overturned. Today, since rebuilding and regrading of the road, this fault scarp has been completely obscured.

Proceed to the right with U.S. 287 and 191 across the surface of the West Yellowstone Basin.

The road dips down to cross the Madison River about 4 1/2 miles from the junction, and then climbs up again on a forested terrace, all the way to the city limits of West Yellowstone (elevation 6,660 feet). This city is primarily a tourist town—motels, restaurants, and souvenir shops taking up most of the main street.

Log 12A: West Yellowstone to
Madison Junction, 14 miles
Map: Figure 3.18

Photo 3.34. Fault Scarp at the old Cabin Creek campground immediately after the 1959 earthquake. The lower surface, at the right, suddenly dropped 17 feet; it had been continuous with the upper level. (Photograph by I. J. Witkind, U.S. Geological Survey).

The west gate to Yellowstone Park is immediately adjacent to the town of West Yellowstone, Montana. The first 6 to 7 miles into the Park is through open forests on a level alluvial surface of the West Yellowstone Basin, with the Madison River soon coming close on the left. A few miles to the right are hills of Yellowstone welded tuff.

The road rather abruptly enters the Madison canyon and then soon crosses the Madison River. For 2 or 3 miles this canyon is cut through a rhyolite lava flow almost a million years old. From the high cliffs to the left, several landslides blocked the road at the time of the earthquake in 1959.

Where the valley widens a little the caldera fault zone curves in from the southwest across the river and now follows the valley to Madison Junction (see Map, Fig. 3.18). Now the rocks along the road on the left, which stand as high cliffs with large talus piles, represent the remains of the actual caldera wall. These cliffs and the mountains above, all the way to Purple Mountain, are composed of older flows with the thick, younger Yellowstone welded tuff on top. Across the Madison valley the cliffs have been cut in a young, thick lava flow that filled the caldera after its collapse. The Firehole Canyon (see Yellowstone Loop Log 15C) is cut through this thick flow a little further to the east. These cliffs across the Madison valley are scarred by dozens of small landslides and rock falls which occurred during the great earthquake in 1959. The scars have darkened with time and are not as apparent as they were right after the earthquake.

Log 13: Blackfoot via Idaho Falls
to West Yellowstone,
U.S. 191, 140 miles
Map: Figure 3.16

Visitors coming north on I-15 from Utah will come through Pocatello and then north toward Blackfoot. Those coming from southern Idaho on I-15W will pass through American Falls and join I-15 just beyond Pocatello, traveling along the southeastern side of the Snake River plains.

At Blackfoot on I-15 is a road junction with U.S. 26 which goes west to Arco. Stay on I-15 past Blackfoot; in 2 miles cross a major bridge over the Snake River. Now the road runs along the irrigated floodplain of the Snake River with many large irrigation canals.

(1) Almost 7 miles from the bridge the road starts across the lava fields of the Hell's Half Acre flow area. These are pahoehoe flows with large pressure ridges up to 100 feet long by 15 feet high. Much fracturing of the lava surface, especially on these ridges, has taken place. Roadcuts through these ridges show the dense basalt inside the flows. About a mile into the flow area is a rest stop with a "geological area" sign on the right. A similar stop on the left-hand lane occurs in another mile. These flows are quite fresh with only widely scattered sagebrush and cedar trees. They are estimated to be about 2,000 years old. The road leaves the flow area 3 1/2 miles after entering it.

It is now 15 miles across the floodplain, with its many irrigation canals, to the junction of I-15 and U.S. 20 west of Idaho Falls. Turn right and proceed into Idaho Falls, crossing the Snake River bridge with a view of the actual falls to the left, immediately upstream. During the Teton flood in June of 1976 the water level was right up to the level of this bridge.

In the center of Idaho Falls, turn left at the junction of U.S. 20 and 191 and follow both routes northward. (NOTE: A side trip to the Ammon pumice quarries is given at the end of this log.)

Continue on route 191 through Rigby to Lorenzo (where a side trip to Menan Buttes will be given later) and to Rexburg. This 30-

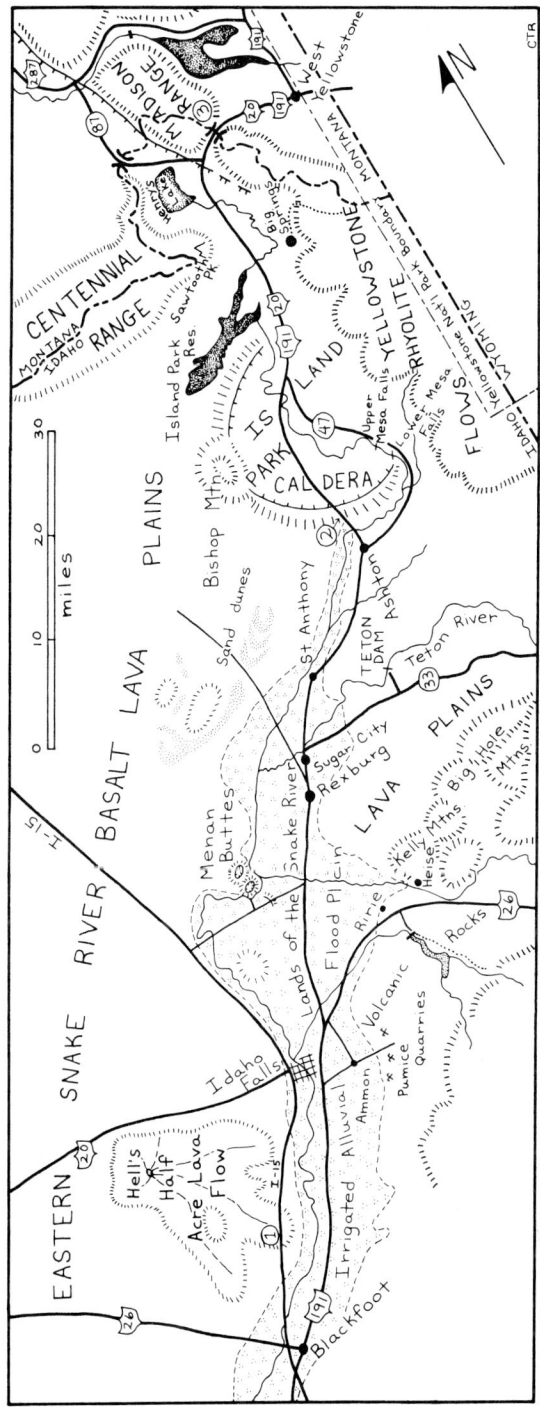

Figure 3.16. Map of the Eastern Snake River Lava Plains from Blackfoot to West Yellowstone, the route of Log 13 and its side trips.

mile route is on the irrigated Snake River plain, with many natural and man-made canals to spread the water to different parts of the plains.

Entering Rexburg the route crosses for the next 5 or 6 miles, through Sugar City, an area which was covered by 6 to 10 feet of water when the Teton Dam failed suddenly in June, 1976.

Just north of Sugar City, Idaho route 33 leads to the right to Teton Basin at the western foot of the Teton Mountains. This route passes, in about 10 miles, a turnoff road to the left to the Teton Dam site.

Continue north on the floodplain of the Henrys Fork of the Snake River. Views to the left for a few miles show a low butte (Juniper Butte) around which small, but well-developed, sand dunes are present. It is possible to drive over and see these dunes; inquire locally (Photo 3.35). To the right the Big Hole Mountains, a low unimpressive range, are in the foreground. Beyond them, and far on the horizon, are the high peaks of the Teton Range. Proceed through St. Anthony, and on toward Ashton. A few miles before Ashton the view ahead shows a low forested ridge extending southwest for

Photo 3.35. Sand dunes west and northwest of St. Anthony on the northeastern Snake River plains, 33 miles north of Idaho Falls. (Photograph by John S. Shelton, with permission.)

several miles. This is the rim of the Island Park caldera.

The junction at Ashton to Idaho 47 turns right through town and goes to the old road into the Island Park caldera past Mesa Falls (see later). Continuing on U.S. 191 cross a bridge over the Henrys Fork of the Snake River, and then start to climb up on the gently sloping outer surface of the caldera rim.

② At 0.8 miles from the bridge is the first good outcrop of the various ash-flow units that make up this outer ridge (Photo 3.36). At the bottom of the outcrop is an exposure of dirty-looking rock, which is the weathered welded tuff of the first major explosive event 2 million years ago. Above this, are unconsolidated ash beds of the 1.2 million year event, and on top is a loosely welded ash-flow tuff of the same period. The white beds in the center of the outcrop are unconsolidated and are composed of small pieces of pumice, clear, colorless crystals of feldspar, and a little quartz. These unconsolidated beds rained down from the sky, as a rather normal kind of ash fall.

The road continues up the grade for a 1,000-foot climb during the next 4 miles, with many more outcrops of the rocks just described, especially the white pumice and crystal beds, and the pinkish, loosely welded tuffs.

On top of the hill is the final outcrop of this material. The road then starts gently down a few hundred feet into forests, crossing the caldera fault. This caldera is about 20 miles in diameter, and is largely filled in its western half with basalt flows. The eastern half of the caldera is completely buried by lava flows that came out of the Yellowstone caldera. The road runs along a flat, forested surface with occasional roadcuts of basalt for nearly 8 miles.

Dr. Robert Christiansen of the U.S. Geological Survey believes, after his many years of field work, that the Island Park caldera was first formed 2 million years ago at the same time a caldera, perhaps connected, formed in western Yellowstone Park; and that both caldera centers were the source of the older welded tuff, the Huckleberry Ridge member of the Yellowstone tuff. This event spread ash flows over much of Idaho as well as Yellowstone Park. This was the source for material now found far to the north in the Madison River valley as well as material far to the south in the Snake River valley graben in Idaho. During the second cycle of volcanic rhyolitic activity in the Yellowstone area, 1.2 million years ago, the Island Park caldera was reactivated, mostly in its southern section, by a smaller event but with both explosive ash falls of pumice fragments and crystals, and with ash flows forming welded tuffs. These materials cover the surface of the old caldera rim formed earlier and partially fill the first caldera, as indicated by the welded tuffs at Mesa Falls. These caldera-forming events were followed by basalt flows, partially filling and covering the inside of the now double caldera. Much later thick rhyolite flows from over in Yellowstone moved westward and buried the eastern half of the Island Park caldera, making it very difficult to see the actual relationships of the older events.

The road enters open clearings, largely sagebrush covered, and crosses the Henrys Fork of the Snake River on the Osborne Bridge. This clearing allows a good view of the low caldera rim ahead, sharply to the left, and back behind. On all three sides the rim is a very low, even, forested ridge. Ahead at about 11 o'clock, behind the caldera rim, are the high Centennial Mountains.

Some 1.4 miles beyond ths bridge, the old road rejoins the present 191 from the right with a sign, *Mesa Falls Scenic Drive.* This is Ida. 47, and it is 14 miles back down this road to the falls.

Photo 3.36. Rhyolite ash deposit outcrops on the outer slope of the Island Park caldera rim along U.S. 20 in Idaho. The lower, darker cliffs are the weathered top of the older Huckleberry Ridge member of the Yellowstone tuff; middle white beds are unconsolidated, well bedded, air-fall ash deposits of tiny feldspar and quartz crystals and small pieces of white pumice; upper darker (pinkish) unit is a poorly welded breccia of pumice fragments of Mesa Falls age, 1.2 million years.

The route continues northward for 9 miles across more of the Island Park caldera floor through forests and open meadows, and past several resorts, until the road crosses the Buffalo Fork River. This is on the approximate trend of the northern caldera rim, but here the rim is completely covered by younger flow units, and it is not visible or recognizable in any way. We have now traveled 21 miles from the south rim in crossing the Island Park caldera.

The next 4 miles are through forests, with several large roadcuts in the youngest member of the Yellowstone tuff which erupted within Yellowstone Park 600,000 years ago.

A junction with Ida. 84 to the right to Big Springs is at the Mack's Inn resort. The road to Big Springs is a good paved road, 5 miles long. At the springs water comes out in quantity from under a thick rhyolite flow. It is an interesting site, and from the bridge across the outlet of the spring it is usually possible to see many trout (no fishing allowed!).

Adjacent to the Mack's Inn resort is the Henrys Fork River which Route 191 crosses on a bridge, proceeding northward. At 1.6 miles from the bridge, an unmarked dirt road to the left leads to a drive up Sawtell Peak. This road turns off to the left, just opposite the Island Park resort. Sawtell Peak has a radio tower and radar globe on its summit; a fairly good gravel road leads all the way up to the summit, at 9,866 feet. The view from the summit is quite spectacular, so a trip up on a nice sunny day can be an added attraction. Sawtell Peak is composed of andesite lavas, and is the remains of an Eocene volcano.

Back on the main road, the route almost immediately comes out into open, flat meadows for the next 8 miles or so, across the Henrys Lake flats. Sawtell Peak is to the left at 9 o'clock. The south end of the Madison Range is almost directly ahead, and low hills of volcanic materials occur to the right at 1 or 2 o'clock. Looking back at perhaps 5 o'clock, across the grassy meadows, one can see the front of high, flat-topped, rhyolite flows that came out of Yellowstone Park.

A view of Henrys Lake is obtained to the left, near the junction, also left, of the road leading for 9 miles to Raynold's Pass at 6,834 feet. The elevation of Henrys Lake is 6,472, so it is obvious that this is a low pass leading over to the Madison River valley and route U.S. 287 to Ennis. Across Henrys Lake is a view of the Centennial Range behind Sawtell Peak (Photo 3.37).

③ The right fork at the junction leads uphill in a valley across the southern end of the Madison Range, and reaches the top of Targhee Pass in 4 miles, at an altitude of 7,072 feet. The big rock outcrops at, and just beyond, the summit are all welded tuffs of the oldest unit of the Yellowstone tuff. The Island Park caldera was first active 2 million years ago, at which time material rushed northward across the low passes. Here, material flowed across this Pass into West Yellowstone Basin. Ash-flow material also rushed across the low Raynold's Pass at the same time, and on northward into the Madison River valley.

The road over Targhee Pass drops down in 2 miles to the level of the West Yellowstone Basin, with views ahead of the Yellowstone Plateau and the notch of the Madison River Canyon cut into the plateau. West Yellowstone is reached 10 miles from the Pass.

GEOLOGICAL SIDE TRIPS ALONG LOG 13

Ammon Pumice Quarries

Several quarries where white pumice has been, and is being, quarried, occur in the low

Photo 3.37. Sawtell Peak, left, and the Centennial Range with early July snow. The foreground shows the flats and low terraces that border Henry's Lake, Idaho.

bare hills 6 or 7 miles east of Idaho Falls, just past the small town of Ammon. These pumice deposits are up to 50 feet thick, massive bedded, and almost unconsolidated. Pumice lumps are up to several inches in size. In places, the pumice deposits are overlain by welded tuff units, occasionally with a glassy basal zone. These deposits are considered to be Pliocene in age.

Those wishing to visit several of these quarries should turn off U.S. route 191, south of Idaho Falls, on either Sunnyside Road, which is 1 mile south of 17th Street, or on York Road, 3 miles south. Both roads lead eastward. Continue east until the roads start up into the hills, and then look for white, dusty roads leading to the right, which go into quarries. There are other quarries in the area, and local inquiries will aid those interested in studying this material.

Menan Buttes

The two Menan Buttes can be seen in the distance from U.S. 191. They are explosion ash cones formed when lava came up through very wet ground, specifically through the Snake River and its saturated floodplain gravels, back in late Pleistocene time (Photo 3.38). To visit these buttes, one leaves U.S. 191 to the left (westbound) 0.2 miles south of the Snake River bridge at Lorenzo. This is just over 4 miles north of Rigby on 191.

Proceed westward on this road from the small community of Lorenzo for 3 miles. Here is a road fork; take either fork. The right fork goes around the low hill called Little Buttes, while the left fork goes on over this butte. Little Buttes are the remnant of a small cone formed at the same time as the larger Menan Buttes to the north. They are

Photo 3.38. Northern Menan Butte showing the low, wide profile of this typical ash cone and its large crater. In the foreground are meanders of the Henry's Fork of the Snake River on its flood plain. In the background are lava fields of the Snake River plain. (Photograph by John S. Shelton, with permission).

composed of material blasted out during the first part of the eruption and deposited in layers of well-bedded, black, glassy ash and white stream pebbles. As the basalt lava came up through the wet gravel, the lava was shattered by steam explosions into glassy ash particles, and stream pebbles were simultaneously thrown up into the air. Combined ash and pebble beds were laid down beyond the explosion site. This material can be seen exposed in pits along the side of either road.

Beyond Little Buttes, continue for 2 miles on either road, and then turn sharp right, before the town of Menan, and proceed northward a little over 2 miles where this road crosses the Snake River. You are now opposite the southern Menan Butte. Continue about a mile and a half and take a little dirt road up between the two buttes to a point where one can see a trail going up the side of the northern butte. This is the best place for a climb up to the rim or summit of North

Menan Butte. These buttes are about 2 miles in diameter at their bases and have craters about a half mile across. The rim of the butte is about 400 feet above the bottom of the crater. The butte is composed of well-cemented or fused black, glassy, basalt grains, many of which are greenish-gray today due to hydration. These buttes are quite unlike ordinary cinder cones. Actually, this is the same kind and shape of volcanic feature as Diamond Head in Hawaii, and it was formed in the same way—by eruption through water or very wet ground. It is recommended for those making the Menan Butte trip that two topographic maps be obtained in advance: the Menan Buttes, and Rigby quadrangles; at a scale of 1:24,000, they show in detail both the Menan Buttes and the Little Buttes and the roads around them (see Appendix B).

Mesa Falls

The upper and lower Mesa Falls may be seen on what was the old road, from Ashton north to West Yellowstone. Today this is Ida. 47, turning off 191 at Ashton and proceeding around along the Henrys Fork River and thus up into the Island Park caldera. After climbing a short grade, one comes up on a high, flat, forested area. Nearly 15 miles from Ashton, a sign announces a scenic turnoff on the left (Grandview Overlook) which permits a view down into the canyon of the Henrys Fork River and the lower falls. The canyon at this point is 500 feet deep, and the falls are a little over 80 feet high with a large volume of water.

A half mile beyond this viewpoint, a road to the left goes down into the canyon and allows one to drive to the top of the Upper Mesa Falls for closeup views of a large, 50-foot waterfall. The rocks at both falls are ash-flow tuffs formed during the middle explosive event of the Yellowstone rhyolites, that is, 1.2 million years ago. These welded tuffs are known as the Mesa Falls member of the Yellowstone tuff. Partway down into the canyon of the Henrys Fork is a flat, terracelike level, 100 feet or so above the river. This terrace level is capped by a basalt lava flow which apparently came down into the Henrys Fork valley when this level was the floodplain of the river. Today, the river has cut on down below, but remnants of the old lava flow on this old floodplain are preserved. The parking area of Upper Mesa Falls is on this basalt capping. There are also older basalt flows on the upper level, on which the main highway is constructed.

The sequence of events here is something like this: (1) Eruption 1.2 million years ago of the Mesa Falls ash flows and caldera collapse to form the inner part of the Island Park caldera; (2) basalt lava within, and partially filling this caldera; (3) canyon cutting by the ancestral Henrys Fork River, forming a valley 300 to 400 feet deep; (4) local basalt flows down on the floodplains of this ancestral Henrys Fork River; and (5) additional erosion to cut the present canyon and waterfalls in the underlying ash-flow tuffs.

ROUTES FROM IDAHO TO SOUTH ENTRANCE

Log 14: Idaho Falls via Snake River Valley to Jackson,
U.S. 26, 110 miles
Map: Figure 3.17

Leaving Idaho Falls, northbound on routes 191 and 26, one reaches a junction in 5 miles. Take the right-hand fork on U.S. 26, and proceed northeastward.

In a couple of miles a low, broad hill on the right at about 2 o'clock, largely crop-covered, is Iona Cone. This is a small, ba-

Trip Guides 175

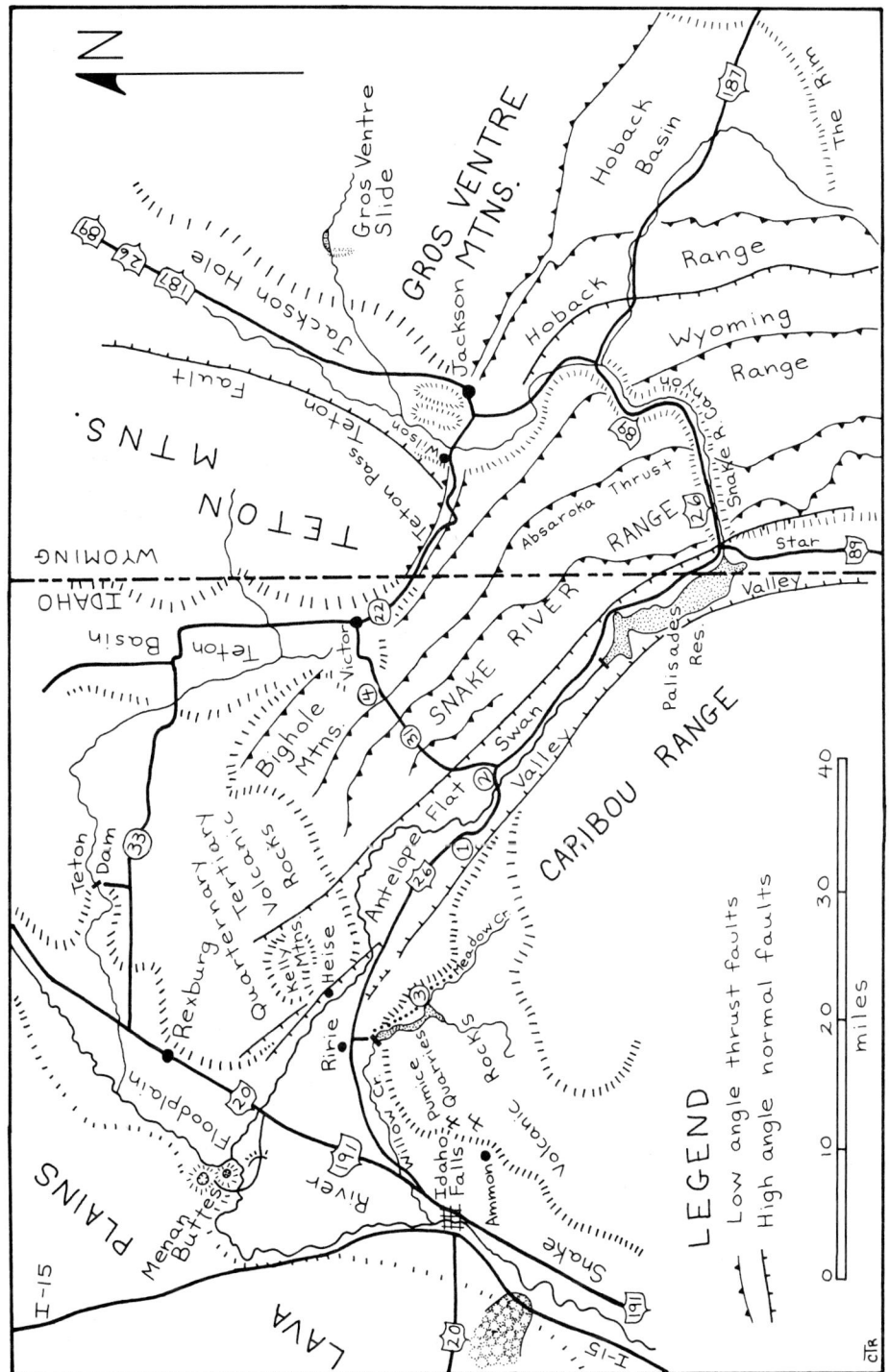

Figure 3.17. Map of the thrust fault belt or the Border Ranges of Idaho and Wyoming from Idaho Falls to Jackson along route of Logs 14 and 14A.

salt, shield volcano of Pleistocene age. Along this same stretch of road Menan Buttes are visible in the distance to the left at about 10 o'clock.

The road continues on the floodplains of Willow Creek and the Snake River canal system, mostly on alluvial or stream deposits.

About 9 miles from the junction, the Ririe by-pass road takes off to the left. Here, one can see the Kelly Mountains to the left across the Snake River valley. These are Pliocene ash flows, welded tuffs, and some rhyolite lava flows.

In another 3 miles a road turns right to the Ririe Dam. (See side trip log at the end of this section.)

① The road continues along a high terrace level, swinging more westward, and at 18 miles from the junction comes to a major rest stop and parking area on the left known as the Snake River Canyon Overlook. Here is a fine place to stop and look at a number of features in the area. Looking down the canyon, to the left at 9 o'clock, are the Kelly Mountains, an uplifted area of Pliocene rhyolite welded tuffs and flows, across the valley and to the right, of the Snake River Range. Immediately below, in the Snake River canyon are basalt lavas which flowed down the canyon after it had been cut partway to its present depth. Immediately across from the overlook, these basalts have been faulted and are situated, therefore, at several levels. On down the river a mile or so, remnants of the old rhyolites in which the valley was first cut stand up as knobs with patches of basalt flow on either side, showing that the basalts are simply part of a flow which came down the canyon (Photo 3.39).

The road now continues gently up over cultivated fields in a wide area known as Antelope Flat. Here one continues in the Snake River graben, a long, narrow, down-faulted valley, or trough, which trends northwest to southeast. The mountains on either side have moved up along the two bounding faults. This graben is nearly 6 miles wide at this point. The Kelly Mountains behind us are actually a local up-faulted block within the graben. The graben is partly filled in the Antelope Flat's section by basalt flows, which in turn, rest on the older welded tuffs from Yellowstone Park, both of which lie in the graben.

Several vent areas for the basalts have been found along the Snake River. One of these is present where the road goes downhill around a couple of sharp curves beyond the flats. Here darkish, thin-bedded, coarse-grained tuffs represent material around an old cinder cone.

② About 15 miles from the overlook, the road crosses the Snake River, and for the next mile or so travels past basalt flow outcrops on the left. These outcrops seem to be broken up into roundish or oval-shaped clumps. These are pillow lavas which form when a lava flow goes into water.

The small town of Swan Valley is reached 3 miles beyond the bridge. Here is the junction of U.S. 26 to the right, and of Ida. 31 to the left (the latter route is Log 14A).

To the right on U.S. 26 the route follows a broad valley in the graben known as Swan Valley. This continues for 11 miles to the Palisades Dam. Near the middle part of this section, notice ledges of welded tuff on either side of the valley, at about 10 o'clock and 2 o'clock respectively. These are outcrops of the 2-million-year-old ash-flow tuff from Yellowstone Park. This tuff lies on river gravels, which in turn, lie on basalts; and all of these materials partially fill the graben, which is only 4 miles wide at this point.

Photo 3.39. The Snake River just below the Snake River Canyon Overlook. The massive rock outcrop in the center along the canyon wall is an old hill of Pliocene rhyolite left standing as the Snake River had cut a Pleistocene valley. A basalt lava flow coming down this old valley on its floodplain went around this hill. The remnants of this flow are preserved and can be seen on either side of the rhyolite hill as the darker columnar jointed cliffs. The Kelly Mountains are in the background.

At the Palisades Dam, a vista point is opposite Calamity Point, a conical hill across the dam which is part of a very thick andesite flow. This same flow can be seen along the road for the next couple miles on the left.

For the next 14 miles the road follows along the left side of the Palisades reservoir to the state line. Toward the latter part of this stretch there are several outcrops of very white pumice tuffs, which are Pliocene in age. They are interbedded with conglomerates and sandstones, also of Pliocene age. Along the reservoir the Caribou Range is across the lake to the right, composed mostly of Mesozoic rocks. The Snake River range is on the left, composed mostly of Paleozoic rocks. Along the foot of the Snake River range on the left is the Grand Valley fault; and along the foot of the Caribou Range across the lake, is the Snake River fault.

These two faults parallel the sides of this down-faulted graben.

The state line is reached 25 miles from the last Snake River bridge, and Alpine Junction, Wyoming is just over 2 more miles. This is the junction of U.S. 27 and 89; the latter comes from the right and from Utah around Bear Lake. Turn left onto the combined 26 and 89, and enter the Grand Canyon of the Snake River.

The next 24 miles of the route are across the Snake River Range, and later the Wyoming Range, to Hoback Junction. This route crosses the so-called thrust fault belt of the border ranges. The route crosses three major groups of thrust faults (see Fig. 2.13). The general structures, to the nongeologists, along this route are steeply dipping sedimentary rocks of various kinds.

Some 8 miles from the junction the route crosses the Absaroka thrust, one of the major thrusts which can be traced from north to south for nearly 200 miles. Here cliffs of Madison limestone have been shoved more or less horizontally over black, Cretaceous shales. It is not easy to see the exact spot unless you are a geologist, but you will drive from a steep narrow valley to a somewhat wider valley in the shales.

Now for many miles the canyon is largely in Mesozoic rocks. Coarse river gravels can be seen along the far side of the Snake River for the next 10 miles or so. These gravels are actually gold-bearing and have been worked on and off during the past century, although not in recent years. The gravels contain 10 to 14 cents worth of gold per cubic yard of gravel! This is not exactly rich, but the gravels are so extensive for so many miles that the total amount of gold involved is quite large.

At Hoback Junction, where the road from Pinedale comes in from the right, turn left and proceed on to Jackson, referring to Log 6 for a description of the next few miles.

Side Trip to Ririe Dam and Meadow Creek Dugway

Turn right on the road sign "Ririe Dam" from U.S. 26 just past the Ririe business route to the left.

The dam is reached in about 2 1/2 miles; go to the right to an overlook. From the overlook, you are on top of a basalt flow which came down the valley when it was quite shallow. This basalt, in turn, sits on the older ash-flow tuff from Yellowstone Park. This tuff is light-colored and slightly pinkish to light gray. It can be seen across the canyon as a light-colored zone. The tuff sits on older basalts which can be seen as a ledge in the canyon wall about halfway down.

Take the road down to the dam itself, and pass the ash-flow tuff along the roadcuts on the right; the basalts are down at dam level.

Leaving the dam, continue on a dusty gravel road about 4 miles beyond the dam, then turn right down into the valley of Meadow Creek on a rather steep, dusty grade; this is the so-called Dugway.

③ Starting down the dugway the first rocks are densely-welded tuffs with a dark, glassy base, a very pretty obsidian. It is Pliocene in age, older than the Yellowstone welded tuffs.

On down the road is a thick section of air-fall and water-laid volcanic tuffs and sandstones. Still further down the road, white pumice tuffs in thin beds of various kinds, some of which fell from the air, and others of which are small ash flows, are present the rest of the way down to stream level (Photo 3.40). These are a continuation, laterally, of the same pumice deposits which are being quarried near Ammon (see Log 13, special side trip to Ammon).

Photo 3.40. Road cuts along the Meadow Creek Dugway. The white foreground exposures are bedded pumice and fine ash deposits. The dark rocks above are part of a Pliocene welded tuff which has a thin glassy basal bed.

Many textures and features can be studied in this section, to give one an idea of how these various rocks were deposited. These include cross-bedding and peculiar concretionary structures, apparently due to cementing action by ground water after deposition.

Log 14A: Swan Valley to Jackson
via Teton Pass,
Ida. 31 and 33, and Wyo. 22, 50 miles
Map: Figure 3.17
(Idaho Falls to Jackson, 90 miles)

Leave Idaho Falls following Log 14 as far as the junction at the town of Swan Valley. Here turn left with Ida. 31, at an elevation of about 5,400 feet. The road climbs up onto the Pine Creek Bench, still within the Snake River graben. This bench is covered with gravels which lie on top of the older Yellowstone welded tuff, which in turn, lies on top of basalts; all of these units are materials which have partially filled the down-faulted graben.

Five miles from Swan Valley the road

crosses the Pine Creek bridge and enters the valley into the mountains. Here the road crosses the Grand Valley fault, along which the graben has been down-dropped and the mountains ahead have been uplifted. In about 1 mile a basalt flow can be seen in the valley of Pine Creek. This is a basalt that flowed into this valley in Pleistocene time from the graben.

Over the next 5 miles one will cross 8 thrust faults! These faults involve progressively younger rocks, starting with Cambrian thrusts over Mississippian, and so forth, to Pennsylvanian over Cretaceous. Almost all of the beds in all fault layers are dipping rather steeply back toward the southwest, so it is not easy to recognize the faults unless one can recognize the actual formations.

(4) About 11 miles from Swan Valley the road crosses the Absaroka fault (seen on Log 14 in the Snake River canyon) just before crossing North Pine Creek. The valley widens here, because the more resistant rocks in the Absaroka fault block overlie softer Cretaceous sandstones and shales ahead. The route continues to climb gently for another 3 miles through sandstones, shales, and a few thin coal beds in Cretaceous formations to Pine Creek Pass at 6,700 feet. This is the crest of the Big Hole range, a rather low range, eroded mostly out of Cretaceous sedimentary rocks and Tertiary volcanic rocks. The route down from the pass goes only 3 miles until the road comes out on the level of Teton Basin at 6,200 feet. In the early days, this was known as Pierre's Hole. It is a late Tertiary down-faulted basin filled with Tertiary sediments. An oil well test hole about 12 miles north of this site reached Precambrian rocks 8,400 feet below the surface.

Directly ahead and to the right is the impressive view of the Teton Range. The highest peaks in the background are Precambrian rocks, more than 7,000 feet above the basin level, or more than 15,000 feet above the Precambrian rocks in the test well north of here. Below the high peaks is the relatively gentle dip-slope on the west side of the Teton Range, developed on the upper Paleozoic rocks.

Continue on to Victor and a junction with Ida. 33. Turn right onto route 33 and drive up the head of the Teton River. In about 2 miles outcrops of welded tuffs from Yellowstone will be seen on Mesozoic rocks. The state line is reached 5 1/2 miles from Victor.

The road climbs a steep uphill grade 6 1/2 miles to the top of Teton Pass. The road will zigzag up a narrow valley, crisscrossing two parallel thrust-fault complexes. On the left is the thrust sheet of the Cache Creek thrust, with outcrops of Triassic redbeds. This fault belongs to the ancestral Teton block and moved toward the southwest. On the right side of the road most rocks are Paleozoic sedimentary rocks in the Jackson thrust sheet, which has been pushed northeastward. Along this valley these two thrusts almost meet. Actually, they must have jammed into each other at an earlier time, but a valley has been eroded out along this collision zone.

At Teton Pass there is an excellent view to the east of the Gros Ventre Mountains across the south end of Jackson Hole. The slope down from Teton Pass into Jackson Hole has been badly scarred by man: an old road, a new road, a power line, ski lifts, and landslides caused by highway construction have ruined the environment!

One mile down from the pass are great cliffs on the left of Flathead sandstone. About the same place on the right are landslides caused by highway construction and snow slides. Beyond these sandstone cliffs are roadcuts in glacial material. Then 2 1/2 miles down from the pass are 100-foot-high cliffs of andesite on the left. Beyond this is more glacial material. Finally, 3 1/2 miles from the pass are 200-foot cliffs of Madison limestone, also on the left.

The small town of Wilson will be reached between 5 1/2 and 6 miles from the pass. Just west of town is a small fault scarp in gravel, which indicates that there has been recent movement along the Teton fault system.

From Wilson the road starts across the Snake River floodplain, crossing a bridge in almost 2 miles. Extensive man-made levees have been built on the west side of the river at this point to prevent its flooding over towards Wilson. (From here to Jackson refer to Map, Fig. 3.13).

About 4 miles from the Snake River the road passes the south end of West Gros Ventre Butte, on the left, which is a normal fault block of Paleozoic rocks. Actually these rocks have been faulted normally in late Tertiary time but are part of the ancestral mountain uplift moved southward by the Cache Creek fault in a much earlier time. To the right of the road, at this point, is a small hill also composed of Paleozoic rocks, but of rather different character. These rocks have been shoved here many miles from the southwest along the nearly horizontal Jackson thrust.

In 3 or 4 more miles the road passes around the south end, on the left, of East Gros Ventre Butte, another normal fault block. This fault is considered still active; a large movement here could cause landslides and destroy the houses being built on its sides.

The route comes to a junction just past the butte with routes U.S. 26, 89, 187, and 189 from the south to Jackson. Turn left 1 mile into Jackson town.

YELLOWSTONE NATIONAL PARK LOOP ROADS
MAP: FIGURE 3.18

Logs are written for going *right* at every entrance point junction and they start at Park Headquarters at Mammoth. As one looks at the map, this is counterclockwise.

The Park Service maintains plenty of signs at all parking sites and side roads indicating what can be seen and the names of particular hot springs, geysers, waterfalls, and so on. Therefore, not a great deal of mileage information is needed here. Significant geological features and data are mentioned in this guide, and some sites which are more general are left to the visitor to find from the Park Service signs and maps.

The Park Service supplies all visitors with a good road map to major features, much like figure 3.18 but without as much geology. At all visitor centers, topographic maps of the Park are for sale as well as many kinds of descriptive books about natural features, geologic and otherwise.

Log 15A: Mammoth to Norris Junction, 21 miles

Mammoth Hot Springs area is Park headquarters with the offices of the superintendent and chief naturalist and a fine museum and Visitor's Center.

Above the various buildings on the hillside are the main hot spring terraces. Drive over to the base of these terraces to one of several parking areas and take one of the trails which lead up onto the terraces.

The terraces are deposits of calcium carbonate precipitated from hot waters that have circulated deep below the surface

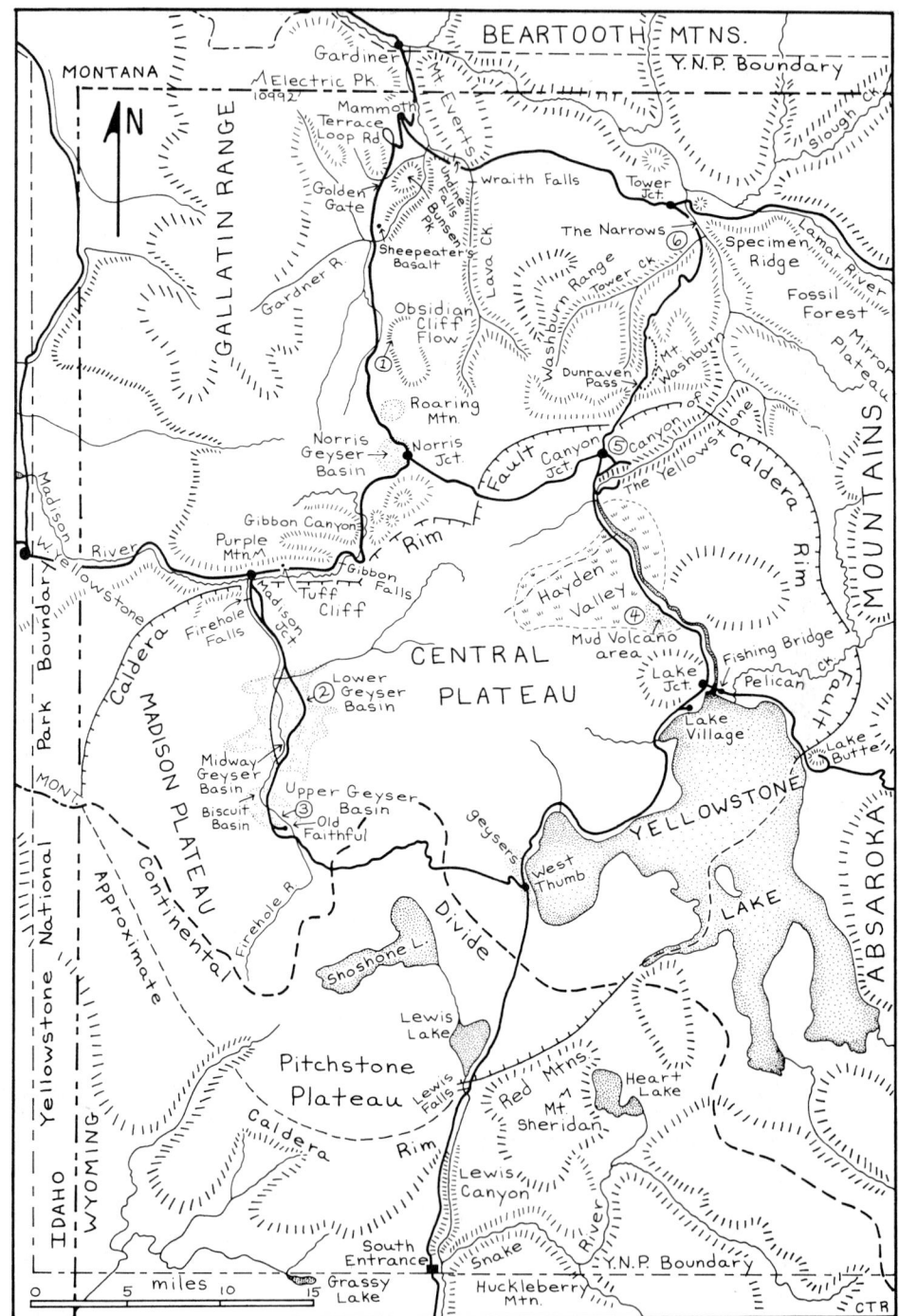

Figure 3.18. Map of Yellowstone National Park showing points of geological interest along the loop roads, Log 15.

through Paleozoic limestones. Here the water has heated and dissolved some of the limestone as calcium bicarbonate in solution in the hot waters. As the water is cooled at the surface it becomes over-saturated and deposits some of the carbonate. Old inactive terraces are dull white to light grayish, while the active terraces with flowing hot water are colorful or shiny white. Most of the colors, however, are due to algae that live in hot waters. The differences in the colors are due to various species of algae which prefer certain temperatures. The color, therefore, is a temperature indicator. The hottest waters have orange and yellow algae; much cooler waters, green or bluish.

During the century that man has been in Yellowstone Park, the actual position of the active springs has changed considerably. Some of the underground cracks and channels become clogged with deposits, and the waters must find a new outlet. Therefore, as one terrace is abandoned, a new one becomes active and is built up. If you visited the Park 25 or 30 years ago, you will see that these changes take place quite frequently.

The main loop highway going south from Mammoth switchbacks around and up above the terraces on the south, affording a fine view across part of them. In a few hundred yards the terrace loop road, a one-way road, turns off to the right and runs up on top of the main terraces past a few parking areas. This is an excellent vantage point from which to look across the terrace areas and take some of the trails which connect with those below on the main road.

From here is a fine panoramic view across the broad valley below to Mt. Everts. This highland rises 2,000 feet above the valley, and its barren face or slope is an exposure of Cretaceous shales and sandstones, the latter of which stick out as ledges. To the left a dark-brown layer is an andesite sill. On top of the mountain on its right-hand half is a thick brown capping of rock, long thought to be a rhyolite lava flow. Now it has been more correctly identified as a rhyolite welded tuff emplaced as a great ash flow (Photo 2.12). This is a remnant of the first great ash-flow event in Yellowstone 2 million years ago and was deposited on a nearly flat surface continuous with the top of Mt. Everts. That means that no valley existed here 2 million years ago!

The terrace road continues around to the left behind the main terrace and goes up a little valley past an active terrace in the open forest. This is the New Highland Spring which started here in 1952 (Photo 3.41). In the past 25 years this terrace has been built on the valley side, burying and killing many trees as can be seen. Here we have a good indication of how long it takes for a terrace to form. This one is more than 10 feet thick in only 25 years.

The terrace road continues around past other older and mostly inactive springs and terrace formations and back to the main loop road.

In a mile or so, the main road passes some jumbled blocks of white rock, some almost the size of small cottages. This is part of an old landslide, and the rock is travertine, or hot spring deposit material of calcium carbonate (Photo 3.42). Up above to the right the edge of a Pleistocene hot spring terrace may be seen; it is from there that these landslide blocks have come. This landslide occurred before white man's records; but notice that new trees among the blocks are quite small. Certainly this slide is not much over 100 years old.

To the left foreground is Bunsen Peak, rising abruptly with long talus slopes coming toward the road beyond the small valley.

Photo 3.41. New Highland Spring at Mammoth Hot Springs built up since 1952 in a forested valley behind the main terrace deposits. These terraces are composed of travertine of calcium carbonate composition.

Photo 3.42. Jumble of landslide blocks of older travertine near Mammoth. This landslide is not much over a century old.

This mountain is an igneous intrusion of Eocene age, related to the Absaroka period of volcanic activity.

In another mile the road is in the narrow valley ascending toward the Golden Gate. At the parking site on the left, one may see the waterfalls in the stream and examine the rocks along the road on the right. These are cliffs of welded tuff of the older Yellowstone ash flow (Photo 2.15). This is the best place to see this material in the Park without a hike. Note how dense and hard the material is, and notice also the presence of little white feldspar crystals in some of the welded tuff. The welded tuff layer on top of Mt. Everts is this same unit. In fact, one may look down the valley and see Mt. Everts in the distance and realize that this site is almost at the level of the tuff on Mt. Everts. The ash flow came through here 2 million years ago, in part, on its way to Mt. Everts. From here to Mt. Everts must have been a nearly level plain at that time. The entire valley below and at Mammoth has been eroded since then.

The road soon climbs above the falls to broad, grassy meadows, an area known as Gardner's Hole, with an excellent view ahead to the right of the Gallatin Mountains. Almost immediately on entering this area, a small dirt road turns to the left. It's a one-way road that swings back around the far side of Bunsen Peak, down a very narrow, steep grade. This road is often closed because of bad road conditions. It does allow one, however, a view down into the Gardner canyon, with its remains of some rather interesting basalt lava flows. (This is not recommended for those who are afraid of narrow roads with steep grades.)

About 3 miles beyond, another little paved road turns off to the left, and goes about a quarter mile to a turn-around and picnic ground along the Gardner River. Here is an outcrop of a basalt lava flow known as Sheepeater's Cliff. The basalt here shows excellent columnar jointing in columns a foot or so in diameter (Photo 3.43). This kind of column is formed when a lava flow cools

Photo 3.43. Columnar jointing in basalt flow of Sheepeater's Cliff along the Gardner River just off the main loop road in northeastern Yellowstone Park.

slowly and uniformly, contracting as it cools, and thus cracking in irregular five-, six-, or seven-sided columns.

① About 4 miles beyond this turnoff, one reaches Obsidian Cliff. A small parking area to the right has a sign explaining the formation of the cliff. Those interested in seeing the material may walk up the main highway across the little creek, and then take a foot trail to the left which leads into the woods up onto the talus piles at the foot of the cliff. Here one may see the material that has fallen down; it is quite banded, with bands of black glass and white crystalline material. There are interesting roundish features, which geologists call lithophysae, which were formed by crystals precipitating from gas in bubble cavities in the still-plastic flow (Photo 3.44). (Remember, no collecting is allowed here, or anywhere else in Yellowstone Park.)

Further south one passes Roaring Mountain, where an entire hillside is covered with fumaroles, or gas escapes, mostly steam,

Photo 3.44. Lithophysae on large block of rhyolite in talus below Obsidian Cliff. These lithophysae are round, flattened gas cavities with concentric layers of tiny crystals arranged with an onionlike structure. The crystals are tridymite (a high temperature form of silica), sanidine feldspar, and a few tiny black to bronzy crystal plates of fayalite, an iron-rich olivine. (Note pencil for scale.)

coming out of so many openings that the hissing becomes appreciable noise. On a cold morning, or a cold day, much condensed steam is seen here, but on a very hot day, the steam is largely invisible. Steam vents broke out in this area early in the past century and have gradually killed the trees on the mountainside as is now apparent.

The highway next reaches Norris Junction. The right road leads to the parking area at the Norris Geyser Basin. Proceed there, park, and walk down the trail to the small museum, with its explanations of geyser activity. The trails leading off to the left, just before the museum, go to a number of geysers and hot springs, most notable of which is Echinus geyser, whose eruptions every hour or so are quite stimulating.

Through the museum, the trail leads down and out to a broad steaming, flat area, known as Porcelain Basin. Here are small geysers of many types. This is an excellent place to see geyser activity at close range (Photo 3.45). A couple of fairly large geysers, just as the trail starts downhill, are Ledge and Valentine geysers. Check with the naturalist on duty to find out what geysers are due to erupt when.

Photo 3.45. Africa Geyser in Porcelain Basin at Norris Geyser Basin. This is an almost continuous geyser, 6 to 10 ft. high (as of 1976-77.)

Log 15B: Norris Junction to Madison Junction, 14 Miles

The loop road continues to the right from Norris Basin through meadows for a few miles, and then enters the Gibbon River canyon. Very soon, Beryl Spring will be seen steaming away on the right.

This canyon is cut in welded tuff of the most recent Yellowstone caldera event, 600,000 years ago. Notice its light, pinkish color, and very massive nonlayered character. On down the canyon is the Gibbon Falls area, still in this welded tuff. A mile or so beyond Gibbon Falls the road swings along to the right and runs along the base of a fairly high ridge on the right. Here, one is driving along the base of the caldera wall which leads to Purple Mountain. To the left, the forests cover part of a lava flow which came out and partially filled the caldera after the latter had collapsed.

Watch for a rather insignificant little parking place, called Tuff Cliff. Here, a short trail leads through the forest to the base of a white cliff, on the side of Purple Mountain. This white material is very loosely consolidated ash-flow tuff with pumice lumps representing material thrown out early in the last eruptive event.

Shortly beyond here, the road reaches Madison Junction with its historical museum and picnic and camping areas.

Log 15C: Madison Junction via Old Faithful to West Thumb, 33 miles

About half a mile after leaving Madison Junction take the road fork to the right which leads up the Firehole canyon on a one-way road. This road is the most scenic drive to Old Faithful; it is a good paved road with many curves, but it is one-way. It leads up the canyon of the Firehole River, with a parking place at the Firehole Falls. This canyon is cut all the way in one thick rhyolite lava flow. The lava was so thick and viscous and moved so slowly, that the upper and outer part of the flow solidified, but continued to be pushed by molten material still rising from beneath. Thus, the solidified part of the flow was fractured and broken into blocks of many sizes, and pushed around so that flow banding now stands vertically. This great confusion of fractured rock material is what a thick flow looks like inside! (Photo 3.46). You will notice many pieces of glassy obsidian, as well as grayish white crystalline rhyolite in this flow.

The road comes back to the main loop highway above the canyon and falls in a very short distance, where the Firehole River has cut no canyon at all. The road continues along the side of the river for several miles before entering the Lower Geyser Basin. An optional dirt road leads off to the right at the beginning of the meadows. Do not take this, but stay on the main paved road to the left.

② In a short distance across the meadows of the Lower Geyser Basin the road comes to a large parking area on the right, best known for the Fountain Paint Pots. Be certain to do the whole walk. The Paint Pots are an area of unconsolidated, fine-grained sediment which, when wet, becomes mud (Photo 2.17). Steam bubbles up through this to give the peculiar boiling mud effect of these pots. A couple of the geysers on beyond the Paint Pots are quite continuous in their activity, and are well worth seeing. Also from here is a good view to the north of the Gallatin Mountains on the horizon.

The white material around the springs and geysers is known as silicious sinter, and is a deposit of silica from the hot waters. These hot waters have circulated deep through rhy-

Photo 3.46. Flow breccia, the fractured outer part of a thick, viscous rhyolite lava flow typical of the structure of the Plateau Flows. The large dark blocks are obsidian.

olite and have dissolved silica, and are depositing it at the surface when the temperature drops. This silicious sinter is sometimes called geyserite. It forms very slowly, so please do not damage it.

Continuing on the loop road is Midway Geyser Basin with its parking area. The geysers and hot springs are across the Firehole River. The waters flow down into this river and have built a terrace right down to the water level.

A few miles beyond, one comes into the Upper Geyser Basin, so-named because it is upstream on the Firehole River. First, on the right are turnoffs to Biscuit Basin and Black Sand Basin, both with interesting hot springs.

Now in less than half a mile is the main exit to the various parking lots at Old Faithful. The main loop highway, here an expressway, completely by-passes the Old Faithful area and you must turn off to the right and then up an overpass to get to Old Faithful.

Around Old Faithful one sees the historic Old Faithful Inn and Lodge, and a new, modern Visitor's Center. Out in the geyser basin, in addition to Old Faithful itself, are a number of equally spectacular geysers, such as Castle and Grand geysers. Their eruptions are spaced at periods of many hours, and to see them, one may have to wait half a day or more. Grand Geyser is worth a long wait! (Photo 3.47)

③ This is the outstanding geyser basin of the world and, certainly, you should plan to walk some of the trails within a mile of Old Faithful, or even 2 or 3 miles away. The Park Service sells a Trail Map; be certain to follow this. One could spend a day or two here, but don't go without spending at least half a day. One trail leads up the side of the mountain to the east to an overlook point, where you can look down and watch Old Faithful far below.

At the Visitor's Center the naturalists will be able to tell you about when to expect certain geysers to erupt. Old Faithful is most regular, but even its eruptions vary from as little as 30 minutes to as much as 90. The average interval is 65 minutes. When the interval is short the eruption is not as spectacular. When the interval is extra long, the eruption may be unusually high.

When you finally leave this fascinating geyser basin, the loop road passes up into a forested, hilly area for 17 miles, crossing the Continental Divide twice, and then comes down to the edge of Yellowstone Lake at West Thumb Junction. Yellowstone Lake has an elevation of 7,733 feet. The Continental Divide, passed a few miles earlier, has an elevation of 8,262 feet. Consequently, the trip has been on the gently rolling surface of the Yellowstone Plateau.

Log 15D: West Thumb to Lake Junction, 21 miles

The main loop highway turns left at West Thumb, and immediately there are small geysers along the lake shore. The rounded shape of the West Thumb embayment of Yellowstone Lake is actually a flooded explosion crater, or caldera, produced long after the main caldera. The hot waters here are coming up along this caldera fracture. The West Thumb caldera is almost as wide as Crater Lake!

The route leads for 21 miles along, or close to, the shore of the lake, sometimes with views of pebbly beaches. Views across the lake to the west show the Absaroka Range on the far skyline, whereas to the south, one sees the Red Mountains.

Near the end of this trip a road to the right leads to Lake Village, where the Yellowstone Hospital is located, at which first aid care is available.

Two miles beyond is Lake Junction. The road to the right leads across the Yellowstone River at the outlet of Yellowstone Lake on the famous Fishing Bridge. Fishing from the bridge is no longer allowed. This road continues on to the east entrance.

Log 15E: Lake Junction to Canyon Junction, 15 miles

The main loop highway continues through forests near or along the Yellowstone River, on the right, which is flowing along lazily on the plateau surface.

④ Four or 5 miles from Lake Junction is the Mud Volcano parking area on the left. Here are a number of hot springs and bubbling mud areas, some of which are rather noisy. Be certain to take time to walk through this area on the 1/2 hour loop trail and see a variety of rather unusual thermal phenomena.

Beyond this area the road comes out in an open, grassy, terrain called Hayden Valley. This open area is developed on glacial till, which because of its relatively poor drainage

Trip Guides 191

Photo 3.47. Grand Geyser in eruption. An eruption lasts nearly half an hour with many bursts and short quiet periods up to a minute long. In this photograph of an eruptive burst, the steam from a previous burst a couple of seconds before still hangs in the air on the right. Some bursts may exceed 175 feet in height.

properties, is in grass rather than forest (Photo 3.48). The Yellowstone River placidly meanders through this flat area. This is an ideal place to see animals, especially near sundown.

After several miles, the route is again in forest; soon now a right turn over a bridge is the side road to Artist's Point. The first parking area to the left after crossing the bridge gives access to several trails along the edge of the Yellowstone canyon, including a view of the Upper Falls.

At the end of this road in about 2 miles, is the big parking lot and short walk out to Artist's Point. Here, perhaps, is the most famous view of the Grand Canyon of the Yellowstone River. One looks up the canyon at the Lower Falls, 308 feet high, with a fine, unobstructed view of the canyon, both up and down. Spread below you is a yellow and

Photo 3.48. Double meander in a small stream in Hayden Valley meadows as seen from the road. The surface material is fine-grained glacial till and lake clays.

reddish canyon cut in an altered rhyolite lava flow (Photo 2.14). Hot waters came up through fractures; you can still see fumaroles and hot springs down in the canyon. The hot water activity has altered and decayed the rhyolite and changed its color from the usual darker ones to the whites, yellows, and red stains prominent here. This altered rhyolite being softer, has eroded more rapidly. At the Falls is a ledge of unaltered solid resistant rhyolite against the softer altered rhyolite.

Return to the main loop road, and soon another side road to the right leads to parking, where a short trail goes down steps to the actual top of the Upper Falls, 109 feet high.

⑤ The road continues a mile and a half from here to Canyon Junction. The right turn goes into Canyon Village with its restaurants, stores, Visitor's Center museum, and cabins. However, this road continues past the Village to the north side of the Grand Canyon of the Yellowstone, as a 2- or 3-mile one-way loop road to several observation points; such as Inspiration Point, Lookout Point (Photo 3.49), and others. Trails run along the canyon rim, and

Photo 3.49. The Lower Falls and the Grand Canyon of the Yellowstone River as seen from the north rim.

partway down into the canyon. The best of the latter is the Red Rock trail, which starts at Lookout Point. This goes down to about the level of the top of the Lower Falls and gives a close, spectacular view of the Lower Falls; the trail is wide, easy-graded, with steps in steeper places. Near the bottom of the Red Rock Trail one sees an area of sandy-looking beds, which are lake sediments, deposited the last time the canyon was a lake because of a glacial dam downstream.

This north canyon rim road leads back to the main loop highway, where you double back to Canyon Junction.

Log 15F: Canyon Junction to Tower Junction, 19 miles

Following the main loop highway from Canyon Junction, the road climbs up in 3 or 4 miles to Dunraven Pass, crossing and climbing up the caldera wall. From the pass is an excellent view back out over the great Yellowstone caldera, the central plateau. A view to the east, on your left, shows the Absaroka Range on the skyline; while across the Yellowstone Plateau, more to your right, and far to the south (75 miles away) the Teton Mountains are visible on a clear day.

From Dunraven Pass it is possible to hike up the old road, now closed to traffic, for 3 miles to the summit of Mt. Washburn and its lookout tower. This is a fine hike, giving views in all directions, although perhaps it should not be taken when thunderstorms are threatening. From the summit one sees not only the Absaroka Mountains to the east, and the plateau and caldera to the south, but also the Beartooth Mountains to the north, and the Gallatin Mountains to the northwest.

If you do not feel up to a 3-mile hike, it is possible to get to the summit of Mt. Washburn on a bus, coming up another route, as mentioned in a moment.

From Dunraven Pass the road travels along the west side of Mt. Washburn, with volcanic breccia outcrops on the right. In a few miles, at a right turn, a side road goes up to a parking area, where you can board a bus for the summit. There is, of course, a charge for this bus trip, but the panoramic view from the summit is well worth the expense. One may hike up this way also at no charge!

Just beyond this Washburn Junction, the main loop road passes around two tight switchbacks and a cut through an outcrop of greenish bouldery materials. These are Absaroka volcanic rocks of the alluvial facies; that is, water-deposited and mudflow materials on the flank of the old Washburn volcano.

The road continues on downslope and finally comes to the very large parking area on the right at Tower Falls. Here, Tower Creek makes a free drop of 132 feet before running into the Yellowstone River in the canyon immediately below.

⑥ A mile beyond the big parking area is an area of much more geologic interest, but with very limited parking. The road runs beneath a big cliff on the left, known as Overhanging Cliff (Photo 3.50), with parking for 3 or 4 cars, or on up the road a hundred yards there is another little parking area for a few cars. Here we have a narrow canyon in the Yellowstone River, an area appropriately called the Narrows. Along the highway is the thick lava flow of Overhanging Cliff. Across this narrow canyon are two thin lava flows with well-developed columnar jointing, interbedded with gravel depos-

Photo 3.50. The Overhanging Cliff basalt lava flow with short thick columns below and long, narrower, irregular columns above; this is all one flow. The columns formed during cooling contraction. Along the Narrows of the Yellowstone River near Tower Falls.

its, and glacial till on top of the upper flow (Photo 3.51). The rocks on the two sides of this canyon do not match very well. Actually, the big thick basalt of Overhanging Cliff is older than either of the lava flows visible across the canyon. At the parking area on up the hill beyond the Overhanging Cliff, is a thin lava flow, which does match the upper flow across the canyon.

You will notice that back to the right, the Yellowstone River is in a fairly wide canyon, but just about where Tower Creek joins, the Yellowstone valley makes a sharp bend and goes into this very narrow canyon. Here an older Yellowstone valley, the wider part visible in the background, has been blocked by moraines from a glacier in the Lamar valley, and by the deposition of gravels and lava

Photo 3.51. View across the Narrows of the Yellowstone River near Tower Falls showing two thin lava flows with well-developed columnar jointing. The material between the flows is a series of stream gravels; above the top flow is glacial till.

flows before that. The last blockage, however, was the glacial damming, which forced the river to turn and cut a new canyon. These Narrows are a younger stretch of the Yellowstone valley than the canyon above.

In a few miles the road reaches Tower Junction; the right-hand road comes in from the northeast entrance.

Log 15G: Tower Junction to Mammoth, 18 miles

Check your odometer at Tower Junction, and in just 1.4 miles a little road to the left leads up to a single petrified tree in a fenced-in enclosure. This is the only petrified tree standing in place which can be seen without a hike and climb. This tree grew at the time the Absaroka volcanics were being deposited and was buried by one of the great mudflows sweeping down from those ancient volcanoes. It became filled and partially replaced by silica to form the present petrified wood.

The main road continues and in another mile and a half passes Garnet Mountain on the right, carved out of Precambrian rocks, the very southernmost exposure of the Beartooth uplift. Now the road travels above the Yellowstone River, a mile away and several hundred feet below. In a few more miles only volcanic rocks are visible on either side of the road, and the road swings left, away from the Yellowstone valley.

In another 6 or 8 miles as the road comes gently downhill through open sage, following a valley, watch for a small parking area to the left with a sign, Wraith Falls. A quarter mile walking trail leads to these falls on Lava Creek. Here is a big exposure of the youngest member of the Yellowstone welded tuff.

The road crosses Lava Creek in about a quarter mile with a little picnic area on the left. This is the place to park for those who wish to hike up Mt. Everts to see the welded tuff on its summit. (NOTE: See a description at the end of this log.)

A half mile further is a parking lot on the right with a view of Undine Falls. Lava Creek cascades over a basalt lava flow, which was deposited in the valley as an intra-valley flow sometime after the welded tuff event.

Beyond here the road rapidly goes down the valley of Lava Creek, with views of the exposed face of Mt. Everts to the right. The road crosses a long high bridge across the Gardner River, and then up to Mammoth, completing the circuit around the Park.

Log 15H: Norris to Canyon Junction, 11 miles

This route is a shortcut across the Park. Leaving Norris Junction, the road travels across swampy meadows for two miles.

Take a junction with a one-way road to the right to Virginia Cascades, while the main road goes uphill to the left. The Virginia Cascades road is paved, though a little narrow, but being a one-way road is quite safe. One traverses along the side of a small valley, with continuing rock exposures of the youngest member of the Yellowstone welded tuff. We are very close here to the north edge of the caldera rim; actually, we are up on the rim, where the ash-flow material was poured out toward the north.

This one-way road ends in a couple miles, returning to the main road; continue on to the right. The route is on a tree-covered plateau, and soon the roadcuts will show black, crumbly outcrops of obsidian. This is a lava flow in the caldera, and the road has crossed the caldera wall where the flows have filled up even with the top of the caldera. There is no topographic expression of the caldera wall, but the change in rock type makes it obvious that the route has now passed into the filled part of the caldera. (Note this relationship on Map, Fig. 3.18.) The rest of the trip is on this flow until the road comes downhill, and out into some meadows just before Canyon Junction.

Hiking Trip on Mt. Everts

A geological hike, about 2 miles each way, to see the base of the oldest member of the Yellowstone tuff on top of Mt. Everts starts at the Lava Creek picnic ground. Walk back across the road bridge on Lava Creek and then start immediately to the left across country, climbing the long, sagebrush-covered slope. Keep to the left, but stay out in open country until you are above the actual cliffs along the face of Mt. Everts. Then, walk to the left on top of these cliffs for more than a mile. Finally, one comes to a valley cut down through this cliff. Climbing down through this valley, it is possible to come out at the base of the cliff. First is an exposure of the youngest member of the Yellowstone tuff, filling an erosional valley cut into the older tuff. The material is moderately welded, pinkish in color, and very uniform throughout. Following along the base of the cliff and climbing uphill, one comes ultimately to the contact between the two major welded tuffs, where some interesting blocks of the older tuff are incorporated in the lower part of the younger one. Continue farther for perhaps a quarter mile along the base of the high cliff in the older tuff unit. Finally, you reach a place where the actual base of the entire unit is exposed. Here are some Tertiary stream gravels, with white, thinly-bedded, very fine-grained ash deposits on top of the gravel. These grade up into somewhat coarser beds, and then finally the actual welded tuff sits on top of the ash (Photo 3.52). This tuff is massive material with about one foot of black glass at the base. This is the best exposure in the Park of the actual base of the oldest unit of the Yellowstone tuff, the Huckleberry Ridge member.

SPECIAL TRIPS

Log 16: Craters-of-the-Moon National Monument, Idaho
Map: Figure 2.14

The youngest lavas on the Snake River Plains are exposed in the Craters-of-the-Moon National Monument. These recent lava flows are striking features of the landscape, are almost as fresh looking as many Hawaiian lavas, and are of much interest to the layman. To reach the area from previously described routes, go west on U.S. 20 from Idaho Falls, or west on U.S. 26 from Blackfoot. (See these junctions on Figure 3.16.) Either route will end at Arco.

On the way across the plains a few interesting buttes are passed. Nearest Idaho Falls are the Twin Buttes. East Butte rises about 1,100 feet above the plain and is apparently the weathered remains of a rhyolite volcanic center. West Butte is darker in color, composed of basalt lavas, and is assumed to be a fault block of older lavas pushed up and partly buried by the younger lavas on the surface. Farther along toward Arco, Big Southern Butte will be seen to the left. This butte is nearly 5 miles in diameter and rises 2,500 feet above the plain. It is composed of a variety of light-colored volcanic rocks, mostly rhyolites, and is an old eroded volcano partly buried by the younger flat-lying basalts of the plains.

At Arco the barren mountain is the southern end of the Lost River Range, and the rocks with all the school dates are limestones of Mississippian age, roughly the equivalent of the Madison limestone. From Arco it is about 20 miles to the Monument on U.S. 20 and 26.

At the entrance to the Monument, check in at the Visitor's Center for maps and other information on what to see. Take the 7-mile loop road and make many stops to see various cones and flow features. Several short hikes will allow one to look into craters, walk over flow surfaces, and visit at least one major lava tunnel, all on trails. Hikes to look into North Crater and Big Craters are especially recommended (Photo 3.53).

The flows from the Monument area have spread out over a very wide region, about 600 square miles, as can be seen on Figure 2.14. However, almost all the vents and cones are situated in a strip of land less than 2 miles wide which extends southeastward for many miles toward American Falls. This is known as the Great Rift Zone, a series of cracks in the earth up which the lavas ascended to the surface. Along this rift zone are some 55 cones which have given rise to lava flows from 14 fissures. Approximately 27 of these cones are cinder cones that rise from 50 to 800 feet above the surface. The largest cinder cone is Big Cinder Butte, visi-

Photo 3.52. Base of the Huckleberry Ridge member of the Yellowstone welded tuff on top of Mt. Everts. Seen from the bottom up: (1) late Tertiary stream gravels on an old land surface, (2) white, thin-bedded, very fine-grained ash or tuff beds, (3) darker, coarser-grained bedded tuff beds, and (4) massive unbedded unit which is the actual welded tuff (the upper third of the picture).

Photo 3.53. Big Craters, a large cinder-spatter cone formed by an eruption with high lava fountaining. The crater is 800 feet wide and 1,200 feet long; this is about the same size as the main crater at Kapoho, Hawaii, formed in 1960. Big Craters is about 2,200 years old.

ble from the loop road. The other cones are lava spatter cones (Photo 3.54), or combined cinder-spatter cones like the Big Craters. Many of the cones are breached on one side, that is, one side is missing. It was from such gaps that lavas poured out. Sometimes lava flows have come out from under cones without carrying the cone material away. On the North Crater flow, on the otherhand, pieces of the crater wall can be seen as large masses sticking up into the air as they were rafted along on the flow. These cone wall remnants on the flows are called "monoliths" by some.

The Big Craters is easily climbed from the main loop road at the Spatter Cone parking lot. This volcano is one of the youngest in the Monument and its crater (Photo 3.53) and surrounding cinder-spatter cone is almost identical in size and shape to the Kapoho Crater, formed in Hawaii in 1960 by a flank eruption of Kilauea volcano.

Lava tunnels, called caves locally, are common in the Monument, and several of these are open to the tourist. They are remnants of the channel ways through which lava rivers flowed underground during the emplacement of large pahoehoe flows. As

Photo 3.54. A spatter cone about 35 feet high near Big Craters with a small pahoehoe lava flow in the foreground.

the extrusion of lava ceased at its source area, lava drained out of these underground rivers, leaving the open tunnels. The floor of the tunnels is the solidified top of the lava which remained in the tunnel. Lava stalactites may be seen hanging from the walls and ceilings of these tunnels. Many of the tunnel roofs have collapsed since the eruptions, and large depressions filled by broken rock occur on the surface today.

The lavas are basalt in composition. Most of the surfaces are relatively smooth with ropy appearances; such surfaces are called *pahoehoe*. However a few of the flows have a blocky, clinkery surface almost impossible to walk on which is called *aa*. This latter type of surface is formed from slightly cooler and more viscous lava. Pahoehoe flows often change into aa flows down "stream" where the flow cools as it proceeds.

The flows are older than they appear. Originally it was believed that some flows were between 500 and 1,000 years old, judging from their general appearance. However, a few years ago an old tree on the youngest flow died, and its rings were counted at 1,400 years. Most recently, Dr. Fred Bullard of the University of Texas reports radiocarbon dating ranging from 2,085 to 2,255 years for the youngest flows. He dug out charcoal formed from tree and sagebrush roots under the ends of flows on which to perform the dating by the carbon 14 method. The oldest flows in the Great Rift Zone may go back as much as 5,000 to 10,000 years. This has been an active volcanic area for a good many years; it is probably not extinct, only dormant!

Log 17: The Crystal Ice Caves on the King's Bowl Rift, Idaho

The Crystal Ice Caves are an open part of the King's Bowl Rift, where an entrance and descending tunnel allow visitors to view the permanent ice formations about 150 feet below the surface. This was first opened to the public in 1965 and was declared a National Landmark in 1968. Most interesting to the geologist, however, is the small lava field associated with the rift where the entire history of a short eruptive event can be studied.

To reach the area one starts from American Falls. From the center of town proceed west and cross the Snake River at the American Falls Dam on Ida. 39. Follow this route 6 miles and then turn left onto North Pleasant Valley Road with signs to the Crystal Ice Caves. Now the route is straight for 9 miles past the end of pavement, across a cultivated area where windblown loess soil lies on the basalt lavas. Groundwater is abundant to supply sprinklers, and wheat, sugar beets, and potatoes are grown here. Next take a right turn and go one mile; then left for two miles, and now right again for three. Now the road curves left and leaves the irrigated land and becomes a dirt road through sagebrush-covered lavas. The road is an all-weather road and is passable to all cars; it's just a little dusty in dry weather.

The King's Bowl lava field is small, less than one square mile, but is distinctly separate from the much larger Wapi lava field. (See the Wapi flows on figure 2.14; the King's Bowl is about 2 miles north of the Wapi.) The King's Bowl lavas are symmetrically related to an open rift along a distance of about 3 miles (Photo 3.55). This rift is apparently along the extension of the Great Rift Zone which starts in Craters-of-the-Moon to the northwest.

The rift can be entered from the bottom of the King's Bowl and from a man-made tunnel about 1,000 feet to the north. This latter is the entrance for the public to the Crystal Ice Caves. In other parts of the rift climbers have gone down as far as 800 feet in the past. This rift is open to greater known depths than any other recorded rift on earth.

The origin of the King's Bowl itself is partly due to explosion, as there are ejected blocks on the lava surface to the west of the rift and white windblown ash on the lava immediately to the east (the white area on Photo 3.55). However, it is probably true that subsidence and collapse was also a factor. It is quite clear at many places that much lava drained back down the rift. This suggests that after the eruption had been underway a short time, the main fracture or rift opened much wider, due to deep-seated tensional forces. The rise of lava then ceased, and surface lava which was still liquid began to flow back into the fracture. This has often happened in Hawaii at Kilauea volcano.

Many small circular mounds are scattered near the King's Bowl in a roughly circular pattern. These are all about the same height, an average of 10 feet. They seem to be the remnants of a wall or rampart around a lava lake which was destroyed by a new surge of lava and then left when the drainback occurred.

Based on many observations and by analogy with eruptions at Kilauea, the sequence of events around the King's Bowl may be summarized as follows:

Photo 3.55. Vertical aerial photograph of the King's Bowl Rift and lava field. The King's Bowl crater is near the center of the rift trace and of the photograph. Immediately to the right of this crater is a whitish ash covering on the lava that was blown downwind during a small explosion from the crater. A series of dark spots around the crater are low mounds, believed to be remnants of the rim or rampart around a small lava lake. Note the many open cracks or small rifts on either side of the main rift beyond the lava flows but parallel to the main rift. At the time of this photography, no road existed to the Ice Caves; this road has been added as a black line. The black 0 is the location of the various buildings at the cave headquarters.

(1) The rift fracture developed about 2,000 years ago. Basalt lavas rushed up this rift and shot up at the surface in lava fountains, building many small spatter cones and ramparts along the rift, still present today.

(2) Near the center of the rift where the ground is flat, lava did not flow very fast but accummulated as a shallow lava pond or lake about 1,000 feet wide and 2,000 feet long parallel to the rift. By slowdown of flows a natural rim of solidified lava formed at the edge of the pond. As more lava flowed out it splashed on this rim and built it higher; thus the lava lake became deeper and better developed.

(3) After repeated surges of the eruption, new lava flooded the lake and suddenly overflowed the lake walls, washing away part of the rim. Thus a row of mounds remained in a roughly circular pattern where the lava lake rim had been, and flows moved beyond a few thousand feet.

(4) Suddenly the rift fracture opened so widely that all rise of lava stopped; lava near the open rift began to rapidly drain back down the fissure, and the lava lake largely drained away. This rapid withdrawal of lava and tensional opening of the rift at depth allowed some surface collapse, thus forming the initial King's Bowl crater. Access of groundwater into the open rift shortly afterward resulted in a steam blast eruption, throwing out the angular blocks and fine dust and enlarging the new crater.

The eruption could not have lasted more than a few hours or, at most, a day or two. Thus, the features at an eruptive rift which are usually completely buried under a large cinder-spatter cone, are still visible here, since lava drained back and the rift was left open. On the trail down into the rift to the ice caves, remnants of the first lava to come up are preserved as a dike.

Circulation of air into the rift is very poor. Therefore, cold air remains in the lower openings year-round, and the ice never melts. At 150 feet below the surface the summer temperature is about 30°. Groundwaters running down the rift freeze to form permanent ice stalactites.

Log 18: *The Stillwater Igneous Complex, Montana*
Map: Figure 3.8.

The Stillwater Igneous Complex is an extensive body of Precambrian igneous rocks some 30 miles long and 17,000 feet thick. It is a banded igneous intrusion composed of zones and layers of different mineral and rock compositions, due to the separation of crystals at varying times during the long crystallization of the magma. The average composition of the rocks is gabbro but the lower layers, about 4,000 feet thick, form an ultramafic zone composed essentially of two minerals: a bronze-colored pyroxene and olivine. Such rocks are called *pyroxenites* and *peridotites;* they are coarse-grained and contain a few thin layers of the mineral *chromite*. The thickest of the chromite layers is about 6 feet thick and was mined for its chrome content during World War II. The Stillwater Complex is one of a half dozen such complexes in the world; the most famous other complex is the Bushveld in South Africa and Rhodesia which supplies a large percentage of the world's chromium and platinum ores.

Chromite was mined at two sites, the Benbow and Mouat Mines, for about 6 months during World War II. Platinum is present in several zones in very small traces; it has been prospected in recent years and may be mined in the future. Associated with the base of this Igneous Complex are veins and disseminations of nickel and copper sulfide minerals, similar to the association of nickel-copper ores with the Sudbury gabbro in Ontario. These nickel and copper minerals, though sparsely disseminated in the Stillwater Complex, add up to many millions of tons. They may be mined some day if certain smelting and environmental problems can be solved.

The upper 14,000 feet of the Complex contains a series of inter-layered gabbros and *anorthosites* (rocks with more than 95% of plagioclase feldspar). In this zone the calcium-rich plagioclase is unusually light-colored (white) and very coarse-grained making rocks which look almost like marble from a distance! Some of the gabbros have closely spaced banding due to the alternation of augite and plagioclase crystal layers. The Stillwater Complex can be divided into several zones based on its mineral and rock composition and on the order in which the various mineral layers settled out of the liquid magma. These zones are briefly described in the following table.

The mineralogy of the Complex is simple; just 5 minerals make up 99% of the entire mass. They are bronzite pyroxene, augite pyroxene, chromite, olivine, and calcium-rich plagioclase feldspar. But these 5 minerals occur in simple combinations, and

TABLE 3.1
Generalized Section of the Stillwater Igneous Complex

Zones and Thicknesses		Rock Types Most Abundant, Ores	Minerals Most Abundant
Eroded upper surface of the igneous complex		Sandstones of the Flathead formation	Quartz
Banded and upper zones 14,000 feet max.		Interlayered gabbros and anorthosites; a platinum mineral layer.	Augite pyroxene, plagioclase feldspar, a trace of olivine.
Ultramafic Zone	Bronzitite member 1,200 feet	Thick, massive pyroxenite (Bronzitite type).	Bronzite pyroxene, small amount augite, and plagioclase.
	Peridotite member 2,300 feet	Interlayered pyroxenites and peridotites with thin layers of chromite ore.	Bronzite pyroxene, olivine, small amount chromite.
Basal zone averages 700 feet		Gabbros with some thin pyroxenites; fine-grained at actual base. Nickel-copper ores in lower part and below.	Plagioclase, bronzite.
Below the Complex: Contact metamorphosed quartzites and iron formation rocks; very massive			Quartz, biotite, augite, plagioclase, cordierite, magnetite.

alone, to form some very unusual rock types. These rare rocks are quite handsome as specimens.

The original flat-lying layers of settled crystals have been tilted to near vertical during the period of Rocky Mountain uplift. The Stillwater rocks were partially eroded in Precambrian time and then buried under Cambrian and other sedimentary rocks, which are also tilted and lie against the Stillwater rocks toward the mountain front. The complex igneous rocks have suffered very intricate faulting during the mountain building period. The resulting vertical, highly-faulted structure makes mining of the chromite and other economic minerals extremely difficult and therefore expensive. Mining today is not economical in competition with South African ores.

Several different radiogenic techniques have been applied to Stillwater igneous rocks to compute their age. These studies indicate various ages in the range 2.75 to 3.1 billion years; however, most experts favor an age over 3 billion years!

To visit the Complex, either turn off at Columbus on Mont. 419 southbound toward Absarokee, or take Mont. 307 westward from Red Lodge as indicated on figure 3.8. From Red Lodge it is 20 miles to the bridge over East Rosebud Creek near Roscoe and another 11 miles to the junction with route 419. At this junction turn sharp left toward Fishtail. This town is reached in 4 miles where the route turns right. In another mile stay right at a junction and continue into a fairly narrow forested valley. There will be glimpses ahead of a roadcut scar on the mountain front. This is the road to the Benbow Mine.

Some 9 or 10 miles from Fishtail the valley opens up into wide grassy meadows. This little basin is the center of an anticline called the Dean Dome. Low rim rocks dip away from the meadows in all directions. This rim rock is the Eagle sandstone of Cretaceous age. A sharp rock pinnacle ahead, as the road swings westward through this area, is an igneous dike of andesite. Just before one passes this dike is a Y junction; take the left gravel road around the dike. This road is maintained by the Forest Service and is reasonably good for most cars in dry weather. In about 5 miles the road starts to climb the mountain front by several switchbacks and will cross vertical beds of various Paleozoic formations. About 10 miles from the Y junction the narrow road comes to the first series of outcrops of the upper and banded zones of the Complex. Here there are excellent exposures of various gabbros and a few anorthosite layers. It is now 2 1/2 miles to the Benbow Mine, the road crossing 2 faults, which repeat the Flathead sandstone, and the big Bronzitite member in outcrops along the road. Stay uphill to the right.

At the Benbow Mine site, the old partially dismantled headframe is still standing (Photo 3.56) with many dumps all around it. These dumps contain the pyroxenites and peridotites of the ultramafic zone as well as samples of the chromite ore. At this site the olivine is completely altered to serpentine which varies from black to various shades of green. The shape of original rounded olivine grains can still be seen, however. The rock outcrops behind the foundations of former mine buildings are badly sheared, but specimens on the dump are still quite fresh, and collecting is good.

Return to the Y junction at the paved road and continue on the pavement (left at this time) on the right side of the dike pinnacle. The road climbs a low hill, and then on the

Photo 3.56. Headframe of the old Benbow Mine built and operated about 1942. The rock piles or dumps around the shaft, especially on the far side below the building, offer good rock collecting from the ultramafic zone. Elevation about 8,600 feet.

right is a great cliff of Eagle sandstone with some fallen blocks. Ahead a few miles in the middle distance are beds of folded volcanic sediments of late Cretaceous age; this is the Livingston formation. The road swings down into the Stillwater River valley past some very large bouldery moraines, both lateral and terminal. At 7 miles from the Y junction, just after crossing the Stillwater River, is a little store, Carter's Camp, on the left opposite a gravel road to the right. This is the Nye post office. Six miles from here the road will come to the old burned-out Mouat Mine mill site on the right. Ahead is a steep granite gneiss rock wall along a fault. To the left is the remains of a stockpile of chromite concentrate from the old mill. The stockpile is owned by the U.S. Government and is being trucked away. It was about one-third gone in 1977.

Turn right up in front of the old mill and follow what soon becomes a very rough gravel road. It takes 2 quick switchbacks up behind the ruined mill and then a long steep climb up the valley side, facing away from the mountains. There are spectacular views down into the valley and on up into the Stillwater Canyon in the high Beartooth Mountains beyond. Continue on the rough but passable road and pass in about a mile the famous inch-scale layering outcrop in gabbro (Photo 3.57). The dark layers are augite crystals, and the white layers are plagioclase feldspar crystals. This layering is somehow related to crystal settling, not to metamorphism. This is one of the most unusual outcrops in the Stillwater area. To turn cars around proceed about a half mile up to a wide place at a switchback and road fork.

On uphill at this switchback the road leads to a locked gate still about 2 miles before the actual Mouat Mine. In recent years it has been very difficult to get permission to enter this area, although some fine specimens of the olivine-rich rocks of the ultramafic zone can be collected at the Mouat Mine dumps in

Photo 3.57. The famous inch-scale layering in gabbro in the upper and banded zone on the Mouat Mine Road. Dark bands are augite pyroxene crystals and the white bands are plagioclase feldspar crystals. Note hammer near middle of picture for scale.

which the olivine is fresh and not altered to serpentine.

At the same wide switchback and road junction, the branch road to the right is a Forest Service road and leads around to the canyon of the West Stillwater River. This canyon is cut across the Complex and affords some good exposures of those rocks including a tunnel run into the canyon wall in 1975 along a platinum-rich layer in the banded zone. However, this road is rough with high centers. It is only recommended for 4-wheel drive cars or trucks.

One other access to the rocks of the Complex is another road recommended only for 4-wheel drive cars or pick-up trucks. This starts at the gravel road turnoff opposite the Nye store and proceeds up to Limestone (a few houses); turn left and on up Picket Pin Creek for several miles. Finally the road comes out on top of the Beartooth Plateau near Picket Pin Mountain and runs to Iron Mountain. Here there are excellent outcrops of the upper and banded zone and further along, the ultramafic zone and finally, some iron-rich rocks below the Complex rocks. Several major mining companies have had exploration programs here for iron, platinum, nickel, and chromium.

Appendix A.1
Geological Time Scale

Era	Period	Epoch	Tentative Absolute Age
Cenozoic	Quaternary	Holocene	11,000 yrs.
		Pleistocene	2 million yrs.
	Tertiary	Pliocene	8
		Miocene	26
		Oligocene	37
		Eocene	53
		Paleocene	70 m.yrs.
Mesozoic	Cretaceous		135
	Jurassic		190
	Triassic		230 m.yrs.
Paleozoic	Permian		280
	Pennsylvanian		
	Mississippian		350
	Devonian		400
	Silurian		430
	Ordovician		500
	Cambrian		600 m. yrs.
Precambrian			600-3600 m.yrs.

---------- Lost Interval ----------

| Origin of Earth | | | 4600 m.yrs. |

Appendix A.2
Paleozoic Stratigraphic Section
Beartooth Mountains and Clarks Fork Valley

Age	Formation	Description
	(Chugwater fm.—Triassic)	
Permian	Phosphoria fm.	Gray limestones & dolomites, + calc. ss.
Pennsylvanian	Tensleep ss.	Grayish to tan massive sandstones, locally cross-bedded.
?	Amsden fm.	Reddish shales and siltstones, + gray lms and dol; locally gray cherty ss.
Mississippian	Madison lms.	Chiefly massive light-gray to tan and buff coarsely crystalline to fine-grained limestones, some dolomites and local cherty zones; a few thinly-bedded limestones.
Devonian	Three Forks fm.	Platy gray to brown & yellowish dol & lms with some grayish-green sh.
Devonian	Jefferson lms.	Thinly-bedded buff-brown to grayish-brown limestones and dolomites with fetid odor; locally sandy or conglomeratic at base.
Devonian	Beartooth Butte fm.	Thinly-bedded red & buff limy shale with some gray lms and basal lms cgl.
Ordovician	Bighorn Dol.	Massive, mottled grayish-buff to cream-colored dol with a middle unit of mainly thinly-bedded fine-grained lms.
Cambrian	Grove Creek fm.	Yellowish-green sh, lms & intraform cgl.
Cambrian	Snowy Range fm.	Interbedded grayish-green shales & greenish intraform cgl, with few thin sandstones.
Cambrian	Maurice fm. (Pilgrim)	Massive coarsely xln limestones, some oolitic, with basal unit of grayish-green coarse intraform cgl & sh.
Cambrian	Park sh	Gray, greenish, & purplish sh with interbedded tan platy ss & sltst; some fine-grained lms & intrafm cgl.
Cambrian	Meagher lms.	Wavy-bedded limestones; some greenish sh.
Cambrian	Wolsey sh.	Greenish to purplish shales.
Cambrian	Flathead ss.	Light-colored ss, locally conglomeratic.
Precambrian	(Complex of granitic gneisses and migmatites intruded by mafic dikes, etc.)	

Vertical scale: 1 inch = approximately 350 feet (Compiled by Erling Dorf)

Appendix A.3
Mesozoic Stratigraphic Section
Bighorn Basin—Beartooth Mountains, Wyoming-Montana

Age	Formation	Description
	(Fort Union: Polecat Bench fm–Paleocene).	
Cretaceous	Lance fm.	Gray to greenish-gray shales interbedded with grayish-buff sandstones and occasional coal beds.
	Lennep ss.	Brownish thinly-bedded ss; some sh.
	Bearpaw sh. (Meeteetse)	Dark gray soft shales with numerous zones of fossiliferous calcareous concretions.
	Judith River fm.	Light-colored sandstones, interbedded with sandy shales and siltstones, and occasional dark gray shales.
	Claggett sh.	Dark gray soft shales, with some zones of concretions, and with more sandy beds toward top.
	Eagle ss.	Massive light gray sandstones at base grading upward into thinly-bedded ss, sh, and occasional coal beds.
	Telegraph Creek fm.	Thinly-bedded grayish shales and sandstones.
	Cody sh.	Light to dark gray soft shales in lower part to brownish or olive shales and thin platy sandstones in upper part; more sandy shales near top; interbedded calcareous concretionary zones.
	Frontier fm.	Massive grayish sandstones interbedded with thinly-bedded ss and sh.
	Mowry sh.	Brownish to gray hard shales, sandy in lower part; interbedded bentonite beds.
	Thermopolis sh.	Dark gray soft shales interbedded with numerous bentonite beds; 20-foot sandstone unit in lower part.
	Cloverly fm.	Basal conglomerates or pebbly ss; reddish sh in middle; grayish ss at top.
Jurassic	Morrison fm.	Variegated reddish, purplish, and gray sh interbedded with light gray ss.
	Sundance fm.	Basal brownish limestones at base, calc. sh in middle, greenish sh & ss at top.
	Gypsum Spr fm.	Thin lms, reddish sh and gypsum.
Triassic	Chugwater fm.	Typical red-beds: shales, siltstones and sandstones.
	(Phosphoria formation—Permian.)	

Vertical scale: 1 inch = approximately 1,000 feet (Compiled by Erling Dorf)

Appendix A.4

		Cenozoic History and Stratigraphy— Absaroka-Yellowstone Volcanic Provinces
PLEISTOCENE		Minor faulting—Recent. Pinedale glaciation—Late Wisconsin. Erosion and minor faulting
	3rd volcanic cycle	*Plateau Flows*—rhyolites; at least 1,500m, filled the calderas. Dated from 560,000 to 70,000 years on K/Ar by U.S.G.S. The Obsidian Cliff Flow is one of these; dates at 75,000 years. *Osprey Basalts* and gravels: post canyon cutting; late in Plateau flow time Canyon cutting cycle; correlates with Yarmouth interglacial. *Swan Lake Flat Basalts*—Sheepeaters Cliffs; before erosion. Early Plateau. *Lava Creek Tuff* of *Yellowstone Group* (0.6 m.y., 300m thick, Near age of Kansan Glaciation. Yellowstone Caldera formed by collapse of magma-chamber roof after eruption. *Undine Falls Basalt.* 6m thick. *Mt. Jackson Rhyolite Flows:* 2 major flows, 400m at type section. 0.6 to 0.8 m.y.
	2nd	*Mesa Falls Tuff* of *Yellowstone Group* (1.2 m.y.) Associated with the Island Park Caldera in Idaho.
	1st cycle	Sediments and *basalts* of the *Narrows* at Tower Falls; fills late Pliocene valley, gravels have about 10% of rhyolite welded tuff clasts. *Huckleberry Ridge Tuff (Yellowstone group):* 2 m.y. 170m at type locality. Major caldera in central to southwest Yellowstone, now partly filled. Local Late Pliocene basalts: *Junction Butte Basalt, Overhanging Cliff Basalt.* prepaleovalley at Tower, underlying gravels have no rhyolite clasts.
		Long erosion: regional uplift and deformation, intermittent local eruptive activity (great amounts in Jackson Hole). Oligo. thru Pliocene.
EOCENE	Absaroka Volcanic Super-Group	*Wiggins, Tepee Trail, Two Ocean, Langford fms* of *Thorofare Creek Group* (2,000m, 44-48 m.y.), Volcaniclastics and andesite lavas. *Late Acid* and *Basic Breccias* of Hague. *Mt. Wallace, Wapiti fms., Trout Peak Trachyandesite* of *Sunlight Group.* Volcaniclastics, flows (3,000m, 48 m.y.). *Early Basic Breccia* and *Early Basalt Flows* of Hague. *Sepulcher, Cathedral Cliffs, Lamar River fms.* of *Washburn Group.* (1,000m, 49 m.y.), Volcaniclastics, lavas. Early Acid and Basic Breccias of Hague.
		Willwood Formation in Bighorn Basin and Shoshone River areas (Early Eocene); Crandall conglomerate, local stream channel deposits in Clarks Fork Valley and Sunlight Basin. Fort Union Formation—Paleocene.

Appendix B
Topographic Maps

The U.S. Geological Survey has prepared topographic maps for a major portion of the United States on various scales. These maps are issued in quadrangles, which are rectangular areas bordered by latitude and longitude directions. These topographic maps show natural water features in blue, topography or land form features in brown (usually by contour lines), and cultural or man's features in black. The latter include roads, boundaries, certain buildings, and place names. Some maps show forested areas in green overprint and major highways and cities in red.

State index maps of the topographic maps available with quadrangle names are issued free by states. The standard maps are issued in 15-minute quadrangles at a scale of 1:62,500, about one inch to one mile; and in 7 1/2-minute quadrangles at a scale of 1:24,000, one inch equals 2,000 feet or less than half a mile. There is also an interstate series prepared with Army Map Service cooperation, on a scale of 1:250,000, or one inch equals 4 miles. This scale might well be a great help in the area of this guide, as these maps show all the main roads and most major land features. These maps sell at $2.00 a sheet.

All maps west of the Mississippi River are sold from the Branch of Distribution, U.S. Geological Survey, Box 25286 Federal Center, Denver, Colorado, 80225.

Special maps of the National Parks are also available; specifically of Yellowstone National Park, Grand Teton National Park, and the Craters-of-the-Moon National Monument. These can be purchased at the various park headquarters' Visitor's Centers.

	Bozeman, MT NL–12–8 *	Billings, MT NL–12–9	Hardin, MT NL–13–7
Dubois, ID-MT NL–12–10	Ashton, ID-MT-WY NL–12–11	Cody, WY NL–12–12	Sheridan, WY NL–13–10
Idaho Falls, ID NK–12–1	Driggs, ID-WY NK–12–2	Thermopolis, WY NK–12–3	
Pocatello, ID NK–12–4	Preston, ID-WY NK–12–5	Lander, WY NK–12–6	

*Dashed lines show the approximate location of Yellowstone National Park.

Names and numbers of the 1:250,000 scale maps, one inch = 4 miles: To order, give this scale, the name, and state.

Appendix C

Glossary

AA Aa lava has a blocky and clinkery surface.

ABRASION The mechanical wearing of solid materials by impact and friction.

AGGLOMERATE A fragmental volcanic rock consisting of large, somewhat rounded stones in a finer matrix, much like conglomerate in appearance but wholly volcanic in constitution.

AIR-FALL An air-fall of ash occurs after an explosive volcanic eruption has thrown much fine debris high into the air and ash and dust falls like snow: *an ash fall*.

ALLUVIAL FACIES As used here, the alluvial facies consists of deposits around a volcanic area composed of broken volcanic debris that have been moved again after an eruption by stream flow or flood action or as mudflows and thus redeposited in layers at a moderate distance from the volcano.

ALLUVIAL FAN See fan.

ALLUVIUM Unconsolidated gravel, sand, and finer rock debris deposited principally by running water; adjective *alluvial*.

AMPHIBOLITE A metamorphic rock composed largely of the black mineral hornblende.

ANDESITE A kind of fine-grained igneous rock between rhyolite and basalt in composition and usually greenish or grayish in color. Very common in the Absaroka and Yellowstone areas.

ANGULAR UNCONFORMITY An arrangement in which older deformed stratified rocks have been truncated by erosion and younger layers have been laid down upon them with a different angle of inclination.

ANTECEDENT STREAM One which maintained its course in spite of localized uplift across its path; the stream anteceded the structure.

ANTICLINE A fold in stratified rock convex upward. Beds on the flanks are inclined outward.

ANTICLINAL CORE The mass of older rock in the heart of an anticline.

ANTICLINAL NOSE The place where beds at the axis of a plunging anticline pass beneath the ground surface.

ASH See volcanic ash.

ASH CONE A volcanic cone composed of glassy grains of sand-sized material. These cones are broad rings with large craters and are formed by volcanic eruptions through water or very wet ground.

ASH FLOW An eruption of red-hot volcanic ash in a more or less horizontal direction which is lubricated by its own gases. The ash-gas mixtures move across surfaces and down valleys as a fast moving flow in direct contrast to ash falling from the air.

ASH-FLOW TUFF Deposits of volcanic ash, usually well consolidated, that were erupted by the ash flow mechanism. (See also welded tuff.)

AXIS The central line of an elongated geological structure such as an anticline or syncline.

BADLANDS An area of usually horizontal clayey and sandy sedimentary rock which has been deeply gullied in an intricate fashion by erosion in a semiarid climate and without vegetation.

BARCHAN An isolated, crescent-shaped dune, convex upwind.

BASALT A fine-grained black lava relatively rich in calcium, iron, and magnesium. The extrusive equivalent (in composition) of gabbro.

BASEMENT Old crystalline rocks upon which younger rocks have been deposited.

BATHOLITH A very large igneous body intruded into the earth's crust at considerable depth where it cooled slowly to form coarsely crystalline rock.

BEDDING The layered structure of sedimentary rocks.

BEDROCK Consolidated rock material of any sort.

BENCH A high, level, or gently sloping, surface with steep slopes to lower levels. Benches are remnants of old elevated river terraces, outwash plains, or pediment surfaces.

BENCH MARK An established mark, the elevation of which is accurately determined with respect to sea level.

BIOTITE This is the black variety of the mineral mica.

BRECCIA A rock containing abundant angular fragments of rocks or minerals. These are sedimentary breccias, volcanic breccias, tectonic breccias, landslide breccias, and other types.

BUTTE A small hill rising abruptly above the surrounding area and having steep sloping sides and a small flattish top.

CALCAREOUS Rich in calcite.

CALCITE A common mineral composed of calcium, carbon, and oxygen ($CaCO_3$). The principal source of cement.

CALDERA A very large volcanic crater or volcanic depression usually formed by the collapse of the central part of a volcano or volcanic area.

CALICHE A calcareous deposit formed within dry-region soils by weathering.

CARBON-14 See Radio-carbon.

CARBONATE ROCKS Those composed of the minerals calcite (calcium carbonate) and dolomite (calcium-magnesium carbonate).

CHALCOPYRITE See pyrite.

CHROMITE A heavy, black, metallic mineral composed of chromium, iron and oxygen. The ore mineral of chrome.

CINDER CONE A volcanic cone composed of cinders; usually steep and with a small crater at its top.

CINDERS See volcanic cinders.

CIRQUE A basin or hollow or natural amphitheater with 3 steep or cliffed sides at the upper end of a mountain valley. Cirques are formed by the gouging action of glacial ice.

CLEAVAGE The facility to break along parallel smooth planes, especially in minerals, but also in rocks.

COLUMNAR JOINTS These are cracks in volcanic rocks, usually in lava flows along which the rocks split into elongate polygonal blocks which are 4, 5, 6, or 7-sided. In a cliff exposure these cracks are usually vertical and appear to separate the rock into parallel columns. Such cracks have formed during contraction of the rock as it cooled and shrank.

CONE See ash cone, cinder cone, lava cone and spatter cone.

CONGLOMERATE A sedimentary rock consisting of larger rounded rock and mineral fragments embedded in a finer, usually sandy matrix and all cemented together.

CRATER The opening of a volcano from which lava, ash, and gas is erupted to the earth's surface.

CROSS BEDDING A feature in sedimentary rocks, usually in sandstones, in which many small, thin layers are at an angle to the larger beds or main strata. They have been formed when a sudden drop in the velocity of fast-moving water or wind has resulted in the rapid deposition of sand or silt.

CRYSTAL A regular, solid, geometrical form bounded by plane surfaces expressing an internal ordered arrangement of atoms.

CRYSTALLINE Substances having fixed internal atomic arrangements.

CRYSTALLINE ROCKS A term commonly applied to mixed igneous and metamorphic rocks, or to either separately.

DEBRIS Broken-up and usually partly decomposed rock materials.

DEBRIS CONE A cone-shaped accumulation of rock debris at the mouth of a gully or small canyon, usually smaller, steeper, and often rougher than an alluvial fan.

DEBRIS FLOW A flow of usually wet, muddy rock debris of mixed sizes, much like a slurry of freshly mixed concrete pouring down a chute.

DECOMPOSITION The chemical breakdown of rocks and minerals.

DEFORMATION The folding and breaking (faulting) of rocks due to movements within the Earth, as occurs during mountain building.

DESERT PAVEMENT An armor of closely fitted stones, one layer thick, on the surface of alluvial material. Basically a residual accumulation of larger fragments owing to removal of fine particles.

DIKE A sheetlike body of igneous rock formed by intrusion along a fracture.

DIORITE A coarse-grained intrusive igneous rock about midway between a granite and a gabbro in chemical and mineralogical composition.

DIP The direction and degree of inclination (from horizontal) of a sedimentary bed or any other geological planar feature.

DIP SLOPE The relatively smooth and gentle slope of a ridge or a mountain range down the direction of dip of the rocks composing the ridge or range.

DISINTEGRATION The physical breakup of rocks and minerals.

DOLOMITE A sedimentary rock composed of the mineral dolomite, a calcium-magnesium carbonate.

DOME A topographic dome is a roughly circular, upwardly convex land form. A structural dome in sedimentary rocks involves an outward dip or inclination of the beds in all directions. A volcanic dome is a domelike extrusion of highly viscous lava.

EARTH FLOW A form of mass movement in which relatively unconsolidated surface material, usually weathered, flows down a hillside.

END MORAINE A moraine deposited at the lower end of an ice stream or outer end of an ice lobe.

EPICENTER The spot on the earth's surface directly above the subsurface point at which an earthquake shock originates.

EROSION The removal of rock material by any natural process.

ERRATICS Large boulders lying on the surface where they were deposited as a glacier melted away.

EXTRUSIVE ROCK Rock extruded onto the earth's surface, usually in molten condition (lava).

FAN A deposit, usually alluvial, of rock debris at the foot of a steep slope (mountain face) with an apex at the mountain base (canyon mouth) and a radial, fanlike, divergence therefrom.

FANGLOMERATE The consolidated deposits of an alluvial fan; a variety of conglomerate which is coarse, ill-sorted, and contains angular stones.

FAULT A fracture along which blocks of the earth's crust have slipped past each other.

FAULT SCARP A straight scarp or mountain front along the uplifted side of a fault. See also scarp.

FAULT ZONE A zone in the earth's crust consisting of many roughly parallel, overlapping, closely spaced faults and fractures; may be up to several miles wide.

FELDSPAR An abundant rock forming class of minerals composed of aluminum, silicon, oxygen, and one or more of the alkalies, sodium, calcium, and potassium.

FLATIRONS Relatively smooth triangular surfaces pointing upwards along a mountain front or scarp formed by erosion in steeply dipping sedimentary rocks and given triangular shape by cross cutting canyons.

FLUVIAL Features of erosion or deposition created by running water.

FOLIATION A crude banding formed in rocks by metamorphism, less regular than the bedding of sedimentary rocks.

FORMATION A geological formation is a rock unit of distinctive characteristics which formed over a limited span of time and under some uniformity of conditions. To a geologist it is a rock body of some considerable areal extent which can be recognized, named, and mapped.

FUMAROLES Hot gases, mostly steam, escaping from holes or cracks in recent volcanic areas, sometimes with a loud hissing sound.

GABBRO A dark, coarse-grained intrusive igneous rock richer in iron, magnesium, and calcium and poorer in silica than granite.

GEOPHYSICAL EXPLORATION Subsurface exploration of rocks and structures carried on by indirect means such as gravity or magnetic variations.

GEOTHERMAL Involving heat from within the earth.

GEYSERITE See siliceous sinter.

GEYSERS Hot springs that intermittently erupt columns of hot water and steam.

GLACIAL TILL See till.

GNEISS A coarse-grained metamorphic rock with irregular banding (foliation).

GORGE A narrow, steep-walled passage cut into rock by a stream.

GRABEN A sizeable block of the earth's crust dropped down between two faults steeply inclined inward, giving a keystone shape to the block, longer than it is wide.

GRANITE A common, coarse-grained, igneous intrusive rock relatively rich in silica, potassium, and sodium.

GRANITIC A term commonly used for many coarse-grained igneous intrusive rocks not strictly of granite composition.

GRANODIORITE   A coarse-grained, igneous intrusive rock half way between a granite and a diorite on the scale of rock composition.

GRAVITY FAULT   A large block or thick sheet of rocks breaking along a nearly horizontal surface, usually a bedding plane, and sliding horizontally on a very low slope under the impetus of gravity. Individual blocks may be a few miles wide and up to 2,000 feet thick.

GULLY   A small ravine cut by running water.

GYPSUM   A soft, white (sometimes colorless) mineral found in sedimentary rocks; may occur in extensive strata and is then "rock gypsum." Chemically it is hydrated calcium sulfate.

HANGING VALLEY   A tributary valley the floor of which is much higher at its mouth than the floor of the trunk valley.

HOGBACK   A ridge composed of a resistant layer within steeply tilted eroded strata.

HOODOO WEATHERING   A type of weathering and erosion common in volcanic pyroclastic rocks that developes sharp spires, pinnacles, and rock minarets. Formed by erosion along vertical cracks or joints in rocks that are only moderately cemented.

HORN   A sharp, steep mountain peak that has been carved by glaciers on 3 sides. The Matterhorn in Switzerland is the type example.

HORNBLENDE   A shiny black mineral with two directions of cleavage found in igneous and metamorphic rocks.

HYDROTHERMAL   Involving hot waters within the Earth.

IGNEOUS ACTIVITY   All the processes associated with molten rock (magma) both within and on the Earth.

IGNEOUS ROCKS   A class of rocks formed by crystallization from a molten state.

INCLUSION   A fragment of older rock inclosed (included) within an igneous rock.

INCOMPETENT   A rock which is relatively weak and responds readily to pressure by crumpling or by flow.

INTERMITTENT STREAM   One which does not have a continuous or perennial flow.

INTRUSIVE ROCKS   Rocks or rock masses which have been intruded or injected into other rock, usually in a molten state.

LACCOLITH   An intrusive mass of igneous rocks that has a mushroom-top shape and is perhaps 1,000 feet to 3 miles in diameter.

LATERAL FAULT   One on which the displacement is sidewise rather than up-down.

LATERAL MORAINE   A ridgelike deposit of bouldery ill-sorted debris laid down along the lateral margin of a valley glacier.

LAVA   The term is used both for molten rock material extruded onto the earth's surface and for the consolidated (crystallized) rock.

LAVA CONE   A small gently sloping to almost flat volcanic cone formed by basalt lava flows and perhaps 2 to 10 miles in diameter.

LAVA FOUNTAINS   Upward jets of very liquid red-hot lava from a crack or fracture or central crater during an eruption. Resembles in shape and behavior (only) a gigantic water fountain. Typical of Hawaiian eruptions.

LAVA STALACTITE   An irregular cylindrical deposit projecting downwards from the roof of a tunnel and formed as liquid lava dripped down and froze.

LAVA TUNNEL   A long underground tunnel through which fluid lava rivers have flowed during the spreading out of large lava flows. They vary from a few feet to tens of feet in width and height. After the end of the lava activity, parts of the tunnel roof often collapse leaving isolated lava caves.

LIMB   One of the two sides of an anticline or syncline.

LIMESTONE   A sedimentary rock composed wholly or almost wholly of the mineral calcite.

LOESS   Deposits of fine silt blown and deposited by the wind.

MAGMA   Molten rock within the earth's crust.

MARBLE   Recrystallized limestone or dolomite; a metamorphic rock.

MARINE   The ocean environment; marine sediments are those deposited in the ocean.

MASS MOVEMENTS   The movement, usually down slope, of a mass of rock or rock debris by gravity, not transported by some other agent such as ice or water.

MATRIX   The fine-grained constituents of a rock in which coarser particles are embedded.

MEANDER   Sharp bends and aimless curves of a river on its floodplain.

MESA   A flat-topped tableland with steep sides.

MESOZOIC   One of the eras of the geological time scale (*see* Appendix A) extending from 70 to 230 m.y. ago.

METAMORPHIC ROCKS   Those which have undergone such marked physical change because of heat or pressure or both as to be distinct from the original rock. The process is *metamorphism*.

METAVOLCANIC   Rocks formed by metamorphism of volcanic materials.

M.Y.   An abbreviation for a million years.

MINERAL   A homogeneous, naturally occurring, solid substance of inorganic composition, consistent physical properties, and specified chemical composition.

MONOCLINE   A fold that dips in only one direction: that is, nearly flat beds are folded so they bend down and then level out again.

MONOLITHOLOGIC BRECCIA   A breccia formed of fragments of only one kind of rock.

MONOMINERALIC ROCK   One composed of only one mineral; for example, limestone and dolomite.

MONZONITE   An igneous rock whose composition lies between granite and diorite. In the Beartooth Mts. they usually have the texture of a porphyry.

MORAINE   A deposit of coarse, ill-sorted rock debris laid down by glacial ice without intervention of any other agent, such as running water.

MUD FLOW   A form of mass movement involving the flow of mud, usually containing coarser rock debris, in which instance the term debris flow is equally applicable.

MUD POT   A shallow, hot-spring pit filled with bubbling mud.

MUDSTONE   A fine-grained sedimentary rock which is hard to characterize as shale or siltstone because of massiveness or poor sorting.

MUD VOLCANO   A steam escape or hot spring through wet clay or mud whose boiling activity has built a low mound of mud around its opening. Sometimes this pile of mud looks like a model of a volcano.

NORMAL FAULT   A fault that is due to a tensional or pulling apart stress and has a steep dip where displacement has been mainly vertical.

NOSE   *See* anticlinal nose.

OBLIQUE AIR PHOTO   One taken with the axis of the camera tilted from vertical. If the horizon shows, it is a high-oblique photo.

OBSIDIAN   Natural volcanic glass. Lava which cooled so rapidly that it didn't crystallize.

ODOMETER   An instrument for measuring distance.

OLIVINE   A green, glassy mineral found in dark-colored rocks like basalt and in ultramafic rocks.

ORE DEPOSIT   An accumulation of metallic minerals that can be mined at a profit. The minerals are termed *ore minerals,* and the aggregate is termed *ore*.

OUTCROP   An exposure of bedrock at the surface.

OUTWASH PLAIN   A nearly level plain formed of stream deposits from the meltwater from a glacier.

PAHOEHOE   Lava with a relatively smooth or highly folded or ropy surface, sometimes in irregular roundish forms but never clinkery in appearance. Name comes from Hawaii.

PALEOZOIC   A major era of the geological time scale embracing the interval from 230 to 600 m.y. (*see* Appendix A).

PALISADES   Nearly vertical beds of sedimentary rock rising abruptly along a mountain front or scarp.

PEDIMENT   A relatively smooth, gently sloping surface produced by erosion at the foot of a steeper face, usually a mountain.

PEGMATITE   A very coarse-grained igneous rock formed by the fluids given off in the late stage of crystallization of an igneous body; most often close to granite in composition.

PERMAFROST   Ground or soil that remains permanently frozen year after year with summer melting of the surface down only a foot or two. Common in Alaska and in high mountain areas above timberline.

PILLOW LAVA   A lava flow composed of rounded or elongate masses piled on each other, especially in the lower part of a flow. These form as a flow enters water or very wet ground and is rapidly chilled. Pillows vary from a foot to over 6 feet in diameter.

PLACER DEPOSIT   A water laid accumulation of rock debris containing a concentration of heavy, physically and chemically resistant, valuable minerals such as diamond, gold, or platinum. Such minerals are described as *placer minerals*.

PLEISTOCENE   An epoch within the Cenozoic Era of the geological time scale, (*see* Appendix A). Usually taken to embrace the last 2 million years.

PLUG   A small, cylindrical, near-surface, igneous intrusive body.

PLUNGE   The inclination from horizontal of the long axis of a fold or warp.

PLUVIAL PERIOD   An interval of cooler, wetter conditions in a dry region, coincident with a phase of glaciation in colder, better-watered areas.

PORPHYRY An igneous rock that has large scattered crystals surrounded by a dense groundmass or matrix material of fine or microscopic grains. The term may be used as an adjective to describe an arrangement of large crystals in fine crystals as in "porphyritic basalt."

POTASSIUM-ARGON A method of absolute dating of rocks and minerals using the ratio of radioactive potassium to its daughter product, the argon 40 isotope.

POTHOLE A narrow cylindrical hole worn into solid rock by a fixed vortex in a stream.

PRECAMBRIAN All rocks older than Paleozoic (*see* Appendix A).

PRESSURE RIDGE Small ridges 5 to 20 feet high and 20 to 100 feet long in pahoehoe lava flows formed by tension which caused the surface to buckle up in small folds. The tensional stress is probably caused by liquid lava continuing to move under a thick solidified crust.

PUMICE Frothy rock glass, so light that it floats.

PYRITE AND CHALCOPYRITE Iron sulfide and copper-iron sulfide minerals with a brassy to yellowish metallic appearance. These two minerals sometimes go by the name "Fool's Gold"!

PYROCLASTIC Hot or fiery (pyro) fragmental (clastic) debris thrown out of an explosive volcanic vent.

PYROXENE A common igneous- and metamorphic-rock family of minerals, often green to black, and ranging widely in composition.

QUARTZ One of our most common minerals, hard and chemically resistant, composed of silicon and oxygen (SiO_2).

QUARTZITE A rock formed by metamorphism of sandstone, which is hard, coherent, and consists of quartz.

RADIOACTIVE The property of some elements to spontaneously change into other elements with the emission of charged particles, usually accompanied by generation of heat.

RADIOCARBON The radioactive isotope of carbon (^{14}C) which disintegrates at a known rate. It is used to determine geological ages up to about 40,000 years.

RADIOGENIC This applies to radioactive elements or isotopes which disintegrate at a known rate and can therefore be used to determine the ages of minerals in the range of millions and billions of years. The most widely used radioactive pairs in geology are uranium-lead, potassium-argon, and strontium-rubidium. (see also radioactivity and potassium-argon.)

RECESSIONAL MORAINE Parallel ridges of terminal or end moraines and of lateral moraines, which indicate successive positions of the ice front or sides as a glacier gradually melts or retreats.

RELIEF Topographic relief is the difference in elevation of contiguous parts of a landscape, valley to peak.

RHYOLITE An extrusive igneous rock of granitic composition, fine-grained, often light-colored to red.

RIFT AND RIFT ZONE A rift is a crack in the earth's surface and a rift zone is a long narrow belt with many parallel cracks. Used here especially for the cracks and fractures in the lava plains in Idaho (as the Great Rift Zone) up which basalt magmas have come to the surface and then flowed out as lavas. (See also fault zone).

ROCK An aggregate of minerals.

ROCK CLEAVAGE The facility to break along parallel smooth planes within a mass of rock.

ROCKFALL The relatively free fall of rock masses from steep bedrock faces.

ROCK GLACIER An accumulation of large angular blocks of rock, usually lobate in form with steep margins, that moves slowly by creep.

SANDSTONE A sedimentary rock formed by cementation of sand-size particles.

SCARP A straight steep bank or face which can be a few feet to thousands of feet high, like the east face of the Sierra Nevada.

SCHIST A finer-grained and more thinly and regularly foliated metamorphic rock than gneiss.

SCORIA Small fragments of porous volcanic rock thrown out of an explosive volcanic vent. Usually black or red and up to 1 1/2 inches in diameter.

SEDIMENTARY ROCKS A class of rocks of secondary origin, made up of transported and deposited rock and mineral particles and of chemical substances derived from weathering.

SEPTUM   An older mass of metamorphic rock separating two adjacent intrusive igneous bodies.

SERPENTINITE   A rock consisting largely of the mineral serpentine, a hydrous magnesium silicate, produced by alteration of igneous rocks rich in iron and magnesium.

SHALE   A sedimentary rock consisting largely of very fine mineral particles, laid down in thin layers.

SHIELD VOLCANO   A very gently sloping volcano composed mostly of thin lava flows of basalt composition. A greatly enlarged lava cone.

SILICEOUS   Rich in silica, SiO_2.

SILICEOUS SINTER   Hot spring and geyser deposits composed of silica (silicon dioxide). Also called geyserite.

SILL   A layer of igneous rock that lies parallel to the sedimentary layers or either side of it, or above and below it. Molten magma was forced in between beds.

SILTSTONE   A fine-grained, well-bedded sedimentary rock composed of silt, finer than sand and coarser than clay.

SLATE   A weakly metamorphosed rock derived from shale by compaction with the development of closely spaced, smooth, parallel breaking surfaces (slaty cleavage).

SORTING   The arrangement of particles by size.

SPATTER CONE   or lava spatter cone. A volcanic cone composed of globs or chunks of lava which fell to earth still hot and plastic and then partially melted or fused together. Sometimes layers of fused spatter alternate with layers of cinders and the feature is called a **Cinder-spatter Cone**.

SPUR   The subordinate ridges extending from the crest of a larger ridge.

STRATA   Layers of a sedimentary rock. Bedded rocks are *stratified*.

STRUCTURE   Phenomena that determine the geometrical relationships of rock units, such as folds, faults, and fractures.

SUPERIMPOSED STREAM   One which has cut down through an overlying mantle into rocks of different character and structure.

SYENITE   An intrusive igneous rock much like granite but lacking or very low in quartz.

SYNCLINE   A down-fold in layered rocks which is concave upward. Beds on the flanks are inclined inward.

TACONITE   An iron-rich rock, sedimentary or metamorphic, which may be a low grade iron ore.

TALUS   Piles of broken, angular rock fragments that accumulate at the foot of cliffs and steep mountain faces as material breaks off and falls by gravity. These talus deposits are called "**Talus Cones**" if they spread out at the foot of a little gully, or "**Talus Slopes**" if they have accumulated along a cliff front.

TARN   A lake in the deep rock-gouged basin of a cirque in glaciated mountains.

TERMINAL MORAINE   See end moraine.

TERRACE   A geometrical form consisting of a flat tread and a steep riser or cliff. Stream terraces, lake terraces, marine terraces, and structural terraces are distinguished in geology.

TERRESTRIAL   Deposits laid down on land as contrasted to the sea; terrestrial conditions as compared to marine conditions.

TERTIARY   A period of the Cenozoic Era (*see* Appendix A) embracing the time from 70 to 2 m.y. ago.

THRUST BLOCK   Term is used here for blocks of the upper layer of the Heart Mountain Gravity fault, which blocks have moved over the underlying surface.

THRUST FAULT   A gently inclined fault along which one block is thrust over another.

TILL   Ill-sorted, mixed fine and coarse rock debris deposited directly from glacial ice.

TRAVERTINE   An accumulation of calcium carbonate formed by deposition from ground or surface waters, commonly porous and cellular.

TUFF   See volcanic tuff.

ULTRAMAFIC   The term refers to igneous rocks that have little or no feldspar but only the dark-colored iron and magnesium-rich mafic minerals, such as pyroxene and olivine.

UNCONFORMITY   A surface of erosion separating younger strata from older rocks.

U-SHAPED VALLEY   A valley or canyon in mountainous areas that has steep or clifflike sides but a wide, relatively flat bottom. Such valleys have been carved out or widened by glaciers.

VEIN   A sheetlike deposit of mineral matter along a fracture.

VENT FACIES   The pyroclastic rocks composed of fragments as deposited by the original eruptions and not modified by later erosion or stream action.

VENTIFACT   A stone whose shape and surface characteristics have been modified by natural sandblasting.

VERTICAL AIR PHOTO   One taken with the axis of the camera pointed straight down toward the ground.

VOLCANIC ASH   Fine-grained (less than 1/8 inch diameter) volcanic debris, often glassy, explosively erupted from a volcanic vent.

VOLCANIC CINDERS   Like volcanic ash but coarser, 1/8 to 1 inch. Fragments are highly porous.

VOLCANIC TUFF   A compacted deposit consisting of ash, cinders, and occasionally larger fragments of solid volcanic rock. If the latter are numerous, it is known as TUFF-BRECCIA.

V-SHAPED VALLEY   A valley whose sides or walls slope directly to the actual stream with almost no flat ground in the valley. Such valleys have been eroded mainly by running water.

WARP   A part of the earth's crust which has been broadly bent.

WATER GAP   A gap in a ridge, cut and still occupied by the stream that cut it.

WATER TABLE   The level beneath the ground surface below which all openings in rocks are filled with water.

WELDED TUFF   A volcanic tuff which is composed of ash-flow particles that have fused together immediately after deposition and while still very hot. The resulting welded tuff is usually a dense rock with a dull, stony appearance. Sometimes, however, the particles have melted together so completely as to form a solid, glassy black, or even red, rock which can be called obsidian.

WIND GAP   A gap or saddle in a ridge now abandoned by the stream that cut it.

Appendix D
Annotated Bibliography

GENERAL BACKGROUND

BLOOM, ARTHUR L. *The Surface of the Earth.* Englewood Cliffs, N.J.: Prentice-Hall, Inc., 1969.
A simplified up-to-date treatment of processes which shape features of the earth's surface (paperback).

FENTON, C. A., and FENTON, M. A. *The Rock Book.* New York: Doubleday, Doran & Co., 1940.
This old but highly readable book presents material on rocks and minerals in a style attractive to nonprofessionals (hardcover).

HARRIS, ANN G. *Geology of National Parks.* Dubuque, Iowa: Kendall/Hunt Publishing Co., 1975.
A summary of the geology of Yellowstone and Teton National parks as well as many others, in an authoritative but not overly technical manner (paperback).

MATHER, KIRTLEY F. *The Earth Beneath Us.* New York: Random House, 1964.
An introductory geology book written for the educated layman; beautifully illustrated; a fascinating story of geology (hardcover).

MILES, VADEN, ET AL., AND PARSONS, W. H. *College Physical Science,* 3rd edition. New York: Harper & Row, 1974.
An introductory college textbook with the last 9 chapters on geology written simply and nontechnically. Includes an explanation of Continental Drift or Plate Tectonics (hardcover).

PEARL, RICHARD M. *Geology.* New York: Barnes & Noble, Inc., 1966.
An introduction to both physical and historical geology presented in an easily understood style; a brief treatment of the essential basic elements (paperback).

PEARL, RICHARD M. *Rocks and Minerals.* New York: Barnes & Noble, Inc., 1956.
Presents in popular language the entire range of the mineral kingdom covering minerals and rocks, ores and metals, gems and meteorites. Explains how rocks and minerals are classified and identified (paperback).

SHELTON, JOHN S. *Geology Illustrated.* San Francisco: W. H. Greeman & Co., 1966.
A superbly illustrated book dealing with a wide variety of geological features and phenomena (hardcover).

VANDERS, IRIS, and KERR PAUL F. *Mineral Recognition.* New York: John Wiley & Sons, Inc., 1967.
A beautifully illustrated book describing mineral properties, and how to recognize the common rock-forming, ore, and gem minerals (hardcover).

YELLOWSTONE, TETON, AND SURROUNDING REGION (General)

BILLINGS GEOLOGICAL SOCIETY GUIDEBOOK, 9th Annual Field Conference, 1958. *Beartooth Uplift and Sunlight Basin.*
Articles on the Beartooth Precambrian rocks and the Absaroka Volcanic rocks with road logs across the Beartooth Plateau into the Sunlight Basin.

BILLINGS GEOLOGICAL SOCIETY GUIDEBOOK, 11th Annual Field Conference, 1960. *West Yellowstone Earthquake Area.*
Descriptive and technical articles on the 1959 earthquake and landslides, the Madison Range and Madison Valley, the Fossil Forests of the Yellowstone area, and other features near West Yellowstone; with road logs.

BLACKSTONE, DONALD L. *Traveler's Guide to the Geology of Wyoming,* Bulletin 55. Laramie: Geological Survey of Wyoming, 1971.
Geologic history of the state with a guide to especially interesting localities. For the nonscientist.

FISCHER, W. A. *Yellowstone's Living Geology.* Vol. 33, Special Issue of the Library and Museum Assoc. of Yellowstone, 1960.
Geological information in simple language about the Park, with emphasis on changes caused by the 1959 earthquake.

KEEFER, WILLIAM R. *The Geologic Story of Yellowstone National Park.* U.S. Geological

Survey Bulletin No. 1347, 92 pages, 1971.

An authoritative but nontechnical explanation of Yellowstone's geology for the nonscientist; excellently done with good diagrams.

LOVE, J. D., and REED, J. C. *Creation of the Teton Landscape.* Grand Teton Natural History Assoc., 120 pages, 1968.

An excellent geologic story of the Teton Mountains and Jackson Hole in laymen's language from the Precambrian rocks to the numerous glacial deposits in the Hole.

VOIGHT, BARRY, editor. *Rock Mechanics,* Guidebook to 3rd Expedition for Rock Mechanics, Spec. Publication. University Park, Pennsylvania: Experiment Station, College of Earth and Mineral Sciences, Pennsylvania State University, 1975.

An unusual collection of technical articles and road logs covering the Big Horn Mountains, Big Horn Basin, Absaroka Range, Heart Mountain Fault problem, Yellowstone Park, and the Tetons. Articles on geologic structures, landslides, and dam sites. Excellent for the professional.

SPECIFIC AREAS (Technical)

BEARTOOTH MOUNTAINS AND STILLWATER COMPLEX

CASELLA, CLARENCE J. *A Review of the Precambrian Geology of the Eastern Beartooth Mountains, Montana and Wyoming.* Geological Society of America Memoir 115, pp. 53-71, 1969.

A summary of professional studies to date in this area with a bibliography of other published works.

HESS, HARRY H. *Stillwater Igneous Complex.* Geological Society of America Memoir 80, 1960.

A definitive work on these rocks by a famous geologist with theories for the origin of banding and layering of igneous rocks.

PAGE, NORMAN J. *Stillwater Complex, Montana.* U.S. Geological Survey Professional Paper 999, 79 pages, 1977.

A technical description of the rock succession, metamorphism, and structure of the Complex and adjacent rocks with complete bibliography of all work to date.

YELLOWSTONE AND ABSAROKA REGIONS

CHRISTIANSEN, ROBERT L., and BLANK, H. R. *Volcanic Stratigraphy of the Quarternary Rhyolite Plateau in Yellowstone National Park.* U.S. Geological Survey Professional Paper 729B, 1972.

Description and naming of the three volcanic cycles of rhyolite volcanism in and near Yellowstone Park and the associated minor basalt volcanism.

HAGUE, A., WEED, W. H., and IDDINGS, J. P. *Yellowstone National Park.* U.S. Geological Survey Atlas, Folio 30, 1896.

This is the old classic report on the Park whose maps are still quite accurate!

LOVERING, T. S. *The New World or Cooke City Mining District, Montana.* U.S. Geological Survey Bulletin 811A, 1929.

A description of the geology and ore deposits around Cooke City. This is still the only word in print.

SMEDES, H. W., and PROSTKA, H. J. *Stratigraphic Framework of the Absaroka Volcanic Supergroup in the Yellowstone National Park Region.* U.S. Geological Survey Professional Paper 729C, 1972.

A professional description of the various volcanic units of the Absaroka Volcanic Field rocks.

VOLCANIC DEPOSITS

PARSONS, WILLARD H. *Criteria for the Recognition of Volcanic Breccias.* Geological Society of America Memoir 115, pp. 263-304, 1969.

A review of the various ways in which pyroclastic deposits may be deposited under different types of volcanic activity.

SMITH, ROBERT L. *Ash Flows.* Geological Society of America Bulletin Vol. 71, pp. 795-842, 1960.

This is the definitive discussion, description, and explanation of ash-flow type eruptions and their deposits.

HEART MOUNTAIN GRAVITY FAULT

PIERCE, WILLIAM G. *Heart Mountain and South Fork Detachment Faults of Wyoming.* American Association of Petroleum Geologists Bulletin Vol. 41, pp. 591-626., 1957.

A description of the unusual Heart Mountain gravity-type fault and the evidence for its movement. The original, classic article on this fault.

PIERCE, WILLIAM G. *Reef Creek Detachment Fault, Northwestern Wyoming.* Geological Society of America Bulletin Vol. 74, pp. 1225–1236, 1963.

An additional detail of the entire Heart Mountain fault problem.

See also BARRY VOIGHT, previously listed.

SNAKE RIVER LAVA PLAINS

GREELEY, R., and KING, JOHN S. *Geologic Field Guide to the Quarternary Volcanics of the South-Central Snake River Plains, Idaho,* Pamphlet 160. Moscow, Idaho: Idaho Bureau of Mines and Geology, 1975.

Field guide and general description of various features of the plains north of American Falls including the King's Bowl Rift and other craters, lava tunnels, and cones.

STEARNS, H. T. *Geology of Craters-of-the-Moon National Monument, Idaho.* Craters-of-the-Moon National Historical Association, 34 pages, 1963.

A description of volcanic features in the Monument and a comparison of such features with those in Hawaii's Volcanoes National Park. This is written in nontechnical language and illustrated profusely with colored pictures of Hawaiian eruptions of a similar type.

MAP

Geologic Map of Yellowstone National Park, U.S. Geological Survey, Map No. I–711, scale of 1:125,000, 1972.

This is the centennial map of the Park.

INDEX

Aa lava, 201
Absaroka Mountains, 31-38
Absaroka ore deposits, 36
Absaroka thrust, 178, 180
Absaroka Volcanic Field, 15, 32-38, 42, 109-110, 129, 145, 153, 161
Absarokee, 206
Africa geyser, 187
Alluvial facies, 34-35, 110, 145
Alluvial fan, 130, 162
Alpine Junction, 178
American Falls, 166, 202
American Falls Dam, 202
Ammon (town), 172, 178
Ammon pumice quarries, 171-172, 159
Amsden formation, 85, 89, 99, 159
Antelope Flat, 176
Antelope mesa, 128
Archaeological site, 91, 155
Arco, 166, 198
Arctic tundra, 117
Artist's Point, 55, 192
Ash deposits (beds), 169, 198
Ash fall (air-fall) tuffs, 169-170, 178
Ash flows, 50-53, 169-170, 174, 178, 183
Ashton, 168-169, 174
Atlantic City, 28, 30, 140

Badlands, 87, 99
Bald Mountain, 91
Barronnette Peak, 129
Basalt lavas, 74-75, 79, 153, 166, 185, 195
Basalt quarry, 153-154
Basalt volcano, 145
Batholiths, 6
Bear Creek, 162
Bear Lake, Utah, 178
Beartooth Butte, 119-120
Beartooth Mountains, Range, 38-45, 152-153
Beartooth Mountain Summit, 117
Beartooth ore deposits, 43
Beartooth Plateau, 95, 113, 115, 117
Belfrey, 96, 125
Benbow Mine, 204, 206

Benches, 45-46, 113
Bentonite, 124
Beryl Spring, 188
Big Cinder Butte, 198
Big Craters, 198, 200
Big Hole Mountains, 72, 168, 180
Big Horn Basin, 21-23
Bighorn dolomite, 89-91
Big Horn Lake, Reservoir, 21, 94
Big Horn Mountains, Range, 16-21
Big Horn River, Canyon, 21, 23
Big Sky Resort, 160
Big Southern Butte, 198
Big Springs, 171
Billings, 88, 113
Biscuit Basin, 189
Black Butte, 161
Blackfoot, 166, 198
Black Hills, 83
Blacksand Basin, 189
Blacktail Butte, 146
Boysen Dam, 24
Boysen Dam, original, 101
Boysen Peak, 101
Boysen Reservoir (Lake), 100-101
Bozeman, 46, 157
Breakaway fault, 129
Bridger Range, 157
Brown, Dr. Barnum, 99
Bryon anticline, 95
Buffalo Bill Cody, 103, 110
Buffalo Bill Dam, 88, 103, 105
Buffalo Bill Historical Center, 103
Buffalo Fork River, 171
Buffalo Horn Creek, 160
Buffalo (town), 84
Bullard, Dr. Fred, 201
Bull Lake Creek, 142
Bunsen Peak, 50, 183, 185
Burgess Junction, 91, 96
Burlington Railroad, 87, 95, 103

Cabin Creek fault, 164-165
Cache Creek thrust, 69-70, 180-181

Calamity Point, 177
Caldera development, 50-53, 79-80
Caldera fault, 150, 166, 197
Cambrian formations, 91-92, 96, 101, 128-129
Cambrian-Precambrian unconformity, 97-98, 101, 105-106, 119
Cameron, town and terrace, 162
Canyon Junction, 193-194
Canyon Mountain and anticline, 152
Canyon Village, 51, 193
Carbon-14, 12, 122, 155
Caribou Range, 177
Carter Mountain, 95, 102, 107-108
Carter's Camp, 207
Cascade Creek, 149
Casper arch, 24-25
Casper (city), 25, 83, 142
Castle geyser, 58, 190
Cathedral Cliffs, 128
Cedar Creek fan, 162
Cedar Mountain, 103, 107
Centennial Mountains, 79, 169-172
Cheyenne, 83
Chief Joseph, 122, 125
Chimney Rock, 110-111
Chinese wall, 109
Christiansen, Dr. Robert, 169
Chromite, 117, 204-207
Chromite stockpile, 207
Chugwater formation, 86-87, 95, 99, 101, 105, 125, 141
Cinnabar Mountain, 155
Clarks Fork Canyon, River, valley, 37, 120, 125, 128
Clay Butte, 120
Clear Creek, 84
Cloud Peak, 17, 85
Cody, 87, 95, 103, 120
Cody terrace, 95, 103
Colter Bay Village, 150
Colter, John, 105
Colter's Hell, 105
Columbus, 206
Continental Divide, 29, 150, 190
Cooke City, 36, 38-39, 121-122
Cooke City ores, 43, 122
Cooke City Road, 128
Copeman's Tomb, 98
Cora, 136
Corwin Springs, 155
Cottonwood Creek, 124
Crandall Ranger Station, 128
Crater Lake, Oregon, 190
Craters-of-the-Moon, 15, 74, 78-79, 198-202
Cretaceous rocks, 96, 102, 125, 180
Crowheart Butte, 142
Crown Butte (Cooke City area), 122
Crown Butte (Gallatin valley), 160
Crystal Ice Caves, 202-204
Custer Battlefield National Monument, 88

Daisy Pass, 122
Dallas oil field anticline, 141
Dayton, 88
Dead Indian Hill, 125-126
Dead Indian Peak, 109, 125
Dean Dome, 206
Death Canyon, 4, 65, 149
Deep Creek fault, 152
de Maris Hot Springs, 105
Devil's Slide, 5, 155-156
Diamond Head, Hawaii, 79, 174
Dikes, 6, 42, 64, 66, 109-110, 117, 119
Dinosaur bones, 99
Dome Mountain, 154-155
Dorf, Erling, 130
Dubois, 24, 28, 145
Dunraven Pass, 194

Earthflow, 70
Earthquake Lake, 48, 164
East Butte, 198
East Entrance, 110
East Gros Ventre Butte, 145, 181
East Rosebud Creek, 206
Echinus geyser, 187
Ecuador, 34
Eleanor Lake, 110
Electric Peak, 161
Elements, 2
Elephant Head, 110
Elk Basin, 22, 95-96
Elkhart Park, 136
Elk Refuge, 145
Emigrant gold ores, 153
Emigrant Gulch, 37, 43
Emigrant Peak, 153
Ennis Lake, 162
Ennis (town), 46, 161-162
ERTS photographs, 17, 19, 27, 41, 63, 77

Fallen City, 89
Falling Ice glacier, 147
Farson, 132, 138
Faults, 6-9, 66-67, 105-107
Fault scarps, 47-48, 164-165
Faunal Succession, Law of, 13
Firehole Falls, 188
Firehole River Canyon, 53, 166, 188-189
Fishing Bridge, 113
Fishtail, 206
Five Springs Creek, 92-93
Five Springs fault, 92
Flagg Ranch, 150
Flat Creek, 145
Flatirons, 20-21, 94, 99, 108
Folds, 6, 98
Fort Union formation, coal, 86
Fort Washakie, 142

Fossil fish, 120
Fossil Forests, 15, 34, 36-37, 130-131, 154, 161, 196
Fountain Paint Pots, 60, 188
Fox Creek, 120
Franks Peak, 31
Freemont Lake, 30-31, 132-134, 136
Fumaroles, 57-58, 186-187

Gallatin Mountains, Range, 32, 46-48, 157-161, 185, 188
Gallatin River, valley, 157-161
Gannett Peak, 28, 30
Gardiner Fault, 155
Gardiner (town), 46, 155
Gardner Lake, 117
Gardner River, 156, 185, 197
Gardner's Hole, 185
Garland anticline, 95
Garnet Mountain, 196
Geneva, Utah, 140
Geologic Time Scale, 12-14
Geyserite, 189
Geysers, 56-60, 187-190
Gibbon River, Falls, 188
Gillette, 83
Glacial deposits, 132, 146-147
Glaciation, 30-31, 44-45, 54, 68
Golden Gate, 54, 185
Goose Lake, 122
Grand Canyon of the Yellowstone, 53-55
Grand Geyser, 190-191
Grand Teton and glacier, 148
Grand Valley fault, 177, 180
Grand View Overlook, 174
Granite Pass, Creek, 96
Granite Peak, 38
Grass Creek oil field, 102
Grasshopper Glacier, 122-123
Grassy Lake Reservoir, quarry, 150-151
Gravelly Range, 161-162
Grayling Creek, 161
Great Rift Zone, 198, 202
Green Mountains, 25
Green River Basin, 28-30, 73-74, 139-140
Green River formation, 73
Green River Lakes, 29-30, 136, 138
Green River valley, 29, 134, 137-138
Greybull River, 102
Greybull (town), 87, 99, 102
Greys River, 72
Gros Ventre Mountains, Range, 68-70, 135, 180
Gros Ventre River, valley, 70, 146
Gros Ventre slide, 70-71, 146

Half Moon Lake, 136
Halfway House Stage Stop, 102
Hamilton Dome oil field, 102
Hayden Valley, 190, 192
Heart Mountain, 87, 95, 103

Heart Mountain fault, 37-38, 108, 120, 125-126, 128-129
Heat flow, 53
Hebgen Dam, 164
Hebgen Lake Earthquake, 47-48, 164
Hebgen Lake, reservoir, 47, 53, 161, 164
Hell Roaring Creek, 157
Hell's Half Acre flow, 74, 166
Henrys Fork, 168-169, 171, 173-174
Henrys Lake, 171
Hepburn Mesa, 153
High Line Claims, 117
Hoback Basin, 74, 135
Hoback fault, 135
Hoback Junction, 135, 178
Hoback Range, canyon, 72-73, 135
Hogback ridges, 102
Holy City, 110, 112
Hoodoo weathering, 110
Horse Center anticline, 103
Hot springs, 56-59, 181, 183
Hot Springs State Park, 102
Hot water and steam, 56-60
Huckleberry Mountain, 150
Huckleberry tuff, 52, 54, 169, 197-199
Hunter Peak, 128
Hurricane Mesa, 45, 128
Hutton, James, 1

Iceberg Peak, 122
Ice Box Canyon, 129
Idaho Falls, 166-167, 172, 174, 179, 198
Idaho-Wyoming Border Ranges, 70-73
Igneous rocks, 12-13, 204-209
Independence, 36, 43
Index Peak, 120-121
Indian Creek, 162
Indonesia, 34
Inspiration Point, 193
Intrusion, Law of, 13
Iona Cone, 174
Iron Mountain, 209
Ishawooa, 36
Island Park Caldera, 50, 79-80, 169-171, 174

Jackson (city), 135
Jackson Hole, 61-68, 135, 146-150, 180-181
Jackson Lake, 64, 147, 149-150
Jackson thrust, 70, 180-181
Jardine, 43, 155
Jenny Lake, 148-149
Jenny Lake Junction, 148-149
Jim Mountain, 109
Joints, 6-7
Junction Butte, 132
Juniper Butte, 168

Kapoho Crater, Hawaii, 200
Kelly Mountains, Idaho, 176

Kelly, Wyoming, 146
Kendall Warm Springs, 137
Kilauea Volcano, Hawaii, 200, 202
King's Bowl Rift, 202-204
Kirwin, 36
Kitchen Rock, 157

Lake Butte, 110
Lake Junction, 113, 190
Lamar River, valley, 130
Lamar Valley glacier, 53-54
Lander, 28, 141-142
Landslides, 48-49, 70, 89, 96-97, 135, 152, 155, 160, 164, 166, 183-184
Lateral moraine, 136-137
Laurel, 113
Lava Butte, 161
Lava Creek, 197
Lava Creek welded tuff, 150-151, 197
Lava flows, 74-80, 109-110, 132, 153, 166, 194-195, 198, 200-204
Lava tunnels, 200-201
Ledge Geyser, 187
Leigh Lake, 149
Lewis Lake, 150
Lewis River Canyon, 150
Little Bald Ridge, 128
Little Buttes, 172-173
Little Lost River, 79
Little Sheep Mountain, 95
Little Tongue River, 88-90
Livingston, 46, 151-152
Livingston formation, 207
Loess, 75
Logan Mountain, 108
Lone Mountain, 160
Lookout Point, 193-194
Lorenzo, 166, 172
Lost River, 79
Lost River Range, 198
Love, Dr., 65
Lovell, 95
Lower Falls, 192-194
Lower Geyser Basin, 60, 188
Lower Twin Lake, 118

Mack's Inn resort, 171
Madison Canyon, 47, 163
Madison fault, 47, 163
Madison floodplain, 162
Madison Junction, 166, 188
Madison limestone, 85, 92-94, 99, 105-107, 135, 157, 159-161
Madison Range, 46-48, 158, 162-164
Madison River, valley, 47, 161-164, 166
Mammoth Hot Springs, 57, 181-183
Mammoth Village, 156-157, 181
Manderson, 87
Matterhorn, Switzerland, 160

McCullough Peaks, 95
McLaren Mine, 122
Meadow Creek Dugway, 178-179
Meadowlark Lake, 85
Medicine Mountain, 91-92
Medicine Wheel, 91
Meeteetse, 102
Menan Buttes, 79, 166, 172-174, 176
Mesa Falls, 169, 174
Mesa Falls Scenic Drive, 169
Mesa Falls tuff, 169-170, 174
Mesozoic rocks, 14, 22, 69, 88, 99, 105, 135, 141, 155, 179
Metamorphic rocks, 4-5
Middle Rockies, 16-17
Midway Geyser Basin, 189
Mill Creek, 153
Mill Creek fault, 44
Miller Basin, 122
Miller Creek, 122
Minerals, 2
Missouri Flats, 163
Monzonite porphyry, 43
Moose Junction, 146-147
Moraines, 45, (see also *terminal* and *lateral moraine*)
Moran Junction, 145-147
Mouat Mine, 204, 207-208
Mouat Mine mill site, 207
Mount Everts, 156, 183, 185, 197-198
Mount Leidy Highlands, 64, 68-70
Mount Moran, 64, 66, 149
Mount Washburn, 48, 53, 194
Mud Volcano area, 190

Narrows, The, 194-196
National Landmark, 202
New Fork Lakes, 137
New Highland Spring, 183-184
Nez Perce Indians, 125
Norris Geyser Basin, 53, 187
Norris Junction, 187-188
North Crater, 198, 200
North Crater flow, 200
Northeast Gate, 129
Northern Rockies, 16
North Gate, 155
North Menan Butte, 123-124
North Pine Creek, 180
North Platte River, 29, 140
North Pleasant Valley Road, 202
North Snowy block, 38, 44, 152
North Tongue River, 91
Nuclear Reactor Research Site, 74
Nugget sandstone, 141
Nye, 207

Obsidian, 151, 178, 186, 198
Obsidian Cliff, 186
Old Faithful, 52, 59-60, 189-190

Old Faithful Inn, 189
Oregon Basin, 102-103
Oregon trail, 140
Osborne Bridge, 169
Overhanging cliff, 194-195
Overthrust belt, 71-73
Owl Creek Mountains, 23-24, 99-101

Pacific Butte, 140
Pacific Springs, 140
Pahaska Tepee, 110
Pahoehoe lava, 74-75, 78, 166, 200-201
Paleozoic rocks, 101, 119-120, 135, 142, 155
Palisades Dam, reservoir, 176-177
Pass Peak conglomerate, 135
Pat O'Hara Mountain, 124
Pebble Creek campground, 129
Phelps Lake, 149
Phosphate rock, 72
Picket Pin Creek, 209
Picket Pin Mountain, 209
Pierce, William, 121, 126
Pierre's Hole, 180
Pilgrim limestone, 120-121
Pillow lavas, 176
Pilot Peak, 120-121
Pine Creek, 180
Pine Creek bench, 179
Pine Creek Pass, 180
Pinedale, 74, 132, 134
Pinyon Peak Highlands, 65
Plains Indian Museum, 103
Plate tectonics, 8, 10, 72
Pocatello, 166
Point-of-rocks, 153
Polecat bench, 96
Popo Agie River, 141
Porcelain Basin, 187
Powder River Basin, 83
Powder River Pass, 85
Powell (city), 95
Powell terrace, 95, 103
Precambrian rocks, 39, 64-65, 85, 90-92, 101, 105, 115-117, 140, 149, 204-209
Pryor Mountains, 21, 95, 113
Punch Bowl Spring, 59
Purple Mountain, 51, 166, 188

Quad Creek, 115

Radiocarbon dates, 12, 201
Radiogenic isotopes, 12, 39, 206
Ranchester, 86
Rattlesnake Hills, 25
Rattlesnake Mountain, 37, 87, 95, 103
Rattlesnake Mountain anticline, 105-107
Rawlins, 142
Raynolds Pass, 163, 171
Red Canyon fault, 164

Red Grade, 141
Red Lodge, 113, 115, 206
Red Lodge-Cooke City Highway, 38-39, 43, 113, 128
Red Mountains, 190
Red Rock trail, 194
Reef Creek, 128
Republic Mine, 122
Republic Mountain, 121
Rexburg, 166-168
Rhyolite lava flows, 15, 50-52, 188, 193
Rigby, 166
Rim, The, 134-135
Ririe Dam, 176, 178
Ririe (town), 176
Roaring Mountain, 186-187
Rock Creek, valley, 38, 113, 115-116
Rock Creek Vista Point, 115-116
Rock Haven Chapel, 159
Rocks, 2-5
Rock Springs, 132
Rocky Mountain uplift, 14-15
Roosevelt, Pres. Teddy, 103
Roscoe, 206

Saint Anthony, 75, 168
Sand dunes, 75, 168
Sand Turn Observation Point, 89
Sawtell Peak, 171-172
Scenic Views of the Big Horn Basin, 91-92
Sedimentary rocks, 4
Sheepeater's Cliff, 185
Sheep Mountain, anticline, 22, 87, 91, 92, 99, 102
Sheep Mountain (near Cody), 107-108
Shell Creek Canyon, 96-97
Shell Creek Overlook, 97
Shell (town), 99
Sheridan, 87-88
Shoshone Canyon, 37, 103-105
Shoshone River, 95, 103-105
Shoshone River, North Fork, 31, 109-110
Shoshone River, South Fork, 36, 103
Shoshoni, (town), 99, 142
Signal Mountain, 149
Sills, 6, 155-156
Silver Gate, 129
Silver Run Peak, 115
Silvertip Gulch, 96
Sinks, The, 141-142
Skull Creek summit, 124
Snake River, 135, 146-147, 166, 176-177
Snake River Canyon Overlook, Idaho, 176-177
Snake River fault, 177
Snake River floodplain, 166, 173
Snake River graben, 176-178
Snake River Plains, 74-80
Snake River Range, 72, 177-178
Snake River Viewpoint (Jackson Hole), 146-147
Soda Butte Creek, valley, 121, 129-130
Soda Butte glacier, 122

Soda Butte, The, 129
Soldier's Chapel Road, 160
South entrance, 150
Southern Rockies, 16
South Pass, 140
South Pass City, 28, 30, 140
South Pass Viewpoint, 140
South Snowy Block, 42
South Teton Mountain, 148
Spanish Creek, 157
Spanish Peaks, 157
Spatter cone, 200
Specimen Creek, 161
Specimen Ridge, 130
Sphinx Mountain, 160, 162
Square Top Mountain, 138
Squaw Creek and fault, 157
Squaw Lake, 113
Steamboat Point, 88, 90
Stillwater Complex, 43, 204-209
Stillwater River Canyon, 207-208
Storm Castle Peak, 157
Sugar City, 168
Sugarloaf Mountain, 128
Sunlight Basin, 127
Sunlight Basin Road, 125, 127
Sunlight Creek valley, 125-128
Sunlight Peak, 32, 125
Sunlight volcano, 36
Sunnyside Road, 172
Superposition, Law of, 12
Swan Valley, 79, 176, 179
Sweetwater River, 29-30, 140
Sweetwater uplift, 25
Sylvan Lake, 110
Sylvan Pass, 35, 110

Table Mountain, 128, 141
Talus, slopes, cones, 10-11, 110
Targhee Pass, 171
Taylor Creek, 160
Tensleep Creek, Canyon, 85
Tensleep sandstone, 70, 85-86, 99, 105, 107, 125
Tensleep (town), 86
Terminal moraine, 45, 68, 127, 132, 136, 147-149
Terraces, 45-46, 162-163, see also *benches*
Teton Basin, 168, 180
Teton Dam, 168
Teton fault, block, 61, 66-67, 150
Teton glacier, 148
Teton Mountains, Range, 61-68, 113, 145-150, 168, 180
Teton Park Road, 147-148
Teton Pass, 180
Teton River, 79, 180
Teton River flood, 166, 168
Teton Visitor's Center, 147
Thermopolis anticline, 102
Thermopolis shale, 93-94

Thermopolis (town), 101-102
Thousand Springs, 79
Thunderer, 129
Togwotee Pass, 145
Tom Miner Basin, 153, 161
Tongue River Canyon, 88, 91
Tower Falls, 54, 132, 194
Tower Junction, 132, 196
Trout Peak, 31
Tuff Cliff, 188
Twin Buttes, 198
Twin Creek, 141
Twin Falls, 79
Twin Lakes, 117-118

Unconformity, 12-13
Undine Falls, 197
Uniformitarianism, Doctrine of, 1-2
University of Michigan geology field camp, 135
Upper Falls, 192-193
Upper Geyser Basin, 58, 189-190
Upper Mesa Falls, 174
U-shaped valleys, 20, 30, 38, 44, 61, 68, 115-117, 121
U.S. Steel iron mine, 140, 142

Valentine geyser, 187
Vent facies, 34-35, 129
Victor, 180
Virginia Cascades, 197
Virginia City, 161
V-shaped valley, 110, 157

Wapi flows, 74, 202
Wapiti P.O., 109
Washakie uplift, 24, 66, 145
Washburn Range, 50-51
Weathering, 10
Welded tuffs, 50-54, 151, 161-162, 169, 174, 188
West Butte, 198
West Gate, 166
West Gros Ventre Butte, 181
West Stillwater River, 209
West Thumb, 190
West Thumb Junction, 150, 190
West Yellowstone, 47, 161, 164
West Yellowstone Basin, 161, 164, 166, 171
West Yellowstone earthquake, 47, 164-65
White Mountain, 127-128
Whitney Gallery of Western Art, 103
Willow Creek, 176
Willwood formation, 87, 95, 99, 144-145
Wilson, 181
Wind River, 23-24, 142-144
Wind River Basin, 23-26, 99, 142
Wind River Canyon, 23-24, 100-101
Wind River Mountains, Range, 25-31, 132-134, 136, 142

Winkleman Dome oil field, 142
Wood River, 36
Worland, 87, 102
Wraith Falls, 197
Wyoming Creek, 115
Wyoming Fish and Game Commission camp, 128
Wyoming Peak, 72
Wyoming Range, 72, 135-136, 178

Yankee Jim Canyon, 154-155
Yellowstone caldera, 110, 194, (see also *Caldera development*)
Yellowstone Lake, 110, 190
Yellowstone Plateau, 48-60, 110, 185-197
Yellowstone River Canyon, 53-55, 190, 192-194
Yellowstone River floodplain, 152
Yellowstone River valley, 152-155
Yellowstone welded tuffs, 162-163, 166, 197-199
Yellowtail Dam, 21, 95
York Road, 172

/557.872P272M>C1/

DATE DUE

AUG 1 5 1989			
MAY 2 0 1996			

Demco, Inc. 38-293